Library of
Davidson College

Agricultural Productivity in the Socialist Countries

Westview Special Studies

The concept of Westview Special Studies is a response to the continuing crisis in academic and informational publishing. Library budgets are being diverted from the purchase of books and used for data banks, computers, micromedia, and other methods of information retrieval. Interlibrary loan structures further reduce the edition sizes required to satisfy the needs of the scholarly community. Economic pressures on university presses and the few private scholarly publishing companies have greatly limited the capacity of the industry to properly serve the academic and research communities. As a result, many manuscripts dealing with important subjects, often representing the highest level of scholarship, are no longer economically viable publishing projects--or, if accepted for publication, are typically subject to lead times ranging from one to three years.

Westview Special Studies are our practical solution to the problem. As always, the selection criteria include the importance of the subject, the work's contribution to scholarship, and its insight, originality of thought, and excellence of exposition. We accept manuscripts in camera-ready form, typed, set, or word processed according to specifications laid out in our comprehensive manual, which contains straightforward instructions and sample pages. The responsibility for editing and proofreading lies with the author or sponsoring institution, but our editorial staff is always available to answer questions and provide guidance.

The result is a book printed on acid-free paper and bound in sturdy library-quality soft covers. We manufacture these books ourselves using equipment that does not require a lengthy make-ready process and that allows us to publish first editions of 500 to 1,500 copies and to reprint even smaller quantities as needed. Thus, we can produce Special Studies quickly and can keep even very specialized books in print as long as there is a demand for them.

About the Book and Author

With the emergence of collectivization, the communal movement, and the food crisis, the development of agriculture in socialist countries has become a topic of great interest to economists. Focusing on productive efficiency, Dr. Wong estimates an agricultural metaproduction function for nine countries--China, Bulgaria, Czechoslovakia, East Germany, Hungary, Poland, Romania, Yugoslavia, and the Soviet Union--and computes both the partial productivities and total productivity in comparable units. Using the growth accounting procedure, the author performs a quantitative comparative analysis of the differences and the sources of differences in agricultural productivity among socialist countries. Methods of analyzing productivity measures are described, revealing the contribution of land, labor, education, and other factors in agricultural growth. Dr. Wong concludes by discussing the policy implications for development strategy and the effects on the world food market.

Dr. Lung-Fai Wong is legislative analyst and research specialist of the Research Department in the Minnesota House of Representatives.

This book is dedicated
to my wife, Lai-Chun Kan,
and to my parents.

Agricultural Productivity in the Socialist Countries

Lung-Fai Wong

Westview Press / Boulder and London

Westview Special Studies in Agriculture Science and Policy

All rights reserved. No part of this publication may be reproduced or transmitted in any form or by any means, electronic or mechanical, including photocopy, recording, or any information storage and retrieval system, without permission in writing from the publisher.

Copyright © 1986 by Westview Press, Inc.

Published in 1986 in the United States of America by Westview Press, Inc.; Frederick A. Praeger, Publisher; 5500 Central Avenue, Boulder, Colorado 80301

Library of Congress Cataloging in Publication Data
Wong, Lung-Fai.
  Agricultural productivity in the Socialist countries.
  (Westview special studies in agriculture science and policy)
  Bibliography: p.
  1. Agricultural productivity—Communist countries. 2. Agricultural productivity—Communist countries—Case studies. I. Title. II. Series.
HD1415.W54 1986   338.1'6'091717   86-1539
ISBN 0-8133-7152-X

Composition for this book was provided by the author.
This book was produced without formal editing by the publisher.

Printed and bound in the United States of America

 The paper used in this publication meets the minimum requirements of the American National Standard for Permanence of Paper for Printed Library Materials Z39.48-1984.

6 5 4 3 2 1

Contents

List of Tables   xi

List of Figures   xv

Acknowledgments   xvii

Introduction   1

I Agricultural Development in Socialist Countries

1.1 Introduction   5
1.2 Economic Settings of Socialist Agriculture   6
1.3 Agricultural Growth in Socialist Countries   10
Notes   13

II Theory of Productivity and Productivity Indices

2.1 Introduction   15
2.2 Sources of Productivity Growth   16
2.3 Index Number Approach   19
    2.3.1 The Arithmetic Index   20
    2.3.2 The Geometric Index   21
2.4 Production Function Approach   23
2.5 Summary   24
Notes   25

III Metaproduction Function for Socialist Agriculture

3.1 Introduction   27
3.2 The Metaproduction Function and its Problems   27
3.3 Selection of the Form of the Metaproduction Function   30

3.4 Empirical Model Specifications 31
    3.4.1 Problems of Multicollinearity 33
    3.4.2 Agricultural Metaproduction Function for Socialist Countries 35
    3.4.3 Productivity Functions 39
    3.4.4 Centralized vs Less-Centralized Countries 41
3.5 Comparing the Results with Other Studies 43
3.6 Data Quality and Econometric Problems 46
Notes 47

IV Changes in Partial and Total Factor Productivity

4.1 Introduction 49
4.2 Cross-Country Comparison of Partial Productivity 50
    4.2.1 Changes in Labor Productivity 50
    4.2.2 Changes in Land Productivity 57
4.3 Cross-Country Comparison of Total Factor Productivity 61
    4.3.1 Changes in Arithmetic Productivity Index 62
    4.3.2 Changes in Geometric Productivity Index 64
4.4 Trends of Productivity Indices 68
4.5 Summary 80
Notes 81

V Sources of Agricultural Productivity Changes

5.1 Introduction 83
5.2 Contribution of Technical Change in Agricultural Growth 84
5.3 Accounting for Sources of Productivity Growth 90
    5.3.1 Sources of Labor Productivity Change 90
    5.3.2 Sources of Land Productivity Change 95
5.4 Intercountry Comparisons of Productivity Differences 98
    5.4.1 Sources of Labor Productivity Differences 101
    5.4.2 Sources of Land Productivity Differences 104
5.5 Implications of Empirical Findings 108
Notes 110

VI Prospects for Socialist Agriculture

6.1 Introduction 111
6.2 Summary and Empirical Findings 112
6.3 Policy Implications for Productivity Growth 114
6.4 Suggestions for Future Research 120
Notes 121

Appendixes

A: Aggregate Agricultural Output Series   125
B: Time Series Cross-Country Data   141
C: Principal Components Regression   167
D: Trends of Yearly Shift Factors   173

Bibliography   183

Index   191

Tables

Tables

1.1 Resource and Economic Conditions in Socialist Countries   7

1.2 Indices of Aggregate Agricultural Production   11

3.1 Agricultural Metaproduction Functions for Socialist Countries   37

3.2 Per Labor and Per Area Regressions   40

3.3 Comparisons of Centralized and Less-Centralized Countries   42

3.4 Comparisons of Previously Estimated Results   45

4.1 Labor Productivity; wheat units per labor   52

4.2 Indices of Labor Productivity   53

4.3 Land Productivity; wheat units per hectare   58

4.4 Indices of Land Productivity   59

4.5 Arithmetic Indices of Total Factor Productivity   63

4.6 Geometric Indices of Total Factor Productivity   67

4.7 Yearly Shift Factors of Geometric Index   69

5.1 Contributions of Technical Change in Agricultural Growth   89

5.2 Accounting for Changes in Agricultural Labor Productivity Among Socialist Countries   92

5.3 Accounting for Changes in Agricultural Land Productivity Among Socialist Countries   96

5.4 Intercountry Productivity Series (1960 and 1980)   99

5.5 Accounting for Agricultural Labor Productivity Differences, Socialist vs USA (1980)   102

5.6 Accounting for Agricultural Land Productivity Differences, Socialist vs Japan (1980)   106

A.1 Weights for Aggregation; Wheat-Relative Prices   128

A.2 Aggregate Agricultural Output in Wheat Units   130

A.3 Aggregate Agricultural Output for Bulgaria   131

A.4 Aggregate Agricultural Output for Czechoslovakia   132

A.5 Aggregate Agricultural Output for East Germany   133

A.6 Aggregate Agricultural Output for Hungary   134

A.7 Aggregate Agricultural Output for Poland   135

A.8 Aggregate Agricultural Output for Romania   136

A.9 Aggregate Agricultural Output for Yugoslavia   137

A.10 Aggregate Agricultural Output for USSR   138

A.11 Aggregate Agricultural Output for China   139

B.1 Aggregate Output and Input Table for Bulgaria   148

B.2 Aggregate Output and Input Table for Czechoslovakia   149

B.3 Aggregate Output and Input Table for East Germany   150

B.4   Aggregate Output and Input Table for Hungary   151

B.5   Aggregate Output and Input Table for Poland   152

B.6   Aggregate Output and Input Table for Romania   153

B.7   Aggregate Output and Input Table for Yugoslavia   154

B.8   Aggregate Output and Input Table for USSR   155

B.9   Aggregate Output and Input Table for China   156

B.10 Livestock Numbers for Bulgaria   157

B.11 Livestock Numbers for Czechoslovakia   158

B.12 Livestock Numbers for East Germany   159

B.13 Livestock Numbers for Hungary   160

B.14 Livestock Numbers for Poland   161

B.15 Livestock Numbers for Romania   162

B.16 Livestock Numbers for Yugoslavia   163

B.17 Livestock Numbers for USSR   164

B.18 Livestock Numbers for China   165

Figures

Figures

2.1 Difference Between Technical Change and Reallocation of Resources   17

3.1 Simple Correlation Coefficient Matrix   34

4.1 Trends of Productivity for Bulgaria   71

4.2 Trends of Productivity for Czechoslovakia   72

4.3 Trends of Productivity for East Germany   73

4.4 Trends of Productivity for Hungary   74

4.5 Trends of Productivity for Poland   75

4.6 Trends of Productivity for Romania   76

4.7 Trends of Productivity for Yugoslavia   77

4.8 Trends of Productivity for USSR   78

4.9 Trends of Productivity for China   79

5.1 Technical Change and Production Function   85

5.2 Technical Change and Misallocation of Resources   87

5.3 Intercountry Comparison of Productivity Trends   100

D.1 Trend of Yearly Shift Factors for Bulgaria   174

D.2 Trend of Yearly Shift Factors for Czechoslovakia   175

D.3 Trend of Yearly Shift Factors for East Germany   176

D.4 Trend of Yearly Shift Factors for Hungary   177

D.5 Trend of Yearly Shift Factors for Poland   178

D.6 Trend of Yearly Shift Factors for Romania   179

D.7 Trend of Yearly Shift Factors for Yugoslavia   180

D.8 Trend of Yearly Shift Factors for USSR   181

D.9 Trend of Yearly Shift Factors for China   182

Acknowledgments

This book represents the continuation of my interest in socialist agriculture. It is an extension of a doctoral dissertation which represents not only the work of its author, but of many involved. I gratefully acknowledge the many people who made contributions and efforts throughout the various stages of this study. Above all, I would like to thank Dr. Vernon W. Ruttan at the University of Minnesota for his expert and invaluable contributions to its final work.

I am grateful to Maureen Kilkenny for reading and commenting on several parts of the manuscript. My thanks also to Rhea Sullivan for her editorial comments. My appreciation is also extended to those scholars from East European countries who offered their comments on methodology and accuracy of data.

And of course, I would like to express my special appreciation and indebtedness to my family; my wife Lai-Chun and my little daughter Siming who made sacrifices while I was disappearing from them. Their love made the whole thing worthwhile.

It should be noted that this study was conducted by the author independently. The conclusions presented reflect only the views of the author and not the views of individuals or affiliated institutions that supported or assisted the author in any way.

Lung-Fai Wong

Introduction

Importance of This Study

Ever since the emergence of collectivization, the development of agriculture in socialist countries has been of great interest to economists. The recent increase in food purchases by socialist countries in the international market has heightened this interest. Over the past 30 years, several events have attracted attention: the communal movement in China during the late 1950s, the economic reform in the East European countries in the 1960s, the food crisis in Poland during the second half of the 1970s. All of these marked different stages of development and reflected the diversity of economic organization in socialist agriculture. In particular, the productive efficiency of socialist agriculture has concerned economists.

The few events mentioned above only scratch the surface of problems embodied in socialist agriculture. Studies of the general economy and agricultural economy in socialist countries have been undertaken for the last three decades. Most studies have focused on agrarian policies and performance in a particular country or region. A quantitative, comparative analysis of differences and the sources of differences in agricultural productivity among socialist countries has not been available.

It is, therefore, the objective of this study to examine and compare the different aspects of agricultural productivity and the sources of its growth in nine socialist countries: Bulgaria, Czechoslovakia, East Germany, Hungary, Poland, Romania, Yugoslavia, the Soviet Union, and China. While this study is not designed to provide detailed discussion of agrarian policies in these countries, it does analyze socialist agriculture in a quantitative and systematic manner. The growth, trends, and prospects of agricultural productivity in socialist countries do merit special attention. The implications of agricultural productivity are critical to these countries. It affects not only the food supply situation (which urban and industrial development in these countries depended on heavily), it also imposes great stability problems on the political structure in countries such as Hungary, Yugoslavia, and China. It would also be extremely beneficial for the West to be able to understand, evaluate, and project, the future of the lucrative export market of agricultural commodities to these socialist countries, which undoubtedly ties closely to their agricultural productivity.

Research Objectives

One of the objectives of this study is to examine the technical efficiency of socialist agriculture. It will address the issue of performance in socialist agriculture from a direct and technical perspective through the analysis of productivity.

This study seeks to answer the following questions that relate to the agricultural sectors in the nine selected socialist countries:

1. How efficient is socialist agricultural production?

2. What are the technical relationships in socialist agriculture?

3. Are input-output ratios the same as in non-socialist agriculture?

4. Are there common characteristics or patterns of agricultural production and agricultural productivity among socialist countries?

5. What are the differences, if any, between the more-centralized countries and the less-centralized countries?

6. Over the last three decades, what are the trends of productivity changes in these countries?

7. How much is technical change contributing to agricultural output growth in these countries?

Besides comparing the differences among the countries' technical efficiency and productivity, it is also important to be able to identify the sources of the differences within and among these socialist countries. Also, in spite of the fact that agricultural growth rates in these countries are not totally disappointing, it has long been argued that farmers (and other agricultural factors) in socialist countries are less productive than their counterparts in western countries. Therefore, included in the objective of this study is to search for an answer to the following two questions:

8. What are the sources of differences of productivity growth among socialist countries?

9. What are the sources of differences of productivity growth between socialist and non-socialist countries?

Organization of This Book

This study may not be able to provide final answers to all the questions listed above, but all of the questions are addressed in this study. Previous research efforts concerning the structure and policies in agricultural sectors in socialist countries have not provided comprehensive analysis of productivity changes. This study carries the analysis of productivity changes a small, but significant step forward by constructing and comparing several kinds of agricultural productivity measures within and among socialist countries.

The analysis begins in Chapter I with an overview of the characteristics of socialist agriculture. The policy and economic settings that circumscribe the agricultural sector in the nine selected socialist countries are also included in the discussion. The pattern of agricultural growth presented in this chapter serves special purposes in this study.

The theoretical model developed in Chapter II outlines the possible sources of productivity changes and differences between efficiency and technical change. It also provides the methodology and procedures for the construction of productivity indices. The problems and advantages of the index number and production function approaches are summarized in this chapter. In the discussion of total factor productivity, the widely used arithmetic index and Solow's geometric index are considered, together with a brief illustration of the use of the Divisia index.

The primary objective of Chapter III is to estimate an agricultural metaproduction function for the nine socialist countries. The purposes, definition, and estimation problems of the functional form are discussed in the chapter. The development of functional forms of the metaproduction function is reviewed in the chapter. Most important is the presentation of model specification and statistical problems. Data collected for the nine countries is fitted to an empirical model using the statistical techniques of least squares, autoregressive scheme, principal components regression, and mixed estimation regression. The models are verified by comparing the estimates of this study to results obtained by other researchers. At the end of the chapter, several econometric problems that relate to data quality are addressed.

Chapter IV is the core of this study. It contains the computations and comparisons of partial productivity - labor and land productivity. In addition, both the arithmetic and geometric index approaches are employed to construct the total factor productivity index. The comparison and analysis of the total factor productivity index presented in the chapter facilitate the understanding of the trends of productivity and technical changes in the nine socialist countries.

The materials presented in Chapter V add to the value of this study. They reveal the contribution of technical change in agricultural growth. Moreover, the sources of productivity growth among socialist countries are accounted for. The intercountry comparisons of productivity differences between socialist countries and non-socialist countries are also presented in this chapter.

Chapter VI summarizes all of the findings of this study. It also examines the prospects for socialist agriculture more closely, beginning with the discussion of policy implications for productivity growth. Suggestions for further research are also presented.

Finally, one of the most important contributions of this study is the compilation of data on agricultural production for the nine socialist countries for the period 1950-1980. It is a valuable time series cross-country data base that can be used for further analysis of socialist agriculture. The data base is organized and systematically presented in Appendixes A and B.

1

Agricultural Development in Socialist Countries

1.1 Introduction

The agricultural sector in socialist countries is different than other sectors of the socialist economy. Its uniqueness can be seen in four different areas. First, the combined agricultural sectors of the socialist world affect as much as one-third of the world population directly. Second, in the agricultural sector there are three major categories of producers: state, collective, and private. Each is treated differently, particularly the private sector, which is deliberately obstructed by state policy. Third, in the agricultural sectors special planning, price mechanisms and incentive systems are operative. Fourth, the agricultural production process is highly specific with regard to biological factors and organizational-economic and social conditions.[1]

While economic scholars have long recognized some of the problems in socialist agriculture, (i.e. production shortfalls, under-employment, idle resources, and inefficiencies) there is no consensus about the reasons for the different level of performance of the agricultural sector in the centrally planned economy. Some researchers have insisted that agriculture in socialist countries is less efficient than in capitalist countries. Michael Ellman concluded that "The growth of agricultural productivity under state socialism has been very unsatisfactory from a Marxist-Leninist standpoint" (Ellman 1981; 988). From the viewpoint of overall performance, D. Gale Johnson pointed out that the basic shortcoming of Soviet agriculture is that its output growth failed to keep pace with the growth of demand at the prices to consumers (Johnson 1983; 114). While looking at the growth of aggregate agricultural production, Johnson also said: "From a number of viewpoints the agriculture of most centrally planned economies performed well from about 1950 to the mid-1970s" (Johnson 1982; 845). Also on the topic of production, Michael Wyzan has argued that "The empirical evidence suggests that Soviet decisions in the sphere of agricultural production, contrary to the conventional wisdom, are well-founded technologically" (Wyzan 1981; 475).

It is clear that the evaluation of agricultural sectors in socialist countries varies according to the criteria economists use and the focus of their study. Furthermore, the fact that agricultural sector performance differs among socialist countries has provided a wide range of empirical evidence to support competitive hypotheses. This has stimulated the debate about the performance, or lack thereof, of socialist agriculture.

1.2 Economic Settings of Socialist Agriculture

Although the nine socialist countries are generally labelled as the Centrally Planned Economy (CPE), which implies homogeneity, they are in fact different from each other in terms of the degree of centralization, population, economic policy, and resource endowments. For example, China is 111 times more populous than Bulgaria, and the USSR is 239 times more spacious than Hungary (Table 1.1). In addition to differences in their resource endowments, the farm policies and settings in these countries are quite different. An example is a comparison of the different rates and degrees of collectivization of agricultural land in these countries. As shown in Table 1.1, in Poland and Yugoslavia less than one-third of the agricultural land is held by state farms and collective farms, while in other socialist countries, such as the Soviet Union, there is almost no private agricultural sector. As another example, the average farm size in the Soviet Union is 5,000 hectares compared to 4.0 hectares in Yugoslavia. While at the same time the size of private garden plots in China may be as small as half of a hectare. One consequence of these differences in collectivization policy is that the economic settings in socialist agriculture are in many ways not comparable to each other. All this has added to the confusion and difficulties in evaluating socialist agriculture.

It might be helpful here to define the meaning of socialist agriculture. Merely looking at the percentage of agricultural land held by state farms or collectives is not a sufficient criterion for defining socialist agriculture. The economic environment that surrounds peasants in these countries is more important. The economies of the nine

Table 1.1: Resource and Economic Conditions in Socialist Countries

	BULGARIA	CZECHOSL	E.GERMANY	HUNGARY	POLAND	ROMANIA	YUGOSLAVIA	USSR	CHINA
SIZE (MILLION HECTARES)									
1980	11.09	12.79	10.83	9.3	31.27	23.75	25.58	2227.0	960.0
POPULATION (1000 PERSONS)									
1950	7250	12389	18388	9338	24824	16311	16346	180000	551960
1960	7867	13654	17241	9984	29561	18403	18402	214400	662070
1970	8490	14334	17058	10335	32526	20252	20371	242800	829920
1980	8862	15315	16737	10710	35578	22201	22344	265500	987050
NO. OF COLLECTIVE FARMS OF COMMUNES (NUMBER)									
1950	2501	---	---	2185	635	1027	15605	123747	19
1960	932	10816	19313	4265	1668	13685	4233	44944	24317
1970	744	6200	9009	2441	1071	4626	1102	33561	51478
1980	---	1722	4033	1338	2286	4011	598	25900	54183
PERCENT OF SOCIALIZED AGRICULTURAL LAND									
1950	11.4	27.1	5.7	30.6	10.4	23.6	31.6	98.5	---
1960	99.0	87.2	92.4	79.2	13.1	81.9	24.1	99.9	---
1970	---	89.0	93.5	93.2	24.9	90.8	30.1	99.9	---
1980	100.0	95.1	94.5	93.6	31.6	91.0	31.3	100.0	---

countries included in this study are governed by a socialist ideology. Peasants in these countries, regardless of whether they are operating private land or collective land, are largely affected by economic policy that circumscribes their operation. They are particularly affected by the policies concerning land, labor and prices, which shall be discussed in detail.

Land

There are three categories of land ownership in socialist countries: state farms, collective farms, and private farms. Except in Poland and Yugoslavia, most of the agricultural land in socialist countries are socialized. State farms are owned, managed and directly operated by the state appointed farm managers. They are usually larger than collective farms and considered ideologically superior but are less efficient and less popular than collective farms. Many of the state farms received favorable treatment and are used for extensive farming and experiment purposes.

Collective farms are collectively owned and managed by their members. Members select their leadership and set up their own regulations. They are solely responsible for the profits and losses of the farm and get few subsidies from the state. There are many collective farms, especially communes in China, also own and involve in the operation of rural industries. In all cases, the collective farms have to make their own financial arrangements.

Private farms are the most numerous in Yugoslavia and Poland. In the Soviet Union and China, peasants are allowed only to privately operate a small area of garden plot.[2] Peasants operating private farms are solely responsible for their profits and losses. Efficiency varies by country on privately operated farm land. For example, the implementation of the new responsibility system in rural China increased productivity in Chinese agriculture and responsibility may be the most important factor in increasing productivity in China.[3] It is not necessary true that private farms in Yugoslavia and Poland are more efficient than the socialized sector. One of the reasons that private farms in Yugoslavia and Poland are not as efficient as their counterparts in the West is that Yugoslav and Polish peasants are forbidden to expand their farms into economically operational units.

Labor

One of the ideologies of socialism is to achieve an equitable society. The principle is that only labor can be considered as the legitimate source of personal income, and only the state as a whole can benefit from natural resources. That is, the income of agricultural labor in socialist agriculture should not include the income generated from the natural differences in the quality of land or the economic rent of the land. In a socialist economy, labor is not considered a tradable commodity. Nevertheless, agricultural laborers working on state farms are paid wages as hired labor, though are not necessarily paid according to their marginal value of products. On the other hand, members of collective farms are paid according to the financial picture of the farm that they belong to. In the past, commune members in China are paid according to the number of "work-points" they earn in each year.

Prices

The determination of prices in socialist agriculture always poses a problem for the authorities. There is no clear agreement on what the price relations among agricultural commodities, industrial products, and services should be. It is equally difficult to determine the price structure among different agricultural commodities.

On the input side, as implied above, the price of land can only reflect the differences in the productivity of land brought about by man-made improvements. Prices for other agricultural inputs are originally set at some level with respect to border prices and then are usually closely monitored by the state. Because of the distorted labor cost and the isolation from the international market, prices for fertilizer and machinery often do not reflect their production costs and opportunity costs.

The determination of prices for agricultural commodities is governed by both the production cost calculations and delivery requirements. In almost all of the countries included in this study, the state monopolizes the marketing services for agricultural commodities. Commodities produced by state farms belong to the state, therefore, prices serve only as an internal accounting instrument. Prices received by collective farms and private farms are calculated by the state, taking into the consideration of their production costs. In contrast to the marginal cost approach used in the capitalist economies, it is the average cost that is used in the determination of agricultural prices in socialist countries. As a consequence, farms that are more efficient or have good quality land subsidize farms that are less efficient.

Even though peasants might not have any choice but to subsidize other peasants through the prices they receive from the state, they can sell part of their produce in three different markets. These markets each have different procurement prices: the price for compulsory deliveries, the price for above compulsory deliveries, and the price in the open market. The reason for three different prices is to provide incentives for production above the procurement quota. The prices do not necessarily reflect the opportunity costs of the commodities in the domestic or international market.

The policy and economic settings outlined above describe only the basic principles that govern the operation of socialist agriculture. Implementation of these principles differs among socialist countries. In particular, each country uses very different schemes to introduce incentive factors into the system. The existence of huge differences in policy settings and resource endowments inevitably leads to different growth patterns in the agricultural sectors. (Not to mention the different impacts of political crises which arise in these countries from time to time.)

1.3 Agricultural Growth in Socialist Countries

As stated in the introduction chapter, one of the objectives is to examine the technical efficiency of socialist agriculture through the analysis of cross-country comparison of productivity. In order to perform a multi-country comparative analysis, all of the input and output measures used in this study have been converted into comparable units. Agricultural output, for example, is the aggregate production of 53 major commodities measured at the national level and converted into cross-country compatible wheat units (see Appendixes A and B for definitions, sources of data, and conversion procedures).

A summary of the aggregate agricultural output growth indices for the nine countries included in this study for 1950-1980 is presented in Table 1.2. The year 1960 was chosen as the base year for comparison purposes in order to avoid any bias in growth rates that might have resulted from the disruption and recovery after World War II. Hence, the focus is on the period of economic reform in the USSR and the East European countries after the death of Stalin.

Table 1.2: Indices of Aggregate Agricultural Production
(1960=100)

YEAR	BUL	CZE	GDR	HUN	POL	ROM	YUG	USSR	PRC
1950	62	88	69	75	81	58	50	73	82
1951	87	88	82	92	72	78	75	66	90
1952	66	87	86	64	72	70	44	75	104
1953	83	97	86	84	74	85	78	74	107
1954	69	88	90	77	81	79	64	76	111
1955	78	96	83	92	79	96	84	85	119
1956	72	103	85	83	90	75	67	95	125
1957	86	98	88	98	91	96	100	91	129
1958	85	95	91	92	93	80	82	104	133
1959	102	94	86	108	92	104	112	99	115
1960	100	100	100	100	100	100	100	100	100
1961	96	97	76	95	111	104	96	106	98
1962	100	94	88	100	100	96	100	107	104
1963	101	104	88	103	108	100	107	101	116
1964	115	106	93	106	111	105	115	120	131
1965	120	91	98	109	113	115	106	114	142
1966	141	107	98	116	118	132	128	134	154
1967	138	109	108	118	124	130	124	131	157
1968	128	115	107	118	129	127	120	137	153
1969	133	117	99	126	123	131	132	132	155
1970	134	118	103	119	125	114	121	149	173
1971	138	125	102	137	121	141	134	148	178
1972	152	130	113	147	132	159	132	141	177
1973	145	138	113	151	141	149	138	170	192
1974	135	144	124	161	142	153	158	159	200
1975	147	137	117	159	139	156	156	142	210
1976	157	134	112	155	143	196	165	168	215
1977	145	145	121	170	132	190	173	163	218
1978	152	153	127	176	144	193	162	179	238
1979	164	142	127	167	140	201	166	160	259
1980	157	154	127	183	123	201	166	165	266

GROWTH RATE:
60-69	4.38	1.99	2.24	2.92	2.59	3.80	3.39	3.70	6.09
70-80	1.49	2.14	2.10	3.35	0.58	5.06	3.22	1.37	4.42
50-80	3.06	1.91	1.63	2.96	2.33	3.60	3.63	3.13	3.37
60-80	2.40	2.55	2.00	3.36	1.58	3.87	2.95	2.72	4.75

Sources: see Appendix A.

The growth indices presented in Table 1.2 represent the different growth patterns of the socialist countries, even though these patterns may not be a good measure of performance. Among the East European countries, Hungary, Romania, and Yugoslavia can be classified as "fast growth" countries. Growth rates of agricultural production in these three countries in 1960-1980 were in the range of 2.95 to 3.87 percent.[4] These countries are also characterized by their success in maintaining a relatively steady growth rate over the last two decades.

Bulgaria, Czechoslovakia, East Germany, and Poland are slow growth countries. Their growth rates in 1960-1980 were in the range of 1.58 to 2.55 percent. Except for Poland, these countries experienced some stagnation during the early 1960s. Poland apparently was able to maintain steady slow growth in the 1960s. But since 1975, Poland's 1.58 percent growth rate has been the lowest among socialist countries.

Russian agricultural output expanded 65 percent during the same period. Although the 2.72 percent growth rate for the last two decades was short of what had been planned, Soviet agricultural performance compares favorably with East German and Polish performance. But what has been disappointing to the Soviets is that the growth rate dropped from 3.7 percent in 1960-1969 to 1.37 percent in 1970-1980. This declining trend serves as a warning signal to Soviet planners about their future food supply.

Among the nine socialist countries, China is in the earliest stage of development. Yet the rate of growth in agricultural output in China has been high. China achieved a 4.75 percent growth rate which amounts to more than a doubling of its aggregate agricultural production over the last two decades. This rapid growth occurred in spite of the disappointing "Three Red Flags" campaign and setbacks due to drought and floods in the early 1960s. Also, during the tumultuous period of the Cultural Revolution, agricultural production was lower than anticipated. Not until 1972 did Chinese agriculture resume its high growth rate.[5]

Agriculture in these socialist countries shows relatively satisfactory performance when evaluated in terms of overall growth rates. The average growth rate for the seven East European countries was 2.67 for the period of 1960-1980, and the overall average growth for all nine countries is 2.91. This is not low in terms of the historical performance of other developed countries. However, this does not necessarily imply that performance of socialist agriculture was satisfactory from either per worker or per area food production perspectives.

One obvious inconsistency with respect to output growth has been the different rates of growth among countries and within countries over time. For instance, the growth rates in the two sub-periods 1960-1969 and 1970-1980 exhibit contrary growth directions within countries of similar size. For example, among the small countries, the growth rate in Bulgaria dropped from 4.38 percent to 1.49 percent, while the growth rate in Hungary increased from 2.92 percent to 3.35 percent. Within the medium-sized countries, the growth rate in Poland dropped from 2.59 percent to 0.58 percent, while its neighbor Romania experienced a growth rate increase from 3.8 percent to 5.06 percent. The challenge of agriculture in these countries goes beyond the differences in resource scarcity and abundance. The ability to maintain a stable growth rate in agricultural production through growth in productivity, and to improve the efficiency of the agricultural sector are the keys. Therefore, the goal of this study is to examine the trends and the sources of growth of productivity in socialist agriculture.[6]

Notes

1. The same point has been emphasized by Alec Nove, <u>The Soviet Economic System</u>, 2nd edition, George Allen & Unwin Ltd., Great Britain: 1980, page 124.

2. Since 1978, the size and definition of private garden plot in China has changed drastically due to the implementation of the new Agricultural Production Responsibility System. It is getting more common to see Chinese peasants operate on a "contracted" land of 3-6 hectares.

3. In another article, the author pointed out that it is the formation of the new socialist agricultural ladder system that brought about higher productivity in Chinese agriculture (Wong 1985b).

4. All of the growth rates reported in this study are computed by estimating a linear regression of a natural exponential function, i.e., $\log X = a + bT$ where X is the variable to be measured, T is the time variable, and b is the estimated growth rate.

5. The growth indices for Chinese agricultural production are biased upward on two counts. First, the indices are computed using 1960 as the base year which is the worst year in the recent history of Chinese agriculture. Accordingly, indices for other years were exaggerated. Second, the official growth indices are computed using three different constant prices - 1950-1956 used the constant price of 1952, 1957-1970 used the constant price of 1957, and 1971-1980 used the constant price of 1970. As a result of these non-unified constant prices, the reported indices are not consistent and are biased upward, but the estimated growth rate remains neutral and unbiased.

6. This study, however, will not attempt to investigate the overall economic efficiency of socialist agriculture, which would require a much different data set and scale of analysis of the cost structure of different agriculture settings in the nine socialist countries.

2

Theory of Productivity and Productivity Indices

"The story of productivity, the ratio of output to input is at heart the record of man's efforts to raise himself from poverty."[1]

2.1 Introduction

The comparison of productivity growth consists of two important elements - a set of comparable cross-country data and a series of meaningful productivity indices. The comparability of data, the definitions of variables, and the detailed explanation of sources of data can be found in Appendixes A and B. The theory and procedure of the derivation of productivity indices is the focus of this chapter.

To be able to understand the essence of productivity, a series of meaningful productivity indices is essential. Not only do such indices reveal information about output per unit of input, but they also describe the dynamic progress of production. Most economists agree that the problem of inappropriate use of productivity statistics is as serious as the reliability of the data itself. Choosing an appropriate measure requires a proper understanding of the productivity index and its derivation. It is equally important to understand the sources of productivity change.

In this chapter, the possible causes of productivity growth and the differences between technical change and allocation efficiency are discussed. The theory and derivation of two approaches of measuring productivity - the index number approach and the production function approach - are also presented here.

2.2 Sources of Productivity Growth

The dynamic forces in the agricultural sector are both the causes and consequences of agricultural productivity changes. These dynamic forces include technological progress, accumulation of physical capital, improvement of human capital, and innovation of institutional arrangements. Each of these forces has a different role in the process of agricultural development and productivity growth. The primary use of productivity statistics in a study of agricultural sectors is to measure the effectiveness with which producers (economic agents) utilize their resources for the purpose of production. Productivity statistics measure the technical efficiency of resource use and provide insight into the performance of the agricultural sector.

Productivity is not synonymous with efficiency and hence, it is dangerous to identify productivity with efficiency. Productivity is commonly measured by the physical relationships between output and total or partial inputs, while economic efficiency refers to an equality between ratios of marginal products and corresponding factor price ratios. The achievement of efficiency often brings about a productivity increase, but the converse is not necessarily true. This dilemma is especially obvious in the environment of the non-market economy. For example, in order to get a larger bonus, a state farm manager in the Soviet Union would maximize total output instead of the profit of the farm. The result of this behavior is that the application of inputs, such as fertilizer and machinery, are increased to the level where their marginal products reach zero. The output maximizing result is that total output value and labor productivity are increased, but are not efficient in the normative sense.

On the other hand, one can find examples where productivity is defined as efficiency. Kendrick (1961) defines "changes in total factor productivity as changes in productivity efficiency." This confusion did not appear without reason. It is indeed a complex task to identify and separate the causes of production growth. The three major causes of production growth are: improvement in allocation efficiency, technological change, and increase in the levels of inputs. Refer to Figure 2.1, which clarified these causes using an isoquant map of two different kinds of technology.

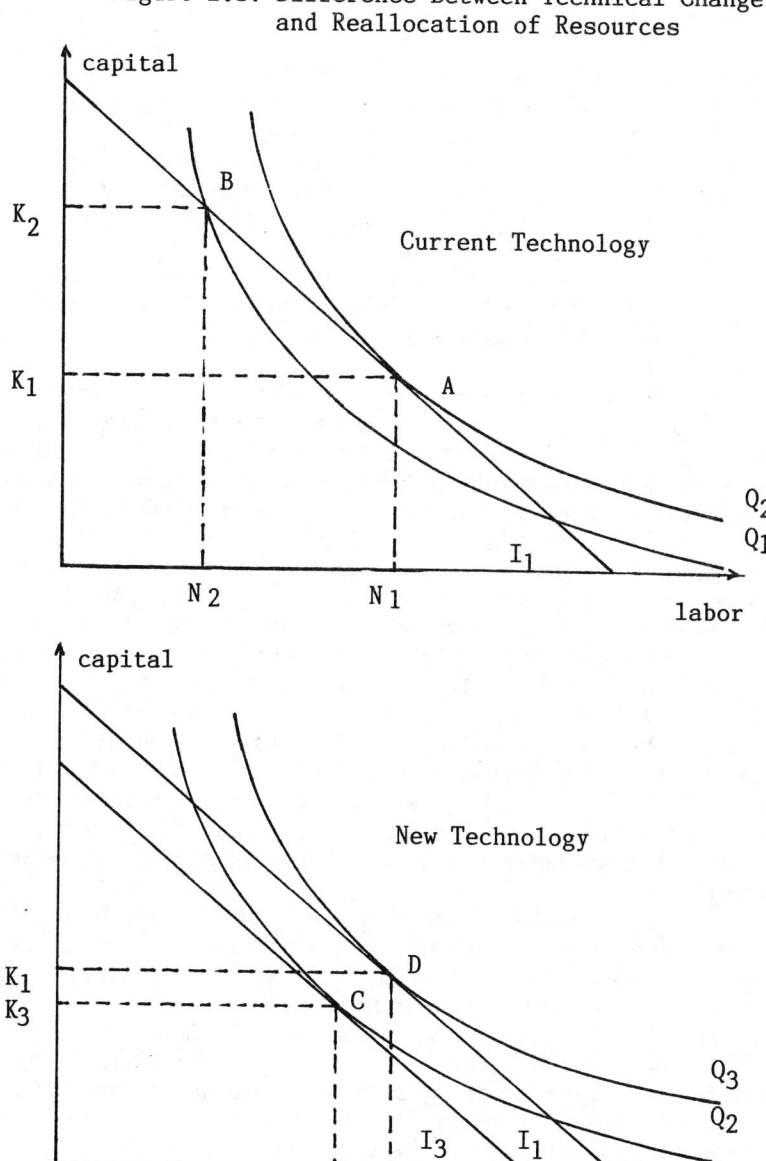

Figure 2.1: Difference Between Technical Change and Reallocation of Resources

The X-axis of Figure 2.1 is the quantity of labor used in production, and the Y-axis is the quantity of capital invested in production, including land. The points on each isoquant (labelled with Q's) represent the different combinations of labor and capital that yield a specified output level. The points on each isocost line (labelled with I's) represent the different combinations of labor and capital that may be purchased for a specified cost. The condition for a profit-maximizing competitive equilibrium is that the value of marginal products of each factor be equal to the marginal cost of that factor. Theoretically, when a firm is minimizing its costs, it equates all ratios of factor prices with marginal product ratios. Graphically, this is denoted as the point of tangency between an isoquant and an isocost line, i.e., points A, C and D.

With the current production technology represented by the isoquant Q_2 and the cost represented by I_1, the firm will choose point A and use N_1 of labor and K_1 of capital. Should the firm choose to produce at point B, the cost of production is the same, but the output level is lowered to Q_1. This clearly depicts the misallocation of resources. An alternative explanation is that as capital (e.g. machinery) was increased without rationally offsetting decrease in labor, the technical efficiency of both machinery and labor was decreased, which caused point B to move away from point A. The inefficient use of machinery and labor in socialist agriculture is not uncommon. There is relatively little incentive for individual workers to be technically efficient or for state farm managers to be economically efficient. To correct the problem, the firm should change the input proportions to those which result in point A. The corresponding increase in output is due entirely to an improvement in allocation efficiency.

Suppose there is technological progress which is Hicks' neutral and does not alter the contribution ratio of input factors (this particular assumption is not necessary to the argument). The new technology allows the firm to produce the same level of output with less cost as at point C. On the other hand, if the firm chooses to use the same level of inputs, the output level Q_3 at point D would be greater than Q_2. This increase in production is due entirely to the change in technology which can be presented graphically as the inward shift of the isoquant from Q_3 to Q_2.[2]

In view of the complexity of identifying the causes of production changes, most productivity statistics measure more than one force of change of input-output proportion. Of course, it would be ideal if one could measure the different magnitudes of all forces that change productivity. But if one considers the improvement of managerial skill, which brings about more efficiency in resource allocation and is viewed as another form of innovation, then most productivity statistics (regardless of their formulations) can be used for measuring technological changes.

One major use of productivity statistics is the measurement of the forces that contribute to production changes; in particular, the force of technical change. Hayami and Peterson (1977; 506) pointed out that "the magnitude of technical change can be measured either in terms of a change in the ratio of output to conventional inputs (usually an index when aggregation is necessary) or a shift in the production function consisting of conventional inputs". Although this definition may also be used to measure technical change in a centrally planned economy, the interpretation may be more difficult than for a market economy. Nevertheless, disagreement remains about how to express productivity statistics mathematically. There are two approaches - the index number approach and the production function approach. Each of these two approaches has its merits and problems. Lave (1966) and Hayami and Peterson (1977) provide good discussion on the differences between the two approaches.

2.3 Index Number Approach

One of the most popular ways to measure productivity is to combine several factors and express them in index form. Because such an index considers more than one production factor, it is called a total factor productivity index or multifactor productivity index. One of the major problems of computing a total factor productivity index is aggregating the inputs and outputs.

In most cases, outputs can be aggregated in terms of their monetary value, but any international comparison of productivity that uses money as a measuring rod will have to suffer the biases caused by exchange rates, different relative resource scarcity, and policy-induced distortions, etc. By the same token, aggregation of inputs requires some kind of weighing scheme, and no weighing scheme is free of biases. The direction and magnitude of biases depend on how close the formulation of the index is to the structure of production. In other words, the biases of the productivity index should be closely related to the biases of the assumed production function. Different assumptions generate different productivity indices. The arithmetic index and geometric index are the two indices based on distinctly different assumptions, which will be discussed.

2.3.1 The Arithmetic Index

Abramovitz (1956) and Kendrick (1961) are two of the early authors who utilized the arithmetic index to measure productivity change. The arithmetic index incorporates inputs weighted by the price of inputs. The validity of this index relies on two assumptions: a. competitive equilibrium and b. a linear and homogeneous production function.[3] Assuming these, the value of the product of an industry is the sum of the factor cost shares as illustrated in equation (2.1):

$$Y_o = w_o L + r_o K \qquad (2.1)$$

where Y_o is the output value, W_o is the wage rate of labor L, and r_o is the return or rental rate of capital K, at a given time t_o. If one considers a static economy where wages, return to capital, and technology do not change, then the percentage change in output is a weighted sum of the percentage change in labor and capital. The value of index C_o in equation (2.2) would then be 1.

$$Y_t/Y_o = C_o[(w_o L_t + r_o K_t) / (w_o L_o + r_o K_o)] \qquad (2.2)$$

or

$$Y_t/Y_o = C_o[W_L (L_t/L_o) + W_K(K_t/K_o)] \qquad (2.3)$$

where W_L = factor share of labor

W_K = factor share of capital

When there are changes in productivity, the value of index C_o will indicate its direction and magnitude. Lave argued that the arithmetic index approach of measurement of technological change is implicit in national income accounting (Lave 1966).

Although the arithmetic index approach does not explicitly assume any form of production function, it implies that the underlying production function is linear, and thus the accurate measure of productivity changes can be obtained only under very restricted conditions. Nevertheless, its simplicity is appreciated by economists. It was used by Kendrick (1961) to estimate total factor productivity in U.S. industries. It has also often been used by the United States

Department of Agriculture to compute different kinds of productivity indices.

The biggest problem in the arithmetic index approach is identifying a single price structure for all inputs involved in the computation. It is clear that the value of the index is affected by the choice between constant prices and current year prices. This problem would not appear if all prices changed in the same direction, thus leaving relative prices intact. Although the arithmetic index can be expressed in terms of factor shares, as shown in equation (2.3), the problems of constant factor share vs current factor share are essentially of the same nature.

2.3.2 The Geometric Index

One of the drawbacks of the arithmetic index approach is its assumption of a linear production function. This assumption is relaxed in the derivation of the geometric index. Robert Solow (1957) used a more general form of production function to define the aggregate production function in terms of aggregate capital, labor and time variable:

$$Q = A(t)F(K,L) \qquad (2.4)$$

With the assumption of neutral technical change (or parallel shift of the production function), the index of technical change between two periods is then given by equation (2.5).

$$\frac{\dot{A}}{A} = \frac{\dot{Y}}{Y} - W_K \frac{\dot{K}}{K} - W_L \frac{\dot{L}}{L} \qquad (2.5)$$

where $\dot{Y}, \dot{K}, \dot{L}$ = rate of change of output, capital, and labor respectively.

Assuming the hypotheses of Euler's theorem and constant return to scale, the index of labor productivity can then be expressed in terms of change of technology over time, change of capital per labor, and the share of capital, as shown in equation (2.6).

$$\frac{\dot{A}}{A} = \frac{\dot{y}}{y} - W_K \frac{\dot{k}}{k} \qquad (2.6)$$

where
y = output per labor
k = capital per labor (K/L)

The interpretation of equations (2.5) and (2.6) is relatively straightforward. The index can be treated as the residual that is not explained by the change of labor and capital, which then naturally measures technical change. It is a "rough profile" of technical change and is an "elementary way of segregating variations in output per head due to technical change from those due to changes in the availability of capital per head" (Solow 1957; 312).

Although Solow did not explicitly employ a specific form of production function, the underlying assumption is that the neutrality of the technological change does not alter the ratio of the marginal product of capital to the marginal product of labor. This is hard to accept over a long period of time. But the elegance of Solow's approach is its employment of factor shares that can be directly derived from the Cobb-Douglas production function. Another advantage of this approach is that it can be applied to the aggregate production function which is estimated in this study.

Unfortunately, there remains the problem of choosing the appropriate factor shares - the constant vs the current. Three proposals have been suggested to deal with this problem. First, one can change the weights or shares to reflect the actual factor shares at each time period (Solow 1957). Second, as suggested by Fisher (1967), one can use an average of the weights for the two periods under comparison. The third approach is to use the Divisia index, which will be discussed.

The first approach is preferable when a series of indices are desired and information is available for the construction of chain-link factor share. Barzel (1963) found that by changing weights frequently, the difference between the Paasche and the Laspeyres indices was reduced from 19 to 13 percent. However, it is not useful when the factor shares are stable over the periods of comparison. This is often the case in developing countries and centrally planned economies.[4]

Irving Fisher suggested using the average of weights in the base period and the comparison period. The resulting index would be a geometric mean of the Laspeyres and Paasche indices. The drawback here is that even though it averages two opposite biases from the Laspeyres and Paasche indices, it does not guarantee the complete elimination of bias.

The Divisia index is a weighted sum of growth rates, where the weights are the input's shares in the total value of input used. It is an exact specification of the homogeneous translog production function and does not impose restrictions on substitution possibilities among inputs. It is therefore more consistent with a wider variety of production functions than either the arithmetic or geometric indices (USDA 1980). However, these desirable properties are valid only if they are being specified in continuous-time form.

In the case of discrete events being observed, the Divisia index can be approximated by equation (2.7). Its goodness of fit depends on how small the time intervals are - the smaller the time interval, the better the approximation.

$$\ln D_t - \ln D_{t-1} = \sum_{i=1} W_i (\ln X_{it} - \ln X_{it-1}) \quad (2.7)$$

where:

D_t = the quantity of output (or input)

W_i = the average of weights of the component's share

X_{it} = the value of component i at time t

One difficulty with the Divisia index approach was spelled out by Hulter (1973). The fact that the Divisia index is a line integral may result in some multiplicity of index values associated with any given point in the set of variables being indexed. Also, although it is generally considered to be the unique index that satisfies the invariance indexing property, the Divisia index is path dependent (Richter 1966). Hence, the problem of how often the weights should be changed would depend on the choice of invariance and independence. The more invariance desired, the more frequent the weights should be changed. The more independence desired, the less often the weights should be changed.

2.4 Production Function Approach

Some economists view technical change as a shift in the production function. Therefore, by introducing a time variable in the production function, the shifting effect can then be captured and a productivity index can be constructed. This approach is particularly useful when the productivity index measures the technical change that occurs in a region, a country, an industry, or a sector of the economy.

There are several good reasons to use the production function approach. It does not require the aggregation of inputs and does not involve the selection of weights. Hence, it avoids the index-number problem. In contrast to the arithmetic and geometric indices, the production function approach does not explicitly assume any specific form of production function prior to the estimation.

The free choice of functional forms implies greater possibilities for specification errors. As early as 1957, Griliches pointed out that the presence of specification bias may cause bias in the estimation of regression parameters. The omission of meaningful variables and/or the existence of measurement error are other possible sources of misspecification. In order to measure the productivity more accurately, instead of using the popular Cobb-Douglas or Constant Elasticity of Substitution (CES) production function, some economists choose more generalized production functions. Examples of generalized functional forms include the Variable Elasticity of Substitution production function (VES), the Generalized Power production function, the Homothetic production functions, and the Transcendental Logarithmic production function.

Unfortunately, a single statistic cannot express every plausible shift of a production function. This is a major statistical problem of the production function approach. In reality, the quality and quantity of the data limit the feasibility of using a generalized production function. For example, VES can be readily used only for a production function that involves not more than two inputs. Other production functions may allow more than two inputs, but as the number of input variables increases, the number of interaction terms involved increases exponentially. This necessitates more observations of these effects than are typically available. As a result, the usefulness of the production function approach tends to be limited by the availability of adequate data (USDA 1980).

Another difficulty is the presence of multi-collinearity among input variables. It occurs most often with time series data. A possible solution, as suggested by Lu (1975), is to use the Analysis of Covariance model on panel data. He also demonstrated the use of time dummy variables for the construction of a productivity index.

2.5 Summary

In this chapter, several major models of measuring productivity indices have been discussed. There are many other models appearing in literature, such as Leontief's dynamic input-output model (1953), the Johansen approach (1961), and the Farrell's approach (1957). For detailed discussion on these models, readers are referred to the original articles.

Measuring the agricultural productivity growth in socialist countries is the main task of this study. To aid in comparison, a series of productivity indices will be constructed independently. Considering the crudeness of the data, the index number approach seems to be the best choice. Because price information is lacking on inputs and outputs for the nine socialist countries included in this study, factor shares will be used for the weights. Without knowing the price structure, factor shares cannot be constructed by the values of total output. The alternative is to estimate factor shares from regression of production function. This is the objective of Chapter III.

Notes

1. John W. Kendrick, <u>Capital in the American Economy: Its Formation and Financing</u>, 1961, page 3.

2. This assumption is true if we assume inputs are not measured in terms of constant quality. If all inputs were measured perfectly, i.e., quality changes made explicit, there would be no productivity gain in terms of input-output ratio reduction.

3. Linear and homogeneous function is not the same as linearly homogeneous function. The former is linear function without a constant term and the latter is function with homogeneous of degree one.

4. For example, the factor shares in Pakistan's agriculture changed slightly during the period 1953 to 1979. The changes were 5.8 % for labor and 4 % for capital and land (Wizarat 1981, 443).

3

Metaproduction Function for Socialist Agriculture

3.1 Introduction

The content of this chapter is both independent from, yet closely related to the last chapter, and it is crucial for the following chapter. In particular, the empirical results presented in this chapter have some extremely important implications for the next two chapters.

The primary purpose of this chapter is to estimate an agricultural metaproduction function for the nine socialist countries selected for this study. The estimated production function will provide two kinds of information: (a) the relationship between inputs and outputs, and (b) the relative importance of different types of input.

This chapter sets out to define what is meant by "metaproduction" function and provides a brief history of its emergence. Several possible functional forms are discussed before presenting the most appropriate and statistically feasible for this study. The specification and statistical problems associated with the empirical model are also included in the discussion. Finally, a summary of our estimates and the results of previous estimates made by other scholars are set forth in the last section of this chapter.

3.2 The Metaproduction Function and its Problems

The agricultural production problem can be viewed as a process of combining inputs and choice of technology. The collection of all techniques utilized for production are often referred to as technology. The decisions of production, allocation, and management which are made at the farm level, affect the outcome of the production process. Agricultural production in socialist countries cannot, of course, escape this generalization. But instead of letting farmers make the decisions, it is the state farm managers or the commune officials who make the decisions. Changes in the decision making process represent changes in the technology set or an alteration of the production process.

Because this study focuses on countries rather than individual farmers, the goal here is to estimate a cross-country production function at the national level. And because of the limited availability of detailed information at the provincial or republic levels, this data had to be omitted from the study. Hence the data utilized in this study is time series data aggregated at the national level. And the reported production function is the cross-country metaproduction function estimated from a panel of time series cross-country data.

A production function for a country or a group of countries is actually a distillation of hundreds of thousands of production processes expressed statistically as a single production function. The estimated function is often called an aggregate agricultural production function and there are always some arguments concerning its legitimacy.

The problem with aggregate production functions stems from the assumption that the input-output relationships in agricultural production between several countries (or even the world) can be readily expressed through a single production function, regardless of differences in cultural background, resource endowments, and economic structure. Although there are many theoretical objections to this assumption, the empirical results of several studies (Hayami and Ruttan, Evenson and Kislav, Nguyen, and Yamada and Ruttan) indicate the existence of an aggregate agricultural production function is not impossible.

Even though the argument over the existence of an aggregate agricultural production function has not been settled, the efforts to estimate metaproduction functions continue. Recently, Mundlak and Hellinghausen (1982) relaxed the assumption: "all countries produce on the same production function" to "all countries have access to the same technology." They show that "the choice of the implemented techniques is determined by the state variables, which represent the physical and economic environment within which the firms operate." With the introduction of state variables and the use of different sample coverage, they came up with a different "global" agricultural production function.

These different results highlight another aspect of the argument - should there be only one unique production function in the world? Biologically, there should be. Statistically, a single production function could be valid only if all the qualitative measures could be adjusted to an identical standard. Hence, the formulation of a universal production function depends on the measurement, formulation, statistical techniques, and data used.

As early as 1955, Bhattacharjee proposed a justification for the cross-country production function. He wrote, "The analogy, that if a production function can be conceived for the agriculture of a single country in spite of the diversity of farms and farming techniques within it, a similar function can also be justified for the agriculture of the world wherein the different countries are like the farms within a nation, is no doubt carried very far, but sounds, in any case, somewhat logical too" (Bhattacharjee 1955; 75).

Nevertheless, some economists feel that to view an aggregate agricultural production function as "the world production function" is too strong of an assumption. Instead, they use the term "metaproduction function" to denote the envelope of several production functions of a group of countries. Hayami and Ruttan (1971; 82) introduced the term to represent the envelope of many individual response curves for 42 market economies. They also labelled it as the "potential production function."

Because of its dynamic characteristics, the metaproduction function is more acceptable than the commonly conceived neoclassical production function. It also describes the innovation possibility curve and the technological frontier for those countries that have not yet adopted the existing state-of-the-art technology. Binswanger considers the metaproduction function as "the envelope of the production points of the most efficient countries". He continues: "As a consequence, the metaproduction function can be measured econometrically. It describes a technological frontier that countries now lying within its border can definitely reach by borrowing or by adaptive research, as appropriate, and by investing in human capital, in extension and in rural infrastructure" (Binswanger and Ruttan 1978; 46).

In the context of this study, the metaproduction function can be viewed as the envelope of all the possible production frontiers of the nine socialist countries. Estimating this function econometrically is the primary objective of this chapter.

3.3 Selection of the Form of the Metaproduction Function

The definition of metaproduction function described above is a general expression. Thus, the actual form of a metaproduction function is not limited by any specific functional form. The relationships between inputs and outputs can be represented by a variety of functional forms, and the final model is conditioned by the measurement, formulation, statistical specification, and data available. The proper procedure to search for an appropriate functional form is to start with a general form. A widely used general form of production function is the Variable Elasticity of Substitution (VES) function as derived by Lu and Fletcher (1968). For a two-input production industry, its production form can then be expressed by VES as follows:

$$Y = r\{\delta K^{-\rho}+(1-\delta)\eta(K/L)^{-c(1+\rho)}L^{-\rho}\}^{-1/\rho} \qquad (3.1)$$

where,

Y = output
K = capital
L = labor
ρ = 1/(b-1), the substitution parameter
η = (1-b)/(1-b-c)
r = the efficiency parameter
δ = distribution parameter

Because of its generality, VES satisfies all theoretical properties of the neoclassical theory of production, such that when c=0, it is the Constant Elasticity of Substitution function (CES); when c=0 and b=1, it is the Cobb-Douglas production function; when c=0 and b=0, it is the fixed coefficient production function; when c=0 and b=infinity, it is the linear and homogeneous function; and when c=1, it is the Linear Elasticity of Substitution function. Thus, an appropriate functional form for the data can be derived by inspection of the parameters of the general form of VES.

However, due to its complex formulation, this approach cannot be readily used for more than two inputs. Since identifying the sources of productivity growth is the objective of this study, it is important to include as many input variables as deemed appropriate, a priori. Due to its limitations, VES is excluded from the search for an appropriate functional form.

Among the various types of functional forms, the Cobb-Douglas type is one of the most widely used production functional form. Although the Cobb-Douglas production function is a very limiting specification, it is especially popular for aggregate production functions because only data collected at the national level is required for estimation. Several major studies (see Table 3.4) found that the Cobb-Douglas functional form was not an unreasonable specification of the metaproduction function. In addition to its simplicity and ease of computing and understanding, it has two features that are important for this study.

First, the coefficients of a Cobb-Douglas production function are elasticities of production with respect to each input and can also be interpreted as the factor shares of the inputs. Second, it allows the principle of diminishing returns to operate within the scale (Bhattacharjee 1955).

Besides these important properties, using the Cobb-Douglas functional form allows comparison of the results of this study with other previous estimates using the same functional form. It is, therefore, the Cobb-Douglas production function which was chosen for this study.

3.4 Empirical Model Specifications

The Cobb-Douglas function allows the incorporation of several variables in the production function. Three categories of variables were chosen that are considered possible sources of productivity change over time, or of productivity differences among countries. These categories are: (a) resource endowments, (b) technical inputs, and (c) human capital. Resource endowments include labor, land and internal capital accumulation in the form of land reclamation and development, such as livestock inventories. Technical inputs include machinery and chemical devices, and biological and chemical materials purchased from the industrial sector. Human capital generally includes education, skill, knowledge and capacity embodied in the population of the agricultural sector. In this study, the capacity of agricultural research institutes is used as the proxy for these elements.

The input variables used in the estimation are agricultural labor (N), land (L), fertilizer (F), machinery (M), livestock (S), and agricultural research (R). The dependent variable is aggregate agricultural output (Y) measured in wheat units (see Appendixes A and B for definitions and sources). The production function being estimated is the unrestricted Cobb-Douglas production form specified as follows:

$$Y = A^a N^{b1} L^{b2} F^{b3} M^{b4} S^{b5} R^{b6} \qquad (3.2)$$

Two kinds of statistical models were estimated. In addition to the metaproduction function which was a pooled time series cross-country model, production functions for each of the nine socialist countries were also estimated. The first model estimated was a group of unrestricted Cobb-Douglas production functions for individual countries as follows:

$$Y_{it} = A^{ai} N_{it}^{bi1} L_{it}^{bi2} F_{it}^{bi3} M_{it}^{bi4} S_{it}^{bi5} R_{it}^{bi6} \qquad (3.3)$$

where b = production elasticity
i = 1,2,...,9 for the ith country
t = 1950, 51,....,80

Production functions for individual countries were estimated separately using equation (3.3). The technique of Ordinary Least Squares (OLS) was first used in an attempt to estimate production function for each of the nine socialist countries. But the results were not satisfactory, mainly because there were too many negative coefficients and many of the coefficients were not significant. In addition, the Durbin-Watson statistics indicated that the disturbance terms, e, corresponding to different observations were correlated over time. The presence of autocorrelation led to the use of the autoregressive scheme. The model used is the first-order autoregressive scheme, AR(1), that can be specified as follows:

$$e_t = Pe_{t-1} + V_t$$

where
e_t = ordinary disturbance term from the estimation of equation (3.3);
V_t = new independent disturbance term;
P = autoregressive parameter, RHO.

Data from each of the nine socialist countries was used and all of the single-country regressions were estimated independently. Because of the lack of sufficient data, the agricultural research variable was not included in the estimates. The results were not satisfactory because there were too many insignificant estimated coefficients, and in many cases, they were negative. Because of their insignificance, the results are not reported here.

3.4.1 Problems of Multicollinearity

The unsatisfactory results of Ordinary Least Squares and Autoregression estimates may be caused by either misspecification of the model, the presence of multicollinearity, or both. The problem of misspecification can be verified by the insignificance of the autoregressive parameters, RHO, that indicates that merely applying AR(1) is not sufficient to decompose both the serial correlation and the multicollinearity.

Multicollinearity is a common problem for regressions that use time series data. Hence, the poor performance of AR(1) is not surprising. Several options can be used to deal with the problem of multicollinearity: (a) dropping variables, (b) using extraneous estimates as prior, (c) using first difference, (d) employing ridge regression, (e) regressing on principal components, and (f) getting more data.

The first solution is not appropriate for this study. As we mentioned before, it is important to include as many variables in this study as possible. Therefore, dropping variables is not an option. More importantly, the interpretation of the estimated production function would become meaningless if any of the five conventional variables were dropped.

Attempts were made to use the first differences, ridge regression, and principal components to counterattack the multicollinearity problem. None of the attempts generated any better results than the AR(1) estimates. As pointed out in Chapter I, a quantitative comparative study of socialist agriculture has not been available; hence, very little extraneous estimates for individual countries can be used to help solve the problem. However, there are several reports appeared in the literature on the estimation of aggregate agricultural production function for non-socialist agriculture. Their results were used as the priors together with the Mixed Estimation econometric model which is presented later in this study.

Getting more data seemed to be the only solution. But as the most recent data available had already been collected for this study, it was extremely difficult to get more data. Some other researchers collected data on Soviet agriculture at the republic level (Clayton, Brooks, and Wyzan). But getting republic or provincial data for the seven East European countries is almost impossible. With only two years (1980 and 1981) of provincial data available for Chinese agriculture, the possibility of getting data for the earlier years is very remote.

Figure 3.1: Simple Correlation Coefficient Matrix for Socialist Agriculture

LABOR	1.0000				
LAND	0.4536	1.0000			
FERTILIZER	0.6856	0.4601	1.0000		
MACHINERY	0.0614	0.8087	0.4385	1.0000	
LIVESTOCK	0.8346	0.8405	0.7334	0.5711	1.0000
RESEARCH	0.1463	0.3764	0.2741	0.4349	0.3478	1.0000
	LABOR	LAND	FERTILIZER	MACHINERY	LIVESTOCK	RESEARCH

While the possibility of finding a solution for the multicollinearity seemed to be exhausted, however, there are other possible statistical formulations can be utilized. The second model that can be estimated is the time series cross-country metaproduction function. There are two reasons for pooling the cross-country data together - to identify the common production frontier for the nine socialist countries, and to increase the number of observations for a single regression. Even so, the results shown that the problem of multicollinearity persists.

A simple correlation coefficient matrix in Figure 3.1 reveals the presence of multicollinearity. The livestock variable is highly correlated to labor, land, and fertilizer variables. The correlations between labor and fertilizer, and land and machinery are also high enough to attribute to the poor regression results.

3.4.2 Agricultural Metaproduction Function for Socialist Countries

The basic criteria for a well-estimated metaproduction function should include at least three conditions: (a) positive estimated coefficients, (b) statistically significant estimates, and (c) inclusion of all conventional inputs in the function. The presence of multicollinearity led to the consideration of other alternatives, such as ridge regression and/or principal components methods. But both approaches have some drawbacks.[1]

Statistically, principal components regression is a restricted regression while ridge regression is a transformed regression. Hence, both regression techniques have biased estimators. But the important thing is that both regressions do not require any elimination of variables. Thus, they may be useful tools for dealing with the problem of multicollinearity.

Pooled time series cross-country panel data from the nine socialist countries was fitted to both regression models. The results of both models are essentially the same. Since the choice of ridge parameter is arbitrary, and there is the problem of choosing a stable ridge parameter, only the results of regression on principal components are presented in regressions R1 to R4 in Table 3.1.

Because the independent variables are measured in different units, this causes high sensitivity to transformations of the components. All Principal Component regressions are therefore performed on the correlation matrix which represents, in effect, the normalized variables. The principal components are chosen according to the criteria that at least 95 percent of variances can be explained. Other statistical interpretations and computational procedures of principal components are presented in Appendix C, which includes a detailed explanation of the principal components regressions.

All regressions presented in Tables 3.1 to 3.3 are estimated time series cross-country production functions. The first four regressions presented in Table 3.1 can be classified into four categories - regressions using annual data, regressions using three-year average data, regressions including agricultural research variables, and regressions including agricultural research variables and trend variables.

The first regression included all nine countries from the period 1950 to 1980 and annual data of the five conventional variables: N,L,F,M,S. As shown in Table 3.1, all estimated coefficients of R1 are positive and statistically significant, except for the livestock coefficient which has an extremely low T-ratio. Other studies have also experienced problems of negative or insignificant livestock coefficients in socialist agriculture (Clayton 1980; and Brooks 1983).

The next three regressions used data from a smaller number of countries and employed three-year averages data. The estimates are based on data for only the seven years for which data on agricultural research is available. Hence, East Germany is excluded from regressions R2 to R4 because of incomplete data for the agricultural research variable. Also, only those years that have data for all six variables are used in these three regressions, which reduces the total number of observations to 56, mostly from the period of 1959 to 1978.

Regressions R3 and R4 include "manyears in agricultural research" in an attempt to capture the effect of technical change, while R2 provides a base for the comparison. With the inclusion of agricultural research in R3, the magnitude of the machinery coefficient drops as much as 58 percent. The magnitude of the fertilizer coefficient drops slightly. Other variables remain quite stable. The significance of the coefficient indicates that agricultural research in these countries makes a significant contribution to agricultural production. Its factor share may even be greater than that of machinery.

Regression R4 is similar to R3, but in addition, a time trend variable is also included in R4. It is included in an attempt to capture some of the unexplained residual effects of technological change, or the shifting of production function over time, elements which are not being captured by the agricultural research variable. Its insignificance suggests

Table 3.1: Agricultural Metaproduction Functions for Socialist Countries

REGRESSION NO.	R1	R2	R3	R4	R5	R6	R7
MODEL	RPC	RPC	RPC	RPC	MIX	MIX	MIX
NO. OF COUNTRIES	9	8	8	8	8	8	8
DEG. OF FREEDOM	266	52	52	52	49	51	50
DEPENDENT VARIABLE	Y	Y	Y	Y	Y	Y	Y
LABOR (N)	.223	.194	.22	.227	.132	.155	.172
	(25.56)	(17.76)	(21.59)	(19.01)	(4.29)	(4.34)	(4.48)
LAND (L)	.143	.133	.127	.142	.186	.042	.043
	(35.75)	(19.48)	(16.1)	(43.75)	(4.89)	(1.13)	(1.10)
FERTILIZER (F)	.182	.263	.217	.171	.252	.239	.212
	(20.22)	(13.61)	(10.78)	(26.19)	(10.68)	(9.17)	(6.83)
MACHINERY (M)	.108	.111	.047	.076	.034	.173	.135
	(7.71)	(5.84)	(2.62)	(5.11)	(.092)	(5.32)	(3.37)
LIVESTOCK (S)	.234	.207	.202	.205	.278	.391	.368
	(.183)	(0.16)	(0.16)	(0.16)	(4.10)	(5.29)	(4.67)
AG. RESEARCH (R)			.095	.081	.007		.07
			(9.37)	(7.40)	(0.23)		(1.77)
TREND (T)				.066			
				(1.18)			
SUM OF CONV. COEF.	.89	.908	.813	.821	.882	1.00	.93
R-SQ.	.98	.99	.99	.99	.99	.96	.96
R-SQ. ADJUSTED	.98	.99	.99	.99	.99	.96	.95

Note: Figures in parentheses are T-ratios for the coefficients

that most of the changes have been explained by the other six variables.

The results using principal components regressions are more acceptable than the results from Ordinary Least Squares and Autoregressive models. They are, however, biased estimators and do not have the property of constant return to scale. As noted in Chapter II, linear and homogeneous assumptions are essential for using the Index Number approach to measure total factor productivity. To overcome these problems, the procedure of Mixed Estimation was adopted. This procedure, in essence combines results from earlier studies with the information provided by the data used in this study.

The prior information we used in our Mixed Estimation model were the coefficients in the agricultural metaproduction function estimated for 38 market economies (Hayami and Ruttan 1971; 93:Q8). The prior information was added to the sample as additional observations and then the Ordinary Least Squares method was applied to the "extended sample" together with linear restriction in operation. The results of using Mixed Estimation are presented in regressions R5, R6 and R7.

Regressions R5, R6 and R7 have the same specifications except that R5 has no linear restriction. The agricultural research variable is included in R5 and R7 but not R6. Comparing these three regressions to regressions R1 to R4, R5 has smaller coefficients in labor and agricultural research variables; R6 and R7 have smaller coefficients in the labor and land variables and larger coefficients in the machinery variable. Others remained fairly stable. Because of their linear property, coefficients in R6 are used in the computation of total factor productivity where the sum of coefficients of conventional inputs is assumed to be one. Results of R7 are used in the analysis of growth accounting where effects of agricultural research are also considered.

Considering the crudeness of the data, the estimates using Principal Components regression or Mixed Estimation models are within a reasonable range. Among the regressions, R3 and R7 have the most interesting results. Besides the fact that most of the coefficients are significant, the significance of the agricultural research variable suggests that investments in the research system can affect the condition of food production in these socialist countries. Although the sums of the coefficients in R1 to R4 are close to one, the sum of the coefficients for conventional inputs is statistically less than unity.

3.4.3 Productivity Functions

Instead of using the absolute value of outputs and inputs, production functions can be estimated in terms of productivity. It can be easily shown that if the sum of coefficients equals one, then the results of regressions of R1 to R5 are obtainable by running regressions on variables that use per area or per labor measures. In some cases, productivity production functions can provide more information in the context of development.

The results of estimating productivity function are reported in Table 3.2. Because of the presence of multicollinearity, another statistical procedure that can scale down the effects of multicollinearity is necessary. Thus, despite it is not unbias, the procedure of principal components regression is used to estimate productivity functions. The first three regressions in Table 3.2 are per labor regressions. The dependent variable is output per labor (Y/N); and the explanatory variables are (A/N), (L/N), (F/N), (M/N), (S/N), (R/N). The results of R8, R9, and R10 are similar. The estimated coefficients for land variable are substantially smaller than those estimated in regressions R1 to R5 in Table 3.1. But the estimated coefficients on machinery and livestock are much larger than those estimated in regressions R1 to R5. This implies that the per labor quantity of fertilizer, livestock, and machinery are important factors in explaining labor productivity (Y/N). A more in-depth investigation and explanation of the sources of changes in labor productivity is the subject of Chapters IV and V. In the meantime, it is also interesting to examine the land productivity function.

The second half of Table 3.2 contains the results of land productivity regressions. The dependent variables are output per hectare (Y/L); and the explanatory variables are also expressed in per area basis, such as (N/L), (F/L), (M/L), (S/L), and (R/L). The results are slightly different from the labor productivity regressions. In particular, the per area livestock variable has higher coefficients than those in labor productivity regressions. Unlike the livestock coefficients in labor productivity regressions, the livestock coefficients in land productivity regressions are highly significant. But on the other hand, the agricultural research variable in land productivity regressions is insignificant.

The discrepancies among these estimates is an artifact of the nonlinear production function. If the production function was a linearly homogeneous function, the results in Tables 3.1 and 3.2 would be identical. Also, because the

Table 3.2: Per Labor and Per Area Regressions

REGRESSION NO.	R8	R9	R10	R11	R12	R13
MODEL	RPC	RPC	RPC	RPC	RPC	RPC
NO. OF COUNTRIES	9	8	8	9	8	8
DEG. OF FREEDOM	276	53	53	275	52	52
DEPENDENT VARIABLE	Y/N	Y/N	Y/N	Y/L	Y/L	Y/L
LABOR (N)	.069 (3.77)			.181 (14.31)	.124 (6.11)	.162 (7.62)
LAND (L)		.054 (1.71)	.057 (2.09)			
FERTILIZER (F)	.178 (27.07)	.187 (11.5)	.271 (14.97)	.132 (12.71)	.23 (8.6)	.188 (6.5)
MACHINERY (M)	.184 (61.54)	.129 (29.81)	.168 35.38	.194 (13.60)	.159 (5.46)	.079 (2.71)
LIVESTOCK (S)	.352 (.412)	.252 (.286)	.34 (.386)	.554 (33.89)	.505 (20.03)	.44 (16.4)
AG. RESEARCH (R)		.149 (20.76)				.122 (.14)
SUM OF CONV. COEF.	.599	.622	.836	1.061	1.018	.869
R-SQ.	.93	.95	.96	.91	.94	.92
R-SQ. ADJUST	.93	.95	.96	.91	.93	.92

Note: Figures in parentheses are T-ratios for the coefficients

principal components in these equations are formulated independently, results of the regressions are less compatible.

3.4.4 Centralized vs Less-Centralized Countries

Earlier in this chapter metaproduction was used to examine the pattern of agricultural production in nine socialist countries. In this section, the different production patterns of two groups of socialist countries that have different institutional characters will be examined.

In order to investigate the different production patterns between centralized and less-centralized agricultures, the four centralized countries - Bulgaria, Czechoslovakia, Soviet Union, and China - were separated from the sample. If data on agricultural research had been available, East Germany would have been included in the centralized group. The other four countries - Hungary, Poland, Romania, and Yugoslavia - are considered less-centralized countries.

Three kinds of principal components regressions are estimated for each of these two groups. It is apparent from Table 3.3 that the estimates for the centralized countries are similar to those in Table 3.1 and Table 3.2, but are quite distinct from the estimates for the group of less-centralized countries. The differences are acute in the labor variable and the agricultural research variable. These differences suggest that agricultural labor in less-centralized countries has a much smaller share than its counterpart in centralized countries, but this does not necessarily correspond to a lower income level.

As the authority of decision making in less-centralized countries is decentralized to the farm level, and because peasants' income is related to their productivity, income maximizing peasants would try to increase their productivity by using more purchased inputs. This behavior eventually would lead to higher labor productivity and farm income. But at the same time, the factor share of non-labor inputs would increase. This is the line of reasoning underlying the claim that labor in less-centralized countries has a smaller factor share.

On the other hand, the agricultural research variable in less-centralized countries has a much higher production elasticity than in centralized countries. This indicates that knowledge generated from the agricultural research system in less-centralized countries is as important as other conventional inputs. This result is rather interesting and important in agricultural development. The implication is that new technology in less-centralized countries is more

Table 3.3: Comparisons of Centralized vs Less-Centralized Countries

	R14	R15	R16	R17	R18	R19	R20	R21
REGRESSION NO.	RPC	RPC	RPC	RPC	RPC	RPC	RPC	RPC
MODEL	4	4	4	4	4	4	4	4
NO. OF COUNTRIES	(CENTRALIZED COUNTRIES)				(LESS CENTRALIZED COUNTRIES)			
DEG. OF FREEDOM	25	25	25	25	25	24	25	25
DEPENDENT VARIABLE	Y	Y	Y/N	Y/L	Y	Y	Y/N	Y/L
LABOR (N)	.208	.220		.179	-.019	.024		-.419
	(25.92)	(47.24)		(13.76)	(-1.03)	(1.21)		(-5.85)
LAND (L)	.159	.153	.065		.125	.150	.771	
	(94.04)	(123.6)	(2.60)		(6.09)	(4.58)	(8.86)	
FERTILIZER (F)	.203	.174	.204	.184	.187	.163	.098	.110
	(80.23)	(134.4)	(11.74)	(31.0)	(10.92)	(6.82)	(5.49)	(8.16)
MACHINERY (M)	.131	.087	.116	.094	.217	.020	.022	.029
	(.09)	(.059)	(33.0)	(10.32)	(.27)	(.26)	(.32)	(.41)
LIVESTOCK (S)	.220	.214	.231	.455	.196	.197	.450	.300
	(72.60)	(86.47)	(.23)	(.45)	(15.0)	(.24)	(15.32)	(2.01)
AG. RESEARCH (R)		.060	.131	.110		.189	.081	.094
		(10.93)	(23.1)	(16.18)		(11.74)	(.14)	(1.88)
SUM OF CONV. COEF.	.921	.848	.616	.912	.706	.554	1.341	.02
R-SQ.	.99	.99	.98	.97	.92	.91	.97	.89
R-SQ. ADJUSTED	.99	.99	.98	.97	.91	.90	.97	.88

Note: Figures in parentheses are T-ratios for the coefficients

productive than in centralized countries. As farmers in less-centralized countries are given more authority to choose inputs and technology, they are more flexible and willingly to adopt new technology. When accompanied by an incentive scheme, this process speeds up the dissemination of technology in the agricultural sector.

An analogous situation also exists for the more-centralized countries. Although state farm managers in these countries have a lot to say about what and how to grow, they may not be able to recognize what is the best available and most appropriate technology for the crops. This knowledge gap between state farm managers and actual field conditions results in the adoption of new technology with less efficiency than experienced by the less-centralized countries. Consequently, the share of agricultural research in more-centralized countries is smaller. A full growth accounting procedure can give an in-depth analysis of these matters, which is the subject of Chapter V.

3.5 Comparing the Results with Other Studies

The controversial results in Table 3.3 raise the doubt of plausibility of the estimated metaproduction functions presented in this chapter. It may be of interest to compare these results with results obtained by other scholars. For the purpose of comparison, the results of several previously estimated production functions are summarized in Table 3.4.

Regressions R6 and R7 in Table 3.1 are chosen to be compared with previously estimated results because they represent the metaproduction functions for the socialist countries and their production elasticities are used in Chapters IV and V. Although the definitions of variables used in other studies are not exactly identical to the definitions used in this study, they are close enough for the purpose of comparison.

As early as 1955, Bhattacharjee estimated an intercountry cross-section aggregate production function. In his study, the machinery coefficient and livestock coefficient were not significant. The regressions estimated by Hayami and Ruttan, Yamada and Ruttan, and Nguyen represent a class of metaproduction functions for a group of developing and developed countries that operate within the framework of a market economy. They also have a small problem with the significance of the land variable, but other than that, their estimates are quite reasonable. In particular, the inclusion of a technical education variable provides some insight on the relationship between human capital and agricultural production.

The inclusion of agricultural research in Evenson and Kislev's estimate is the unique feature of their work. Although their sample of countries is quite different from the sample used in this study, the production elasticity of agricultural research is surprisingly close to the estimates included herein. Mundlak and Hellinghausen expanded the Hayami-Ruttan study and added some "state variables" in an attempt to identify the roles of resource endowments in agricultural production. They obtained some different results - an extremely high labor coefficient.

Since the metaproduction function estimated in this study is for nine socialist countries, it would be more meaningful if the results could be compared with a production function estimated for socialist countries. Regression R28 was estimated earlier by Wong and Ruttan using a similar procedure and sample of socialist countries as R3 (except that data for 1980 was not available at that time), and the results are essentially the same. Clayton estimated a production function for Soviet agriculture by a cross-section of fifteen republics, pooled with a five-year interval time series (1960-1975). Her results summarized in R29 are reasonable except that the livestock coefficient has a low T-ratio. Note that the estimated production elasticity for fertilizer is almost exactly the same as the results reported in this study.

There is no doubt that climate has a substantial effect on agricultural production. Brooks believes that the weather factor is too large to be ignored and has investigated the climate factor in Soviet agricultural production. The time series cross-country production function Brooks estimated included fifteen Soviet republics, ten U.S. states, four Canadian provinces, and the nation of Finland. From the estimated results, Brooks concluded that favorable climate conditions contribute positively to agricultural production and is one of the reasons for the productivity gap between the USSR, the USA, Canada and Finland.

Compared with other studies' results, all of the estimates reported in this study fall into the range of their results. For example, the labor coefficient is within the range of 0.12 to 0.533, the land coefficient is within the range of -.003 to 0.364, the fertilizer coefficient is within the range of 0.1 to 0.3, the machinery coefficient is within the range of -0.04 to 0.153 the livestock coefficient is slightly higher than other estimates, and the agricultural research coefficient is close to Evenson and Kislev's estimate.

Table 3.4: Comparisons of Previously Estimated Results

REGRESSION NO. SOURCES	R22 BHATTAC-HARJEE	R23 HAYAMI-RUTTAN	R24 YAMADA-RUTTAN	R25 EVENSON-KISLEV	R26 NGUYEN	R27 MUNDLAK-HELLING-HAUSEN	R28 WONG-RUTTAN	R29 CLAYTON	R30 BROOKS
MODEL	(1955) OLS	(1971) OLS	(1980) OLS	(1975) OLS	(1979) OLS	(1982) RPC	(1983) RPC	(1980) OLS	(1983) RPC
NO. OF COUNTRIES	22	38	41	36	40	58	8	1	3
ESTIMATED PERIOD	49	55-65	1970	55-68	1970	60-63	59-79	60-75	60-79
DEPENDENT VARIABLE	Y	Y	Y	Y	Y	Y	Y	Y	Y
LABOR (N)	.301 (2.07)	.413 (5.51)	.325 (3.61)	.167 (3.83)	.351 (3.84)	.533 (1.94)	.225 (22.5)	.37 (7.4)	.12 (5.74)
LAND (L)	.364 (1.94)	.076 (1.21)	.019 (.26)	.068 (1.60)	-.003 (-.04)	.190 (1.05)	.129 (16.13)	.20 (4.0)	.34 (13.08)
FERTILIZER (F)	.270 (2.57)	.123 (1.95)	.243 (2.73)	.124 (3.78)	.178 (1.51)	.128 (1.13)	.208 (10.40)	.21 (7.0)	.30 (22.23)
MACHINERY (M)	.027 (0.22)	.116 (1.93)	.113 (1.71)	.049 (1.66)	.153 (1.95)	.082 (.60)	.054 (2.84)	.14 (2.33)	-.04 (-.98)
LIVESTOCK (S)	.037 (0.24)	.235 (2.78)	.234 (4.72)	.359 (6.19)	.323 (3.04)	.228 (.54)	.200 (1.55)	.05 (0.56)	.30 (13.56)
AG. RESEARCH (R)				.101 (3.06)			.097 (9.70)		
TECH. EDUCATION		.142 (2.58)	.135 (1.8)	.084 (3.00)	.169 (2.17)				
CLIMATE									.008 (5.68)
SUM OF CONV. COEF.	.999	.963	.934	.767	1.002	1.161	.816	.97	1.02
R-SQ.	.95	.95	.95	.98	.94		.99	.99	.99
R-SQ. ADJUSTED	.94						.99		

Note: Figures in parentheses are T-ratios for the coefficients

45

With these results, the use of regressions R6 and R7 to represent the production pattern of socialist countries, or as the metaproduction functions for the nine socialist countries is justifiable.

3.6 Data Quality and Econometric Problems

Despite the fact that the results presented in this study are reasonable, there are number of statistical problems that have not yet been overcome. In particular, the data quality problems that have over-shadowed this study merit more discussion. On the output side, produce from state farms, collective farms, and private farms was all included. This should not cause any serious problem per se because the input variables also include the private sector. It causes problems only when the labor input diverted to garden plots was not accounted for, and hence, labor productivity could be overestimated. On the other hand, as illustrated in Appendix A, the output series computed in this study used the price structure of non-socialist countries to aggregate individual commodities. If complete information on price structure in the nine socialist countries had been available, estimates that reflect more closely to the actual conditions in socialist agriculture might have been obtainable.

Problems of data quality also appear in the input variables. The location of the nine socialist countries covers a large geographic area starting from the latitude of 20 degrees north to 70 degrees north. Hence, without adjusting for soil quality and climate condition, it is questionable whether an accurate land coefficient can be obtained. As for the industrial inputs, the quality and distribution of technical inputs such as fertilizer and machinery are related to institutional structure which varies among countries.

Although it takes some time for the effect of agricultural research to show up in the production process, time lags for the agricultural research variable were not imposed. However, this omission would not bias the expected value of estimated production elasticities of the conventional inputs. Hence, the failure to impose time lags for the agricultural research variable should not cause too much bias on other estimated coefficients since the investment of agricultural research in these countries has been increasing.[2]

In spite of the fact that the data used in this study is rather crude, reasonable results were obtained. However, the time series data (annual) failed to provide a satisfactory production function for each of the nine individual countries. The techniques of Ordinary Least Squares and Autoregression performed poorly for the time series single-country estimates as well as for the pooled time series cross-country estimates. The presence of multicollinearity led to the use of the technique of Regression on Principal Components which could only provide a set of biased estimates. The procedure that pooled time series cross-country data together as panel data and the adoption of Mixed Estimation procedures that used prior information had eventually provided a reasonable agricultural metaproduction function for the nine selected socialist countries.

The estimated metaproduction function (R7) has positive production elasticities but a less significant agricultural research coefficient. Prior to applying the linear restriction, the sum of coefficients of the conventional inputs was less than unity. But compared with estimates from other studies, all of the estimates presented in this study fall within acceptable and reasonable ranges.

The estimation of agricultural metaproduction function is an important step towards the identification of sources of productivity changes in socialist countries. In addition to their usefulness in growth accounting, estimated factor shares can also be used in the construction of total factor productivity indices, which is the theme of Chapter IV.

Notes

1. Neither ridge regression nor principal components regression methods have a mechanism to improve the ill-conditioned data; they are simply ad hoc statistic solutions to multicollinearity. Although they can reduce the undesired consequence of multicollinearity, they cannot reduce multicollinearity itself.

2. In the discussion of time lag variables in agricultural research on production, Bredahl and Peterson (1976) show that if a research variable, such as investment in research (R), has been increasing at a constant rate over time, such that $R_{t-1} = kR_t$ where $0<k<1$, then utilizing current year research as the research variable would only bias the expected value of the estimated constant term of the production function upward and would not bias the expected value of estimated production elasticities.

4

Changes in Partial and Total Factor Productivity

4.1 Introduction

As pointed out at the outset of this study, the overall objective of this report is to compare the differences in agricultural productivity changes between the nine selected socialist countries. Hence, measurement of productivity change is extremely important for this study. The theoretical framework of productivity index and the different approaches to constructing productivity statistics was laid out in Chapter II. The results of the empirical model presented in Chapter III provided some insight on the relationships between inputs and outputs. The estimated metaproduction function also provided information on the factor shares of corresponding inputs. All of these analyses were prepared for the construction of the productivity indices in this chapter.

In general, agricultural productivity indices reflect the technical efficiency of the production process and the incomes of the population that are involved in food production. Two kinds of productivity indices are constructed in this chapter - the partial productivity indices and the total factor productivity indices. Although partial productivity indices can be used to measure the physical relationships between individual inputs and outputs, they cannot be used as a means of measuring technical efficiency or performance. In some cases, partial productivity indices can be used to measure the income level of that particular production factor. For example, the labor productivity index reflects certain patterns of farm income. But this interpretation needs to be used with caution.

The total factor productivity index or multifactor productivity index, on the other hand, is commonly used as the indicator of technical change. Its formulation embodies the technical efficiency of several major production factors involved in production. It also shows the trend of the technological change. It should not, however, be used as the measure of economic efficiency of the agricultural sector. Measuring the efficiency of the agricultural sector would require a much more in-depth analysis of the cost structure.

In this chapter, the partial productivity indices for production factors of labor and land are computed. Then, using the estimated factor shares from Chapter III, a series of total factor productivity indices are constructed. Both the arithmetic and geometric index approaches are used for the computation. Analysis of the trends of productivity changes and technical changes are presented in the last section of this chapter.

4.2 Cross-Country Comparison of Partial Productivity

In the literature of agricultural economics, it is not uncommon to find an expression of productivity in terms of output per unit of a single input - a partial productivity index. Although a partial productivity index does not take into account the effects of other production factors, it can still provide meaningful information on net economic progress. An example of this is the labor productivity index which is often used as a major determinant of farm income and wages. This index can be used to measure the production capacity of farmers, or to measure the number of people that a farmer can feed. It is, however, a misspecified measure of technical progress because it confounds both the effects of factor substitution and the effects of technological advances. Land productivity, on the other hand, indicates how much can be produced from a unit of land. Because of differences in stages of economic development and resource constraints, different countries tend to have different patterns of labor productivity and land productivity change.

4.2.1 Changes in Labor Productivity

Following the notation used in previous chapters, labor productivity is defined as wheat units per agricultural labor, including male and female workers. This non-traditional definition has a special purpose for a cross-country comparison study. Not only does it allow comparison between countries that have different price structures, currencies, and output compositions, but the biases stemming from exchange rates can also be avoided.

Using data presented in Appendixes A and B, labor productivity for the nine socialist countries included in this study are computed and summarized in Table 4.1. This table illustrates that the overall picture of labor productivity in these countries has some interesting changes. During the last three decades, the ranking of labor productivity altered vigorously. Although the ranking for East Germany (highest), Yugoslavia, Romania, and China (lowest) remained the same, other countries demonstrated some fluctuation.

The most obvious is the ranking of Hungary. In 1950, Hungary was the fifth among the group; it climbed to second position in 1980. In contrast, during the same period, the ranking of Poland slipped from third to sixth. Bulgaria performed almost as well as Hungary - it gained two positions in the race. The other two countries, USSR and Czechoslovakia, each lost one position.

The ups and downs of ranking are only relative measures. The absolute (in a sense) labor productivity values of all the nine countries were, nevertheless, increasing during this period. Even China, which has the lowest labor productivity, increased 82 percent from 1950-1980. Among these countries, Bulgaria had the highest jump in 1960-1980, a 250 percent increase in labor productivity. Following Bulgaria was Hungary, Czechoslovakia, Yugoslavia, Romania, USSR, East Germany, China, and Poland, in that order.

A summary of labor productivity indices for 1950-1980 is presented in Table 4.2. The year 1960 was chosen as the base year for comparison purposes in order to avoid any bias in growth rate that might have resulted from the disruption and recovery after World War II. This also allows more attention on the period of economic reform in the USSR and East European countries after the death of Stalin. Note that 1960 is a bad choice for base year for China because of the disastrous harvests experienced in 1959-1961. This difficulty was a consequence of unrealistic, ambitious, inexperienced management, and the erosion of incentives associated with egalitarian distribution of income at the commune level (Rawski 1982; 123). Hence, indices for China after this period, using 1960 as the base year, are somewhat exaggerated.

The rate of growth for labor productivity was also computed for the periods 1960-1969, 1970-1980, 1950-1980, and 1960-1980. As shown at the bottom of Table 4.2, most countries (except Romania and Yugoslavia) experienced a higher growth rate of labor productivity in the 1960s than in the 1970s. Overall, the average growth rate for these

Table 4.1: Labor Productivity, wheat units per labor

YEAR	BUL	CZE	GDR	HUN	POL	ROM	YUG	USSR	PRC
1950	2.43	7.16	11.36	5.27	6.08	1.67	1.71	5.51	1.31
1951	3.54	7.66	13.51	6.53	5.42	2.29	2.59	4.96	1.42
1952	2.76	7.87	14.02	4.61	5.42	2.04	1.54	5.68	1.63
1953	3.45	8.74	14.12	6.42	5.58	2.48	2.75	5.65	1.67
1954	2.90	7.76	14.43	5.96	6.12	2.29	2.29	5.85	1.71
1955	3.24	8.31	12.81	6.97	5.98	2.60	3.06	6.60	1.81
1956	2.95	9.11	13.71	6.16	6.83	2.11	2.48	7.44	1.87
1957	3.59	9.00	14.71	7.13	6.92	2.66	3.76	7.19	1.93
1958	3.46	8.98	15.21	6.78	7.09	2.19	3.14	8.29	1.97
1959	4.38	9.15	15.27	8.28	7.03	2.82	4.36	7.67	1.69
1960	4.69	10.69	19.86	7.99	7.65	2.64	3.96	8.00	1.46
1961	4.53	11.00	15.48	8.38	8.46	2.85	3.87	8.70	1.42
1962	5.06	10.96	17.93	8.89	7.61	2.64	4.10	8.93	1.49
1963	5.28	12.27	17.94	9.60	8.21	2.76	4.46	8.57	1.63
1964	6.19	12.78	18.85	10.26	8.39	2.91	4.88	10.10	1.81
1965	7.37	12.13	21.15	12.73	8.70	3.14	4.59	9.52	1.91
1966	8.95	14.32	21.72	13.70	9.11	3.69	5.64	11.28	2.02
1967	8.90	14.96	24.40	14.09	9.62	3.65	5.57	11.14	2.02
1968	8.67	16.03	25.47	14.21	10.04	3.58	5.49	11.74	1.93
1969	9.49	16.52	24.52	15.39	9.58	3.71	6.15	11.47	1.91
1970	9.97	16.81	26.32	14.91	9.76	3.21	5.75	13.06	2.07
1971	10.72	18.07	26.76	17.55	9.47	4.03	6.49	13.07	2.08
1972	12.07	20.04	30.91	19.30	10.42	4.56	6.53	12.48	2.02
1973	11.99	21.93	31.54	20.55	11.10	4.29	6.96	15.00	2.13
1974	11.56	23.06	35.22	22.65	11.12	4.42	8.13	14.02	2.17
1975	13.46	22.45	33.54	22.95	11.64	4.56	8.19	12.69	2.22
1976	15.12	22.42	32.72	22.96	12.21	5.79	8.84	15.05	2.22
1977	14.55	24.83	35.56	25.57	11.50	5.67	9.46	14.73	2.20
1978	15.65	26.69	37.19	26.60	12.81	5.84	9.04	16.18	2.37
1979	16.89	24.96	37.24	25.09	12.89	6.16	9.45	14.60	2.52
1980	16.46	27.12	37.19	27.44	11.61	6.28	9.65	15.14	2.39

Table 4.2: Indices of Labor Productivity (1960=100)

YEAR	BUL	CZE	GDR	HUN	POL	ROM	YUG	USSR	PRC
1950	52	67	57	66	79	63	43	69	89
1951	75	72	68	82	71	87	66	62	97
1952	59	74	71	58	71	77	39	71	112
1953	74	82	71	80	73	94	70	71	114
1954	62	73	73	75	80	87	58	73	117
1955	69	78	64	87	78	98	77	83	124
1956	63	85	69	77	89	80	63	93	128
1957	77	84	74	89	90	101	95	90	132
1958	74	84	77	85	93	83	79	104	135
1959	93	86	77	104	92	107	110	96	116
1960	100	100	100	100	100	100	100	100	100
1961	97	103	78	105	110	108	98	109	97
1962	108	103	90	111	99	100	104	112	102
1963	112	115	90	120	107	104	113	107	112
1964	132	120	95	128	110	110	123	126	123
1965	157	113	106	159	114	119	116	119	131
1966	191	134	109	171	119	140	143	141	138
1967	190	140	123	176	126	138	141	139	138
1968	185	150	128	178	131	135	139	147	132
1969	202	154	123	193	125	140	155	143	130
1970	213	157	133	187	128	122	145	163	142
1971	228	169	135	220	124	152	164	163	142
1972	257	187	156	242	136	172	165	156	138
1973	256	205	159	257	145	162	176	187	146
1974	246	216	177	283	145	167	205	175	148
1975	287	210	169	287	152	173	207	159	152
1976	322	210	165	287	160	219	223	188	152
1977	310	232	179	320	150	214	239	184	151
1978	334	250	187	333	167	221	228	202	162
1979	360	233	188	314	168	233	239	182	172
1980	351	254	187	343	152	237	244	189	164
GROWTH RATE:									
60-69	9.37	5.16	4.61	7.99	2.87	4.38	5.20	4.37	4.11
70-80	5.24	4.33	3.43	5.36	2.62	6.02	5.24	1.81	1.87
50-80	6.80	4.73	4.13	6.04	2.88	3.82	5.44	3.83	1.53
60-80	6.70	5.04	4.36	6.43	2.53	4.51	4.87	3.30	2.40

countries for the period of 1960-1980 was 4.46 percent, which is higher than most people would expect.

One of the explanations for the high growth in labor productivity is the high growth of aggregate agricultural production. As was discussed in Chapter I, the 2.91 average growth rate of production for the period 1960-80 is not low in terms of the historical performance of other developed countries. When the size of the labor force remained constant or decreased, the growth of production naturally translated to the growth of labor productivity.

Another important factor for the growth of labor productivity is the shrinking size of labor forces in the agricultural sector in these countries. All East European countries experienced a large reduction in the agricultural labor force between 1950 and 1980. For example, the agricultural labor force in Bulgaria in 1980 was only 37 percent of the 1950 level - it was a 46 percent reduction for Czechoslovakia; 56 percent reduction for East Germany; 47 percent reduction for Hungary; 80 percent reduction for Poland; and 59 percent reduction for Yugoslavia (see Appendix B).

The causes of the sharp decreases in agricultural labor in East European countries can be traced to both the agricultural and non-agricultural sectors. In the early 1960s, the process of collectivization in agriculture in most of these countries resulted in a massive movement of population to the urban areas. Simultaneously, many East European countries suffered serve economic problems. To counteract the declining economy, policy makers sought to expand production capacity through construction of new factories and an increase in the demand for labor force. This resulted in a massive tapping of male and female labor from the agricultural sector. This situation continued through the 1970s when labor shortage was still a problem.[1] Vais had a good description of the situation of labor shortage in these East European countries and the usage of agriculture as a reservoir of manpower for the non-agricultural sector.

> Thus, at the beginning of the 1970s, two countries - the G.D.R. and Czechoslovakia - achieved high levels of participation of their population, practically exhausted labor reserves among non-working women of working age, and could not rely any more on agriculture as a source of manpower for other sectors of their economies. The labor market in Hungary had very similar characteristics, though the labor shortage was not as acute, as in the two above mentioned countries.

In Poland, Romania, and to a lesser degree, in Bulgaria there were still possibilities for increasing the level of economic activity of working-age women, and agriculture still was a reservoir of manpower for nonagricultural sectors (Vais 1981; 237).

At the beginning of this chapter, it was pointed out that labor productivity is only a physical relationship between labor and production and should not be used as an indicator for performance. However, the growth rate of labor productivity can provide information on the performance of the agricultural sector. For example, Poland, the USSR, and China are countries that consistently had a lower growth rate of labor productivity from 1950-1980. These are also the countries that had poor performance in their agricultural sector.

The rate of reduction of the labor force in the USSR was not as large as in the East European countries. The size of the productivity labor force reduced only 18 percent from 1950-1980, which is a smaller percentage than that of any East European countries. But having a sizeable agricultural labor force per se is not the major cause of low labor productivity. In fact, a large part of the country, especially the European part of the USSR, has been experiencing a shortage of agricultural labor. Also, it is increasingly common in Soviet agriculture to use temporary workers and factory workers during the peak seasons. But this does not stop the out-migration of agricultural labor. The inferior wage rate in the agricultural sector is the major cause of out-migration. According to Brooks' calculation, in nine of the fifteen Soviet republics, the ratios of average non-agricultural wages to agricultural wages in 1965 were close to 2.0 or above. In Georgia republic, the ratio was as high as 2.68 (Johnson and Brooks 1983; 182).

Theoretically, labor mobility is a mechanism for equalizing the differential wage rates that exist in the economy. But this has not happened in the Soviet economy. The educated, young and energetic farmers who were supposed to take responsibility for the process of "complex mechanization", as Soviets refer to it, have migrated out of the agricultural sector and left behind them the unskilled, untrained, aged population of agricultural laborers. This has generated additional problems as tractors and machinery are left idle because of a shortage of trained operators and experienced technicians. Thus, the out-migration of young and trained people from the agricultural sector to the non-agricultural sector is an impediment to the growth of labor productivity and to narrowing the wage gap.

The causes of slow growth in China's agricultural labor productivity are completely different. Unlike the East European countries and the Soviet Union, China has faced a growing rural population which was sizeable to begin with. Statistics show that rural population increased from 500 million in 1952 to 782 million in 1977 (Tang 1980; 43). This added 127.8 million workers to China's agricultural labor force in the period of 1950-1980, which is a 77 percent jump. Despite the resulting decrease in land/man ratio, the labor productivity of wheat units per labor in Chinese agriculture increased 64 percent between 1960 and 1980.

China's labor productivity continued to grow through the 1970s, but the development and adoption of labor-intensive cultivation and the pressure to raise unit area output resulted in the slow growth of labor productivity. Furthermore, the commune establishment in China requires communal members to contribute a significant amount of time to non-farming tasks such as building schools, roads, dams, etc. Consequently, labor productivity in China is the lowest among socialist countries, both in terms of productivity level and growth rate of productivity.

The situation in China indicates that labor productivity and land productivity are closely related. In fact, when there can be only a small increase in agricultural land, net increase of labor productivity can also be achieved through the increase of land productivity. But before turning to the examination of land productivity, some other observations about labor productivity should be pointed out.

From the data in Tables 4.1 and 4.2, three general patterns can be observed. First, the three most industrialized countries (East Germany, Hungary, and Czechoslovakia) have the highest level of labor productivity. Second, the differences in labor productivity between these countries are large and are continuing to grow. In 1960, labor productivity in East Germany was 13.6 times that of China. This ratio grew to 15.56 times by 1980 - a 14.4 percent increase. Third, even though there has been much discussion about the favorable effects of decentralization, labor productivity data cannot be interpreted as supporting the hypothesis that the less-centralized countries (Hungary, Poland, Yugoslavia, and Romania) have out-performed the centralized countries.

4.2.2 Changes in Land Productivity

Land productivity, measured in wheat units per hectare, is presented in Table 4.3. It represents only the physical relationships between production and land and should not be used as an indicator of performance. However, land productivity can be used as a pertinent measure of agricultural productivity and agricultural development in areas where land is a constrained resource, i.e. Asian countries.

In contrast to the fluctuation of labor productivity, the overall picture of land productivity is fairly stable. Figures in Table 4.3 show that from 1950-1980 only four of the nine countries had changes in their rankings of land productivity and they were small changes. Furthermore, ranking of the four highest countries in land productivity and labor productivity in 1980 are identical, which includes East Germany, Hungary, Czechoslovakia, and Bulgaria. Note that the low level of land productivity in the USSR is partly due to the fact that the USSR has a vast area of uncultivated agricultural land which is also defined in this study as agricultural land (see Appendix B).

Although extensive programs of mechanization have taken place during the past three decades, land productivity in all nine socialist countries has increased substantially in that period. A summary of land productivity indices and the annual growth rate for different periods of time are reported in Table 4.4.

The growth rates of land productivity were larger in 1960-1969 than in 1970-1980 for the majority of the nine countries. It also should be noted that in most countries the growth rate of land productivity was smaller than the growth rate of labor productivity. The reasons for slow growth of land productivity are not difficult to identify.

First, the growth of population in all East European countries and the Soviet Union was small, and in some cases the growth rate was negative (such as in East Germany). Thus, the pressure for raising per area production was not as acute as it was in countries in which there was population pressure (such as China). Second, the land/labor ratio in these countries increased in 1950-1980 which implies that a unit of labor had more land to cultivate than before. This eventually led to the adoption of technology which was less labor intensive. Third, the mechanization program in East European countries and the Soviet Union may have opened some new agricultural land, but at the same time it wasted a higher proportion of land. And fourth, because land was owned by the state and rented to state and collective farms

Table 4.3: Land Productivity, wheat units per hectare

YEAR	BUL	CZE	GDR	HUN	POL	ROM	YUG	USSR	PRC
1950	1.18	1.97	2.58	1.50	1.61	0.73	0.69	0.27	0.66
1951	1.67	1.98	3.06	1.85	1.44	0.98	1.02	0.24	0.75
1952	1.27	1.96	3.22	1.29	1.44	0.88	0.59	0.28	0.89
1953	1.60	2.26	3.23	1.71	1.48	1.07	1.03	0.28	0.95
1954	1.33	2.02	3.38	1.56	1.62	1.00	0.83	0.27	1.02
1955	1.52	2.17	3.13	1.88	1.58	1.22	1.08	0.32	1.08
1956	1.40	2.34	3.21	1.70	1.80	0.95	0.85	0.36	1.13
1957	1.69	2.24	3.32	2.01	1.82	1.20	1.27	0.34	1.15
1958	1.68	2.16	3.45	1.89	1.86	0.99	1.04	0.40	1.19
1959	1.97	2.15	3.26	2.22	1.84	1.28	1.42	0.38	1.03
1960	1.92	2.35	3.79	2.07	1.99	1.23	1.27	0.38	0.88
1961	1.84	2.24	2.87	1.98	2.22	1.28	1.21	0.40	0.86
1962	1.91	2.18	3.33	2.11	2.01	1.17	1.27	0.41	0.91
1963	1.93	2.42	3.34	2.18	2.18	1.22	1.37	0.38	1.01
1964	2.17	2.61	3.51	2.25	2.24	1.28	1.47	0.46	1.12
1965	2.25	2.13	3.72	2.32	2.31	1.39	1.36	0.43	1.22
1966	2.64	2.51	3.72	2.48	2.41	1.59	1.64	0.51	1.32
1967	2.56	2.57	4.10	2.52	2.55	1.57	1.60	0.50	1.33
1968	2.37	2.71	4.14	2.53	2.65	1.52	1.55	0.52	1.25
1969	2.40	2.76	3.85	2.70	2.56	1.57	1.70	0.50	1.32
1970	2.42	2.79	4.00	2.56	2.60	1.37	1.56	0.57	1.47
1971	2.50	2.96	3.96	2.95	2.52	1.69	1.74	0.56	1.51
1972	2.74	3.09	4.39	3.17	2.77	1.91	1.72	0.54	1.51
1973	2.64	3.28	4.39	3.27	2.97	1.79	1.81	0.65	1.59
1974	2.45	3.43	4.82	3.51	3.00	1.84	2.07	0.61	1.69
1975	2.69	3.28	4.54	3.47	2.95	1.87	2.05	0.54	1.78
1976	2.75	3.22	4.35	3.39	3.04	2.35	2.18	0.64	1.78
1977	2.54	3.49	4.70	3.73	2.81	2.28	2.29	0.62	1.86
1978	2.66	3.69	4.94	3.88	3.07	2.31	2.14	0.68	1.97
1979	2.87	3.44	4.94	3.71	3.00	2.41	2.20	0.61	2.14
1980	2.76	3.77	4.94	4.08	2.64	2.41	2.20	0.63	2.20

Table 4.4: Indices of Land Productivity (1960=100)

YEAR	BUL	CZE	GDR	HUN	POL	ROM	YUG	USSR	PRC
1950	61	84	68	73	81	59	54	71	74
1951	87	84	81	89	72	79	81	64	84
1952	66	83	85	62	72	71	47	73	101
1953	83	96	85	82	74	87	82	72	108
1954	69	86	89	76	81	81	66	71	116
1955	79	93	82	91	79	99	85	83	123
1956	73	100	85	82	90	77	67	93	128
1957	88	95	88	97	91	98	100	90	131
1958	88	92	91	91	93	81	82	104	135
1959	103	92	86	107	92	104	112	99	116
1960	100	100	100	100	100	100	100	100	100
1961	96	95	76	96	111	104	96	106	98
1962	100	93	88	102	101	95	100	107	103
1963	101	103	88	105	109	99	108	101	114
1964	113	111	93	108	113	104	116	120	127
1965	118	91	98	112	116	113	107	114	138
1966	138	107	98	120	121	129	130	134	149
1967	134	109	108	122	128	127	126	131	151
1968	123	115	109	122	133	123	122	137	142
1969	125	118	101	131	128	127	135	132	149
1970	126	119	106	124	131	111	123	149	167
1971	130	126	104	143	127	137	138	148	172
1972	143	131	116	153	139	155	136	141	171
1973	137	140	116	158	149	145	143	170	180
1974	128	146	127	170	150	149	164	159	192
1975	140	140	120	168	148	152	162	143	201
1976	144	137	115	164	152	191	172	169	202
1977	133	149	124	180	141	185	181	164	210
1978	139	157	130	188	154	188	169	180	223
1979	150	147	130	179	150	195	174	161	243
1980	144	161	130	197	132	195	173	166	250
GROWTH RATE:									
60-69	3.77	2.13	2.50	3.28	3.05	3.48	3.62	3.71	5.49
70-80	1.05	2.45	2.11	3.71	0.90	5.04	3.49	1.35	4.16
50-80	2.67	2.16	1.79	3.31	2.61	3.39	3.65	3.23	3.16
60-80	1.90	2.74	2.18	3.67	1.97	3.75	3.19	2.75	4.48

at no charge, there was little incentive for farmers or managers of state farms to maximize either the utilization of land or the value of marginal product of land. This was not the case when the land was designated to individual farmers as private garden plots.

The situation in China was the reverse. The increasing population in China, from 552 million in 1950 to 987 million in 1980, created enormous pressure on the agricultural sector to produce more food for the newly added population. The increase in total food consumption and the decrease in land/labor ratio led the Chinese to utilize their land with maximum efficiency as possible. With experience that had accumulated over several centuries, Chinese peasants learned how to produce a maximum amount of food from a minimum area of land.

Rawski pointed out that two schemes were used in China in an effort to raise output per unit of land. The first scheme was the intensification of cropping practices. Over the past three decades, the application of resources to each unit of sown hectare, in the absence of changes in the type of crops grown or in the rotation cycle, has been increasing. This intensification increases the level of activity in land preparation, planting, transplanting, and crop management, which absorbs a large number of the underemployed rural population.

The second scheme is the intensification of the cropping cycle. This refers to an increase in the number of crops harvested per unit of cultivated land. According to Rawski, the national index of multiple cropping in China (sown area divided by cultivated area) has risen from 1.31 in 1952 to 1.5 in 1977 or 1978 (Rawski 1982; 125).

There is no doubt that the intensive use of labor and other factor inputs such as fertilizer in Chinese agriculture has been the major cause of the relatively high growth rate of land productivity. In fact, the growth rate of land productivity in China is even larger than the growth rate of its labor productivity.

To summarize this section, several observations are worth mentioning. The three industrialized countries (East Germany, Hungary, and Czechoslovakia) have the highest level of land productivity. The differences in land productivity between countries are smaller than labor productivity and are shrinking over time. Apparently it has been easier to improve labor productivity than to improve land productivity. With the exception of China, none of the countries included in this study have been able to double their land productivity in the last 20 years.

In spite of the common perception that agricultural production in socialized countries is rather slow, analysis presented in this study indicates that the labor productivity of the nine socialist countries, including the highly populated China, has increased by at least 60 percent for the period of 1960-1980. It was also noticed that industrial inputs have played an increasingly important role in agricultural production. For example, from 1960 to 1980 the consumption of chemical fertilizer in Romania and China increased 16 and 19 times, respectively. The number of tractors in Yugoslavia and China increased 12 and 16 times, respectively.

Except for China, the rate of growth of labor productivity has been faster than the rate of growth of land productivity in these socialist countries. Despite the fact that total agricultural area in the East European countries has decreased (or remained unchanged), the USSR and East European countries have emphasized mechanical technology in order to increase their labor productivity, while China has concentrated on labor-intensive technology to intensify land use.

4.3 Cross-Country Comparison of Total Factor Productivity

The biased character of the partial productivity index in measuring technical progress motivated economists to search for alternative measures. As a result of their efforts, the technique of using total factor productivity statistics was developed. Total factor productivity is defined as the ratio of aggregate output to the aggregate of all inputs. Because the total factor productivity measure refers to all conventional inputs, it can be used to evaluate the effects of technical change and factor substitution independently (Peterson and Hayami 1977; 507).

As discussed in Chapter II, there are two commonly used total factor productivity indices - the arithmetic index and the geometric index. Depending on the assumption of the form of production function, each of these two approaches has its own method of aggregating inputs. The objective of this section is to compute and compare total factor productivity for the nine socialist countries, using both arithmetic and geometric index approaches.

4.3.1 Changes in Arithmetic Productivity Index

In the construction of an arithmetic productivity index, the theoretical framework that was presented in Chapter II was employed. Following the same methodology, equation (2.3) in Chapter II can be reformulated to include more than two factor inputs. The formula for the total factor index or multifactor index, using 1960 as the base year, can then be expressed as follows:

$$C_t = (Y_t/Y_{60}) / \sum S_i(X_{it}/X_{i60}) \tag{4.1}$$

where, Y_t = aggregate output in wheat units
X_{it} = i^{th} input quantity at year t
S_i = factor share of corresponding input
C_t = arithmetic index for year t
i = 1,2,3,4,5
t = 1950,....,1980

All of the five conventional inputs (labor, land, fertilizer, machinery, and livestock) are included in the computation of the arithmetic total factor productivity index. The reason 1960 was chosen as the base year was to avoid any bias in growth rate that might have resulted from the disruption and recovery after World War II. And again, as stated earlier, 1960 was a bad base year for China.

Lacking information on factor shares was a serious problem for this study. Had the annual value of factor shares in these countries been available, the divisia index approach could have been utilized to obtain an invariant productivity index (Richter 1966; 740). Complete price information was not available for all nine socialist countries, and if they were available they would be seriously distorted and would fail to reflect the actual resources scarcity. Thus, factor shares cannot be estimated directly. Instead, the results of metaproduction functions estimated in Chapter III were used for the proxy of factor shares. Thus, the factor shares used are the estimated production elasticities of regression R6 in Table 3.1, which are: 0.155 for labor, 0.042 for land, 0.239 for fertilizer, 0.173 for machinery, and 0.391 for livestock. A summary of the computed indices are presented in Table 4.5 together with the annual growth rate of the indices for the period of 1950-1980, the sub-periods of 1960-1970, 1970-1980, and 1960-1980.

The results are somewhat surprising. The decreasing trend of total factor productivity is in sharp contrast to the increasing trends of labor productivity and land productivity.

Table 4.5: Arithmetic Indices for Total Factor Productivity (1960=100)

YEAR	BUL	CZE	GDR	HUN	POL	ROM	YUG	USSR	PRC
1950	88	125	91	109	118	90	79	95	201
1951	122	126	100	149	101	125	121	84	200
1952	93	121	102	99	97	114	70	92	213
1953	115	132	96	118	97	138	121	90	194
1954	94	121	100	110	101	116	94	85	193
1955	104	127	90	117	92	134	116	93	196
1956	89	115	89	104	101	99	85	103	191
1957	102	107	92	122	98	121	120	95	177
1958	99	99	93	109	100	96	89	110	154
1959	96	97	88	115	96	113	110	100	128
1960	100	100	100	100	100	100	100	100	100
1961	93	91	73	90	104	97	91	92	99
1962	94	84	82	84	90	83	89	86	95
1963	90	87	79	79	93	70	87	75	94
1964	89	83	78	77	90	71	91	79	98
1965	84	69	82	77	85	65	84	66	87
1966	87	73	80	79	81	65	96	73	79
1967	76	74	86	71	77	54	93	66	74
1968	62	73	83	64	74	50	88	66	81
1969	67	74	76	66	65	48	89	57	70
1970	70	72	79	55	62	39	80	59	73
1971	71	73	77	57	55	46	78	54	66
1972	75	75	85	60	55	50	70	48	58
1973	71	80	83	56	54	38	71	55	53
1974	68	79	89	55	50	37	71	48	55
1975	67	73	84	49	46	38	64	38	51
1976	71	72	81	52	47	44	63	44	48
1977	61	78	90	54	41	42	60	42	44
1978	64	79	94	55	43	40	51	45	38
1979	65	73	94	53	41	39	49	42	35
1980	62	80	93	61	34	38	48	41	32

GROWTH RATES:

60-69	-4.65	-3.39	-0.75	-4.22	-4.55	-8.31	-0.51	-5.44	-3.94
70-80	-1.54	0.49	1.80	-0.15	-5.03	-0.99	-5.29	-3.31	-7.67
50-80	-1.93	-2.02	-0.34	-3.33	-3.69	-4.76	-2.16	-3.36	-6.32
60-80	-2.21	-0.71	0.56	-2.96	-5.39	-4.70	-3.39	-4.47	-5.65

Except for Czechoslovakia and East Germany, all countries experienced negative growth rates in total factor productivity during all of the periods. The negative growth rate was particularly serious in Bulgaria, Romania, and the USSR. In the 1970s, after some major economic reform in agriculture, the negative growth rate started to slow down. In fact, during the early 1970s, Czechoslovakia and East Germany were able to regain some growth in total factor productivity and achieve positive growth in the sub-period of 1970-1980. A similar decreasing trend for the Soviet Union was reported by Douglas Diamond (1983; 146). He reported that the total factor productivity index in Soviet agriculture declined from 2.1 in 1951-1960 to 1.0 in 1961-1970, and down to 0.2 in 1971-1979.

The declining total factor productivity index in China can be checked with the figures estimated by Anthony Tang (1980; 75). Using a different aggregate procedure and a different set of factor shares (0.54 for labor, 0.27 for land, 0.11 for capital inputs, and 0.08 for current inputs), Tang estimated that the total factor productivity in China's agricultural sector declined 19 percent during the period of 1952-1977 (Tang 1980; 28). On the other hand, using the same weights as Tang's, Rawski also estimated that total factor productivity in Chinese agriculture declined 26 to 36 percent between 1957 and 1975 (Rawski 1983; 132).

The plausibility of declining total factor productivity in East European countries can be checked by comparing these results with the geometric productivity index constructed in the following section.

4.3.2 Changes in Geometric Productivity Index

Solow's geometric index was primarily developed for the purpose of measuring technical change. Assuming a linearly homogeneous production function, competitive equilibrium and neutral technical change, the residual or unexplained growth can be treated as technical change, and can be measured econometrically. A detailed discussion of the formulation of the geometric index can be found in section 2.3.2 of Chapter II in this report.

Using equation (2.6), derived in Chapter II, and expanding to include all five conventional factor inputs, the mathematical expression for the geometric productivity index is as follows:

$$\frac{\dot{A}}{A} = \frac{\dot{y}}{y} - W_l \frac{\dot{l}}{l} - W_f \frac{\dot{f}}{f} - W_m \frac{\dot{m}}{m} - W_s \frac{\dot{s}}{s} \qquad (4.2)$$

where
A = shift factor,
y = output per labor (Y/N),
l = land per labor (L/N),
f = fertilizer per labor (F/N),
m = machinery per labor (M/N),
s = livestock per labor (S/N),
W_i = factor share of corresponding factor

As was illustrated in the last section, the lack of information for prices and factor shares led to the use of estimated production elasticities of regression R6 as proxies for factor shares in equation (4.2). Thus, all countries have the same set of factor shares over the period of 1950-1980.

In the event that discrete annual data is used, equation (4.2) can be approximated by equation (4.3) as:

$$\frac{\Delta A}{A} = \frac{\Delta y}{y} - W_l \frac{\Delta l}{l} - W_f \frac{\Delta f}{f} - W_m \frac{\Delta m}{m} - W_s \frac{\Delta s}{s} \qquad (4.3)$$

where $\Delta y = (y_{t+1} - y_t) / y_t$ and etc.

t = 1950,...,1979

Thus, ($\Delta A(t)/A(t)$) can be obtained from equation (4.3) which is the yearly shift factor of the production function.

The procedure for obtaining a series of annual geometric productivity indices is first to compute the term ($\Delta A/A$) for each year. Then by arbitrary setting A(1950)=1, the time series of cumulated shift factor A(t) can be approximated by

$$A(t+1) = A(t)*[1+(\Delta A(t)/A(t))] \qquad (4.4)$$

t = 1950,..., 1980

The geometric productivity indices A(t) which Solow called "a rough profile" of technical change are presented in Table 4.6. Comparing Table 4.5 and Table 4.6, the geometric indices also show some signs of decreasing trends of productivity in the 1950s and 1960s. But beginning in the 1970s, four countries managed to pull out of the downward trend and bounced back to positive growth rate in the sub-period 1970-1980. Overall, two of the nine countries had positive growth rates in the sub-period 1960-1980. Most noticeable was the 1.82 annual growth rate of East Germany in the sub-period 1970-1980.

Perhaps a critical factor in the reversal of declining productivity in East European countries was due to a series of economic reforms that took place during the 1960s. The reforms were designed in an attempt to make the centralized planning system less rigid and the administration more flexible. The reforms were also intended to change the terms of trade in favor of agriculture. The reforms, which varied by individual country, moved like a wave across Eastern Europe in the 1960s. Describing this "decade of reform", Wadekin writes:

> These second stage reforms, which did not yet concern the collective farm sector, were officially decreed in the GDR in 1963 (June), in Bulgaria in 1964 (January), in Czechoslovakia, Poland, and the USSR in 1965 (January, July, and September, respectively), in Hungary in 1966 (May), and in Romania in 1967 (October). Important changes toward greater liberalization in general ensued in Czechoslovakia during 1967 (not wholly repealed for economic management after the 1968 Soviet intervention) and in Hungarian economics during 1966-67, where the 'New Economic Mechanism' was finally enacted in January 1968 ...... A comprehensive reform of the whole system of the Yugoslav economy was enacted during 1965-67 on the basis of the resolutions of the VIII (1964) Party congress. Instruments of a market economy were applied to a greater degree than in Poland, not to speak of the other countries. For Yugoslav agriculture, the main intent of the reforms was to equalize the conditions of production to those prevailing in the rest of the economy and to eliminate the income and price disparities which existed to the disadvantage of agriculture (Wadekin 1982; 208).

Table 4.6: Geometric Indices for Total Factor Productivity (1960=100)

YEAR	BUL	CZE	GDR	HUN	POL	ROM	YUG	USSR	PRC
1950	185	226	94	264	132	578	192	99	1086
1951	241	230	103	336	108	890	269	86	1020
1952	168	218	105	221	101	731	152	95	732
1953	202	237	97	157	100	875	268	92	476
1954	147	197	101	140	103	518	135	87	407
1955	157	206	91	141	93	595	158	95	340
1956	120	123	89	126	101	260	93	105	265
1957	129	112	91	138	98	302	128	96	226
1958	123	101	93	118	101	100	88	111	167
1959	98	97	86	120	96	115	111	101	136
1960	100	100	100	100	100	100	100	100	100
1961	93	90	71	88	104	96	90	91	99
1962	94	83	80	83	90	82	88	85	92
1963	90	87	78	80	94	69	88	74	91
1964	89	84	77	78	91	71	93	83	95
1965	86	69	81	79	86	68	86	72	86
1966	95	77	80	83	83	72	100	81	82
1967	87	77	87	77	81	64	97	75	78
1968	75	78	84	72	80	60	93	77	79
1969	80	80	78	77	71	60	95	70	72
1970	83	79	80	67	69	50	87	76	76
1971	83	81	79	72	64	61	86	72	72
1972	89	84	87	78	65	67	81	66	66
1973	84	89	86	78	65	56	83	77	65
1974	79	90	92	81	62	56	88	69	66
1975	81	84	87	75	59	57	82	58	64
1976	85	82	84	78	61	69	86	68	62
1977	76	89	93	83	54	64	87	66	59
1978	80	91	96	86	60	64	78	71	57
1979	83	83	96	81	59	64	79	64	56
1980	79	91	95	90	50	64	79	64	53
GROWTH RATES:									
60-69	-2.29	-2.39	-0.31	-2.43	-3.56	-5.48	0.34	-2.96	-3.50
70-80	-0.63	0.87	1.82	2.11	-2.33	1.60	-0.79	-1.30	-3.19
50-80	-3.00	-3.18	-0.26	-3.48	-2.61	-8.83	-2.83	-1.61	-8.79
60-80	-0.90	0.17	0.83	-0.19	-3.35	-1.67	-0.86	-1.69	-3.14

As pointed out earlier, the year of 1960 is not a good base year for China. Thus, the productivity indices for China presented in Table 4.5 and Table 4.6 are somewhat overindexed. But the estimated growth rates are essentially unaffected, regardless of the base year used (since growth rates are estimated by linear trend). In any case, the trend of declining productivity is also parallel to Tang and Rawski's estimates. Although China could not pull out from the declining trend, the rate of negative growth after the 1960s was considerably smaller than in the 1950s. The fluctuation of trends and the inconsistency between partial and total factor productivity indices is intriguing. In the next section, an in-depth examination of the different trends of productivity indices is presented for the nine socialist countries.

One final note about the model of geometric index. When deriving the geometric index, Solow imposed a critical assumption of neutral technical change. His definition of neutrality means that the shifts in production function are pure scale changes, leaving marginal rates of substitution unchanged at given capital/labor ratios (Solow 1957; 316).

To ensure that data used in this study does not violate the neutrality assumption, scatterplots of the yearly shift factors ($\Delta A/A$) against the land/labor ratio (L/N) were examined. From the scatterplots, no trace of relationship was detected between technical progress and input ratios. The statistical technique of Ordinary Least Squares was also used in an attempt to estimate this relationship. The results were that small R-squares and small T-ratios supported the assumption of neutral technical change.[2] Thus, it may be formally concluded that technical change in the nine socialist countries did not alter the marginal rates of substitution between inputs. Therefore, the use of Solow's model for this study does not appear to grossly violate the assumption of neutral technical change.

4.4 Trends of Productivity Indices

One of the favorable features of the geometric index (over arithmetic index) is its provision for year to year changes. Unlike the arithmetic index, which uses a single year as base year, the geometric index actually estimates the yearly shift factor A(t). The yearly shift factors presented in Table 4.7 are important elements for an in-depth study of technical change. In addition, graphs of the yearly shift factors are presented in Appendix D for each of the nine individual countries.

Table 4.7: Yearly Shift Factors for Geometric Index

YEAR	BUL	CZE	GDR	HUN	POL	ROM	YUG	USSR	PRC
1950	0.31	0.02	0.10	0.27	-0.18	0.54	0.40	-0.13	-0.06
1951	-0.30	-0.05	0.02	-0.34	-0.07	-0.18	-0.43	0.10	-0.28
1952	0.20	0.09	-0.07	-0.29	-0.01	0.20	0.76	-0.03	-0.35
1953	-0.27	-0.17	0.04	-0.11	0.03	-0.41	-0.50	-0.06	-0.14
1954	0.07	0.04	-0.10	0.01	-0.10	0.15	0.17	0.10	-0.16
1955	-0.23	-0.40	-0.02	-0.11	0.09	-0.56	-0.41	0.11	-0.22
1956	0.07	-0.08	0.03	0.09	-0.03	0.16	0.38	-0.09	-0.15
1957	-0.04	-0.10	0.02	-0.14	0.03	-0.67	-0.31	0.16	-0.26
1958	-0.21	-0.03	-0.07	0.02	-0.04	0.15	0.26	-0.09	-0.18
1959	0.02	0.03	0.16	-0.17	0.04	-0.13	-0.10	-0.01	-0.26
1960	-0.07	-0.10	-0.29	-0.12	0.04	-0.04	-0.10	-0.09	-0.01
1961	0.01	-0.08	0.13	-0.06	-0.14	-0.15	-0.02	-0.07	-0.07
1962	-0.04	0.04	-0.02	-0.04	0.04	-0.16	0.00	-0.13	-0.02
1963	-0.02	-0.03	-0.01	-0.03	-0.03	0.02	0.06	0.11	0.05
1964	-0.03	-0.18	0.06	0.01	-0.05	-0.04	-0.08	-0.13	-0.09
1965	0.10	0.11	-0.02	0.06	-0.04	0.07	0.17	0.12	-0.05
1966	-0.09	0.01	0.09	-0.07	-0.02	-0.11	-0.03	-0.07	-0.05
1967	-0.14	0.01	-0.03	-0.07	-0.02	-0.06	-0.04	0.03	0.01
1968	0.06	0.02	-0.08	0.08	-0.10	0.00	0.02	-0.09	-0.09
1969	0.04	-0.01	0.04	-0.13	-0.03	-0.16	-0.09	0.09	0.06
1970	0.01	0.03	-0.01	0.08	-0.08	0.20	-0.00	-0.06	-0.05
1971	0.06	0.04	0.11	0.08	0.02	0.09	-0.06	-0.09	-0.10
1972	-0.05	0.06	-0.02	-0.00	-0.00	-0.16	0.03	0.18	-0.02
1973	-0.05	0.01	0.08	0.03	-0.05	0.00	0.06	-0.10	0.02
1974	0.02	-0.07	-0.06	-0.06	-0.05	0.02	-0.07	-0.16	-0.02
1975	0.05	-0.02	-0.03	0.03	0.03	0.22	0.05	0.18	-0.03
1976	-0.11	0.09	0.11	0.07	-0.11	-0.08	0.01	-0.04	-0.05
1977	0.05	0.02	0.04	0.03	0.10	0.01	-0.11	0.08	-0.04
1978	0.04	-0.09	-0.00	-0.05	-0.02	-0.00	0.01	-0.10	-0.00
1979	-0.05	0.10	-0.01	0.11	-0.15	-0.01	0.01	0.01	-0.05
1980	0.00	0.00	0.00	0.00	0.00	0.00	0.00	0.00	0.00
AVERAGE:									
60-69	-.018	-.021	-.013	-.037	-.035	-.063	-.011	-.023	-.026
70-79	-.003	.017	.021	.032	-.031	.029	-.007	-.010	-.034
50-79	-.020	-.023	.006	-.027	-.030	-.036	.001	-.009	-.089
60-79	-.011	-.002	.004	-.003	-.033	-.017	-.009	-.017	-.030

The curves on Figures D.1 to D.9 in Appendix D reveal the pattern of technical change for the period 1960-1979. These curves reveal the different movements of technological change in this period. Because yearly shift factors in the 1950s exhibit some violent fluctuations, they are not included in the curves. In Bulgaria, Poland and China, violent fluctuations continued through the 1960s and 1970s. For other countries for the period 1960-1980, one might almost conclude from the graphs that the yearly shift factors are essentially constant in time, with some random fluctuations around a fixed mean.

As shown in Table 4.7, seven of the nine countries have negative values for the mean of shift factors in the sub-periods 1950-1979, eight countries in the sub-period 1960-1979, and five countries in the sub-period 1970-1979. This indicates, in general, that in the 1970s many countries were able to move back to positive gain in technical change. But the progress was small and varied among countries. In the sub-period 1960-1969, all countries experienced negative technical progress. The range of the average shift factors started from -0.063 in Romania to -0.011 in Yugoslavia. In the sub-period 1970-1979, only Bulgaria, Poland, Yugoslavia, USSR, and China had negative average technical progress. The average range for all countries was from -0.034 in China to 0.032 in Hungary. One may conclude that there is some evidence that technical change in the nine countries may have accelerated in the 1970s.

The upward and downward movements of total factor productivity in different countries can be easily observed in Figures 4.1 to 4.9 for individual countries. In most countries, the differences between partial productivity and total factor productivity index tend to diverge, though not necessarily, in the opposite direction. Furthermore, except for China, the divergence between labor productivity and total factor productivity is faster than the divergence between land productivity and total factor productivity. These divergences are in sharp contrast to the historical experience of other western countries where partial and total productivity moved in the same direction.

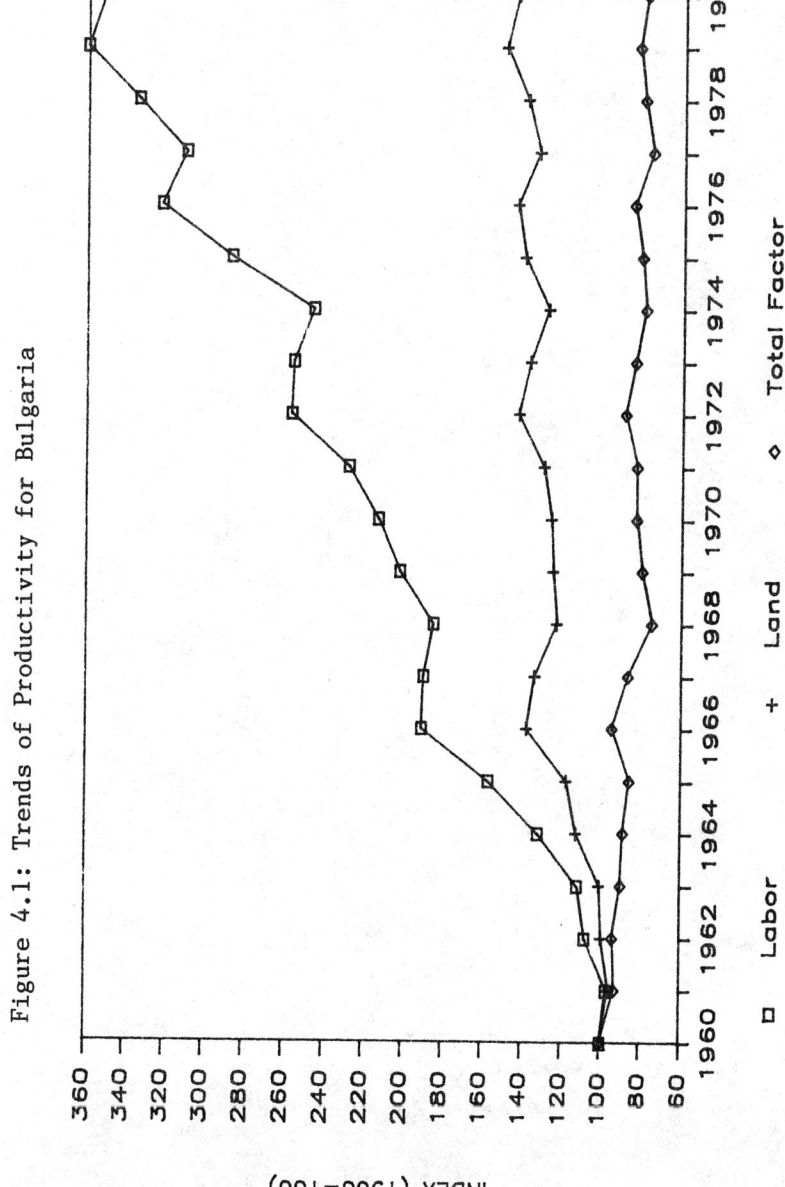

Figure 4.1: Trends of Productivity for Bulgaria

Figure 4.2: Trends of Productivity for Czechoslovakia

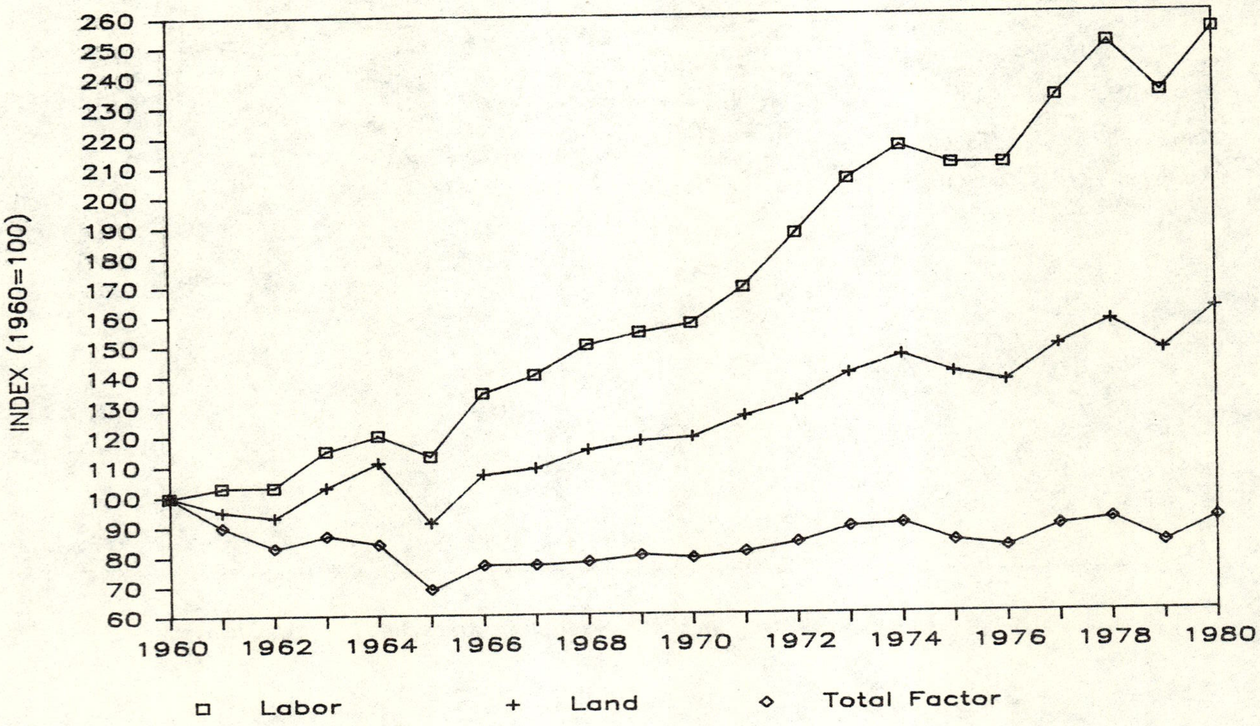

□ Labor   + Land   ◇ Total Factor

INDEX (1960=100)

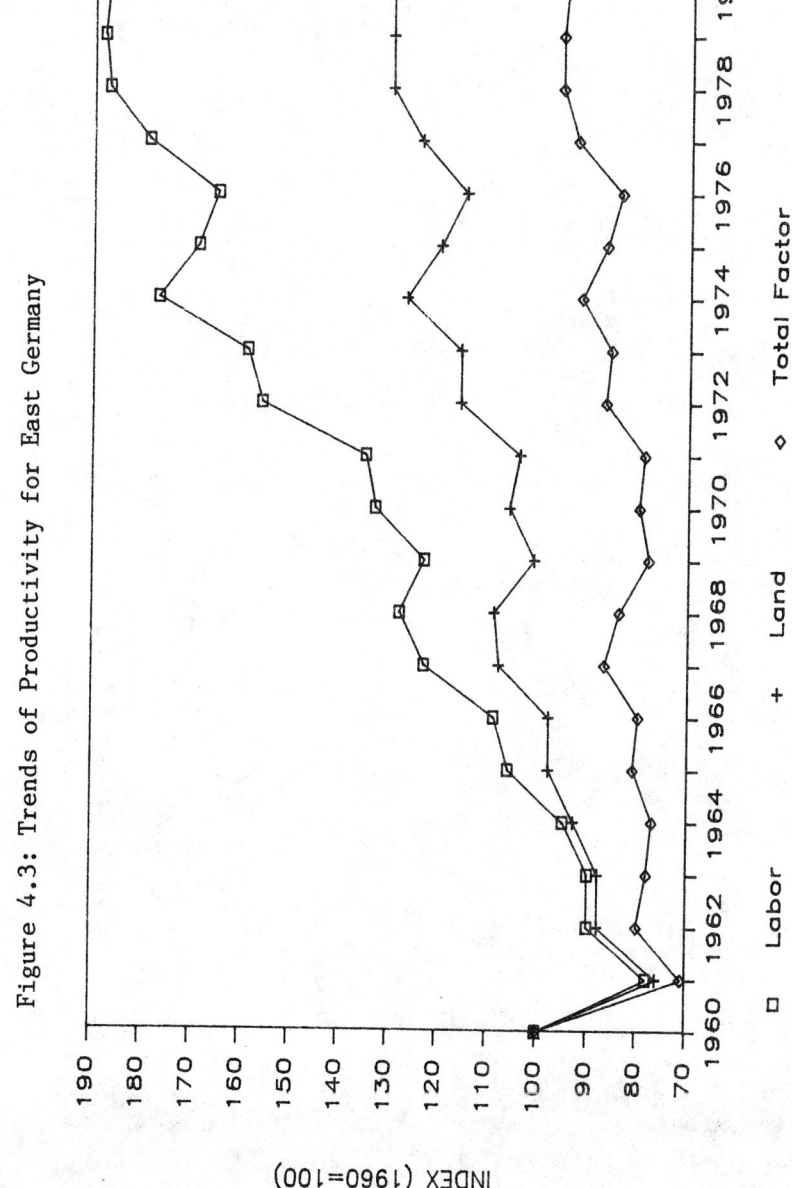

Figure 4.3: Trends of Productivity for East Germany

Figure 4.4: Trends of Productivity for Hungary

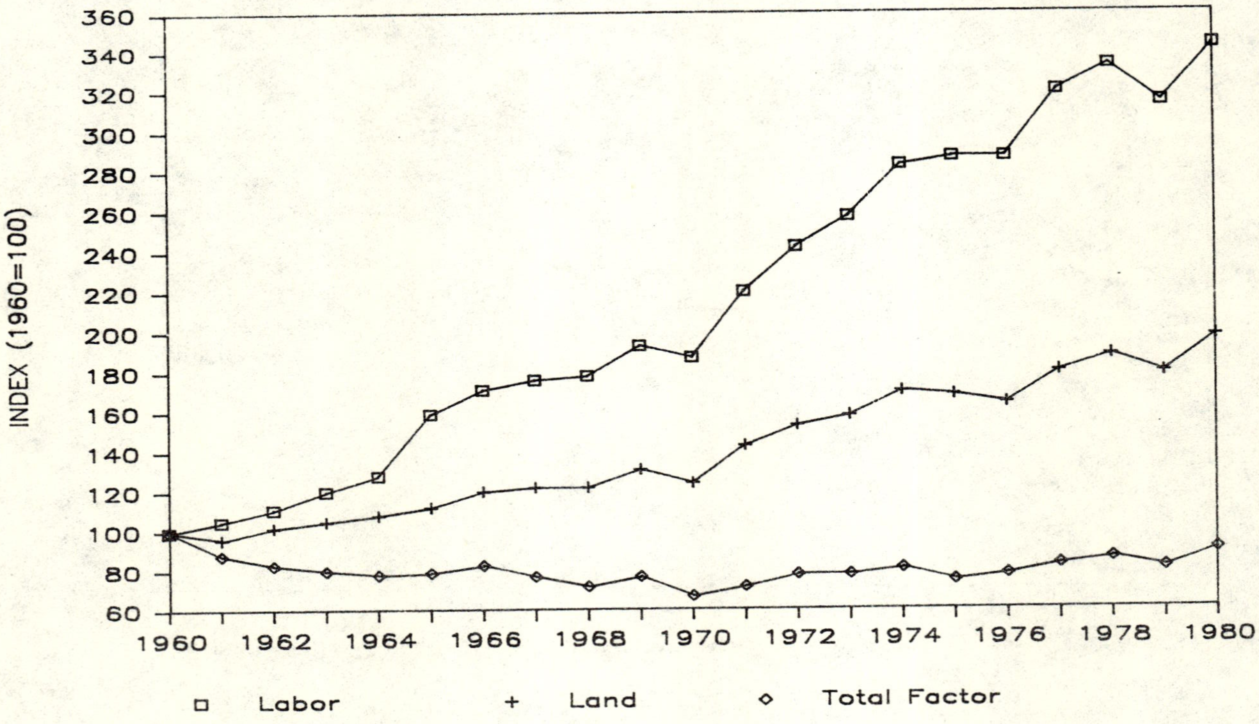

□ Labor + Land ◇ Total Factor

INDEX (1960=100)

75

Figure 4.5: Trends of Productivity for Poland

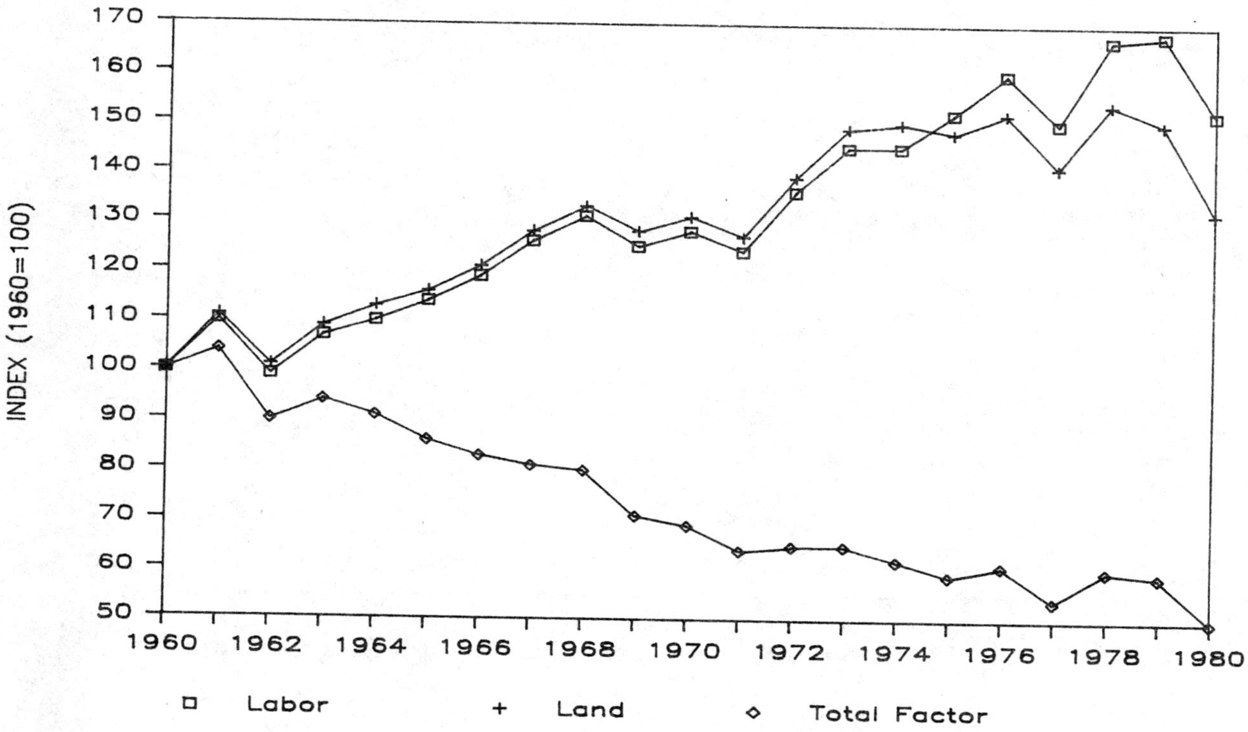

INDEX (1960=100)

□ Labor + Land ◇ Total Factor

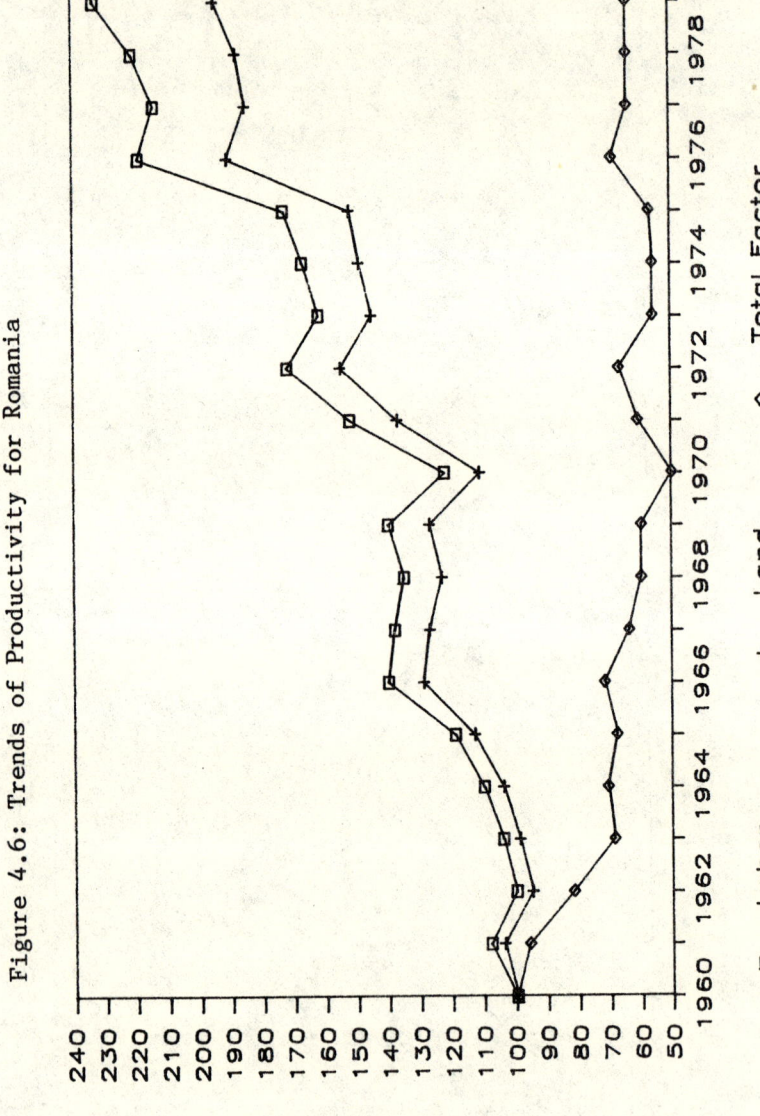

Figure 4.6: Trends of Productivity for Romania

Figure 4.7: Trends of Productivity for Yugoslavia

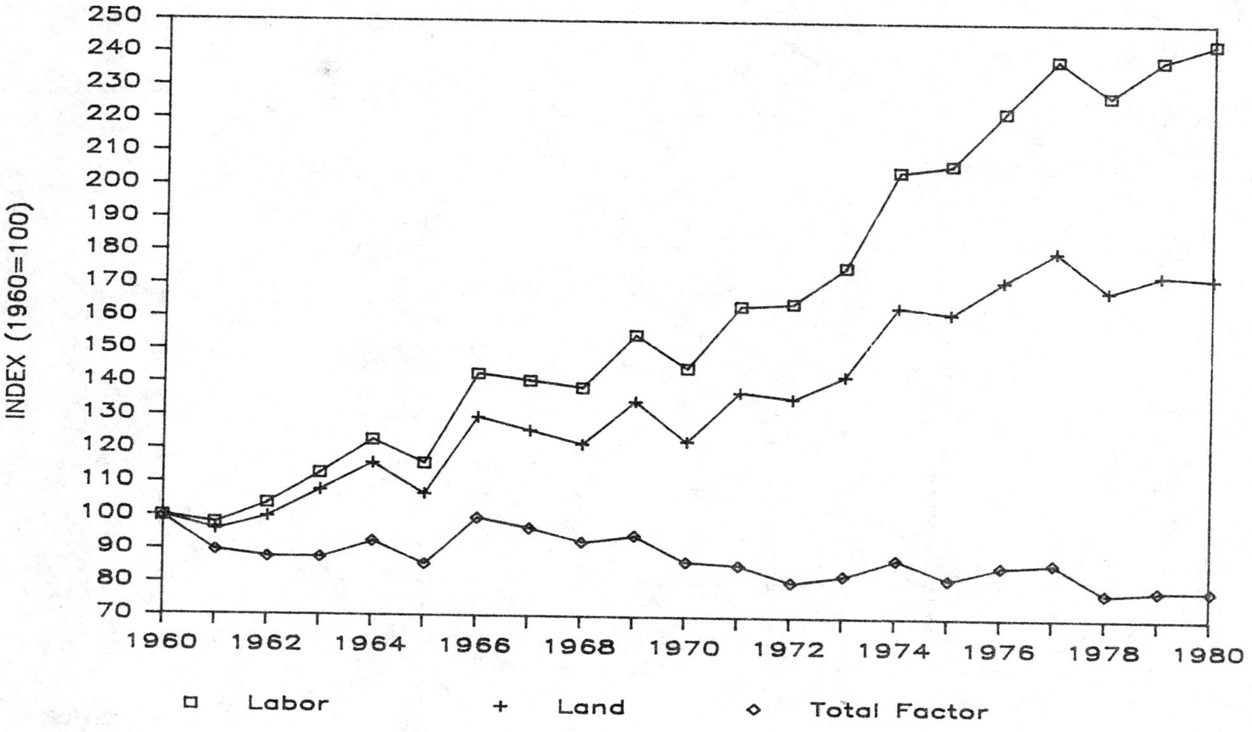

□ Labor   + Land   ◇ Total Factor

INDEX (1960=100)

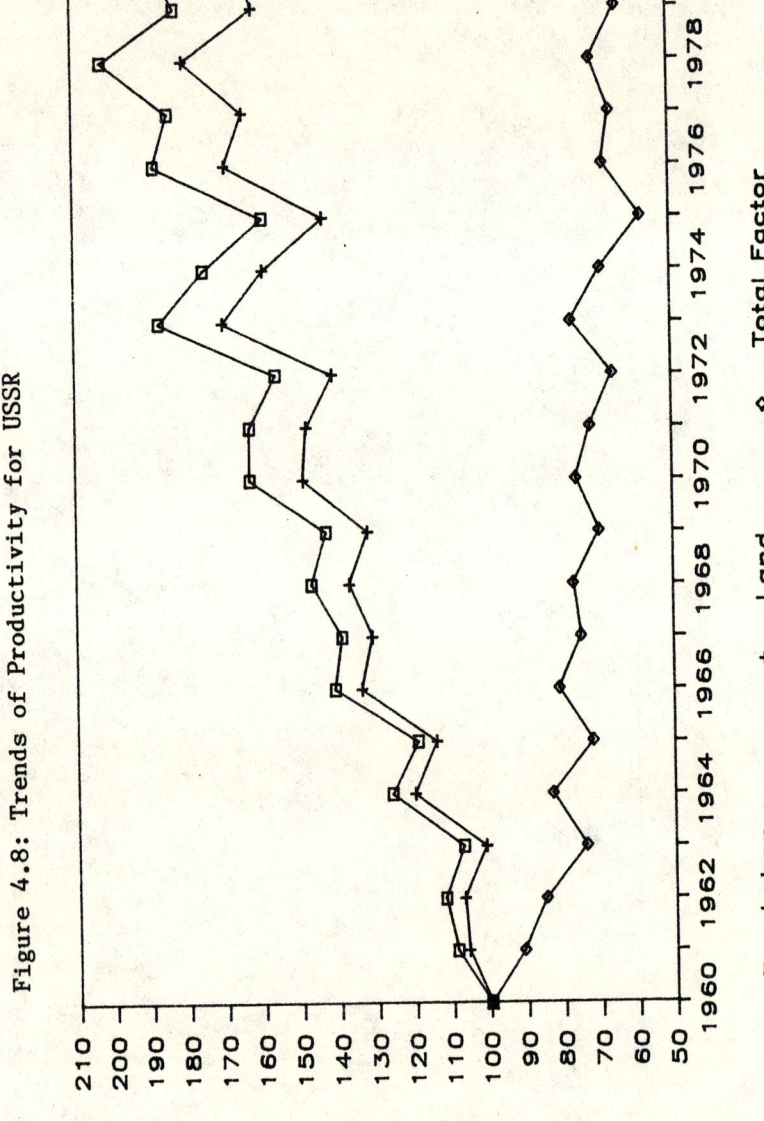

Figure 4.8: Trends of Productivity for USSR

Figure 4.9: Trends of Productivity for China

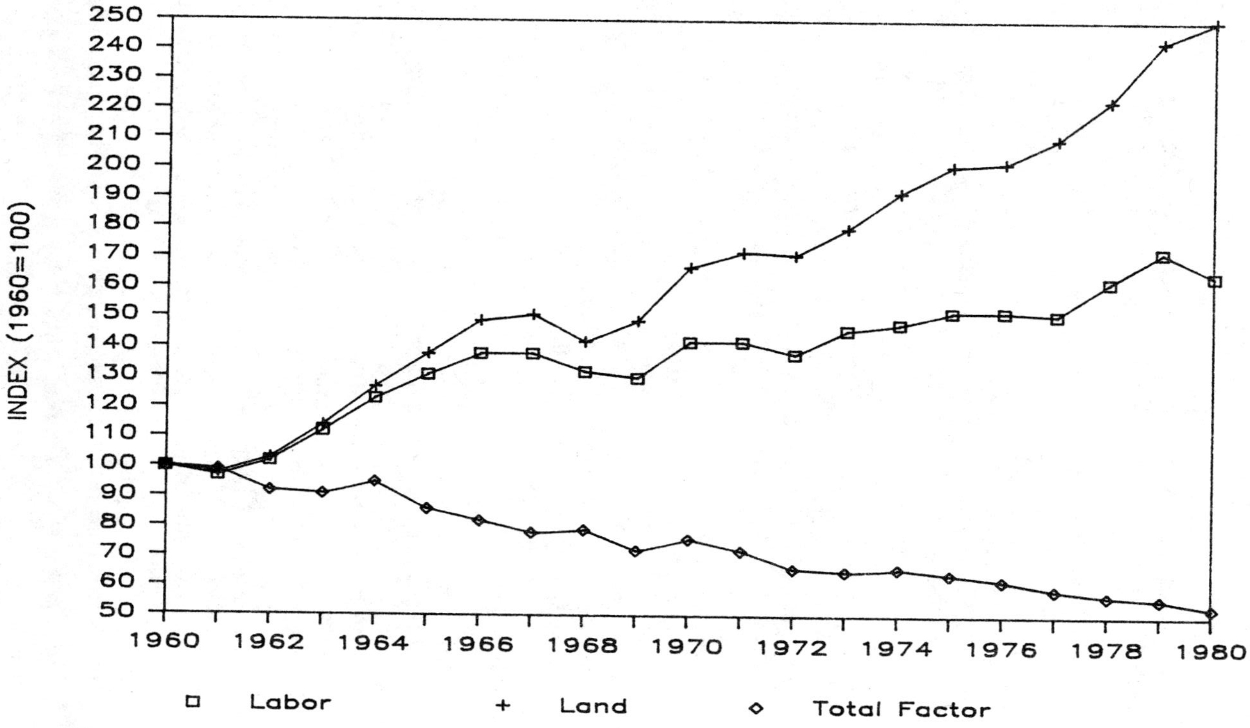

□ Labor   + Land   ◇ Total Factor

4.5 Summary

Several productivity indices - labor, land, arithmetic, and geometric measures - are presented in this chapter. The results indicate strong upward trends of labor productivity and land productivity. Both the arithmetic and geometric total factor productivity indices indicate strong downward trends in the 1950s and some upward and downward trends in the 1970s. Despite the fact that several countries appeared to be able to regain positive growth of total factor productivity in the 1970s, the divergence between partial and total factor productivity continued.

The results of the preceding analysis have both encouraging and discouraging aspects. The upward trends of labor productivity implies that the income of agricultural labor in these socialist countries is rising. But this interpretation is dangerous. The price policy and rigid control of labor mobility in these countries may divert the benefit of increased labor productivity to other parts of the economy instead of to agricultural labor.

The increase in land productivity is another encouraging aspect. It implies that even though these countries experienced food problems and had large scale economic reforms in the last three decades, they managed to increase food production out of an almost constant area. Although increased land productivity did not solve their food problems, it certainly released some of the pressure.

The discouraging aspect is that there are sharp decreases in total factor productivity in the 1950s, continuing through the 1970s. The divergence between partial and total factor productivity indicates that the gain in labor and land productivity may come from the loss of total factor productivity. Worse than that, it also implies that inefficiency and unbalanced cost structure are embodied in the socialist agricultural system. The divergence also indicates that the value of marginal products of fertilizer and machinery is less than their costs, which reduces economic growth of the country as a whole. If this is true, then these countries have paid a high cost for increased partial productivity. To be able to answer this question, the sources of productivity changes are examined in the next chapter. Comparisons of labor productivity and land productivity between socialist and non-socialist countries are also presented in Chapter V.

Notes

1. According to Vais (1981; 239) there are quite a few explanations for the existence of labor shortages in the East European countries. Deficiency in national planning is one of the reasons why labor plans call for greater increase in employment than is possible. The second reason is planners' unfounded optimism with regard to the growth of labor productivity. Thus, when the level of labor productivity is lower than planned, an increase in labor force to above plan level is necessary in order to fulfill output targets. The third reason is that enterprises intentionally underestimate the actual labor demand in order to get an easy approval of their new investment project. Therefore, labor shortage in East European countries is the result of creating more job opportunities than available labor supply.

2. For detailed testing procedures, readers are referred to Lung-Fai Wong, A Comparative Analysis of Agricultural Productivity Growth Among Socialist Countries, Ph.D. thesis, University of Minnesota, Minneapolis: March 1985.

5

Sources of Agricultural Productivity Changes

5.1 Introduction

Decreasing total factor productivity and increasing labor and land partial productivity characterize the performance of agriculture in the nine socialist countries. Moreover, despite the fact that the average annual growth rate of aggregate agricultural production in these countries is not low, several countries have difficulty maintaining growth at a healthy rate. Very often, countries have not been able to fulfill their production plans and have had to turn to the international market for additional food supplies.

Although growth in agricultural production can be achieved by replicating the existing level of factor inputs, this growth would be very costly to the economy. Another source of growth would be to increase productivity, but this does not come easily.

Over the last three decades, there have been several factors identified as sources of agricultural growth in the nine socialist countries. First, the Soviet Union expanded their sown acreage. Second, East European countries and the USSR invested heavily in fertilizer and irrigation systems in an effort to raise yield per hectare. Third, the Chinese intensified their use of land by multiple cropping and labor-intensive farming. Also in the Soviet Union, change in the efficiency of converting feed into livestock products as well as the increase in feed available for output of livestock products due to reduction in use of draft animals were both sources of total agricultural output growth as cited in the literature (Diamond, Bettis, Ramsson 1983; 146).

The sources of growth in agriculture mentioned above are generally well observed by economists. What has been overlooked is the role of technological change in agricultural growth and an accounting of the relative contribution of different factor inputs in the growth of agricultural output and agricultural productivity. Therefore, one of the purposes of this chapter is to examine these two issues.

In this chapter, the contribution of technology to productivity is identified by segregating the effects of increasing factor inputs from the effects of technical change. Then, by using a growth accounting procedure, sources of change in labor and land productivity are identified. The last section of this chapter is devoted to intercountry comparisons of productivity differences between socialist countries and non-socialist countries. The U.S. data is used to account for the differences in labor productivity for 1980, and Japan data is used to account for the differences in land productivity for the same time frame.

5.2 Contribution of Technical Change in Agricultural Growth

Technical change can be regarded as change in production coefficients resulting from the purposeful resource-using activity directed to the development of new knowledge embodied in designs, materials, or organizations.[1] Technical change is an important source of agricultural growth and is a costly, resource using activity. The evidence of declining total factor productivity indicates that technological change may not be the determinant of agricultural growth in the socialist countries. Instead, the increase of agricultural output may be caused mostly by increasing use of conventional inputs.

This conjecture can be easily checked by looking at the estimated metaproduction functions in Table 3.1 of Chapter III. The time trend variable is included in regression R4 to trace the direction of movement of the production function over time. After accounting for the contribution of conventional inputs and the agricultural research variable, this movement naturally represents the contribution of technical change. A significantly positive trend coefficient implies that the production function is shifting upward and a negative coefficient means it is shifting downward, as shown in Figure 5.1.

In the regression R4, the estimated time trend variable is not significantly different from zero. This indicates that technical change did not contribute to the progress of agricultural production in the period 1959-1980 in these socialist countries. A similar result can also be found in Brooks's estimation. Besides the cross-country time series regression that is presented in R30 in Table 3.4, Brooks also

Figure 5.1: Technical Change and Production Function

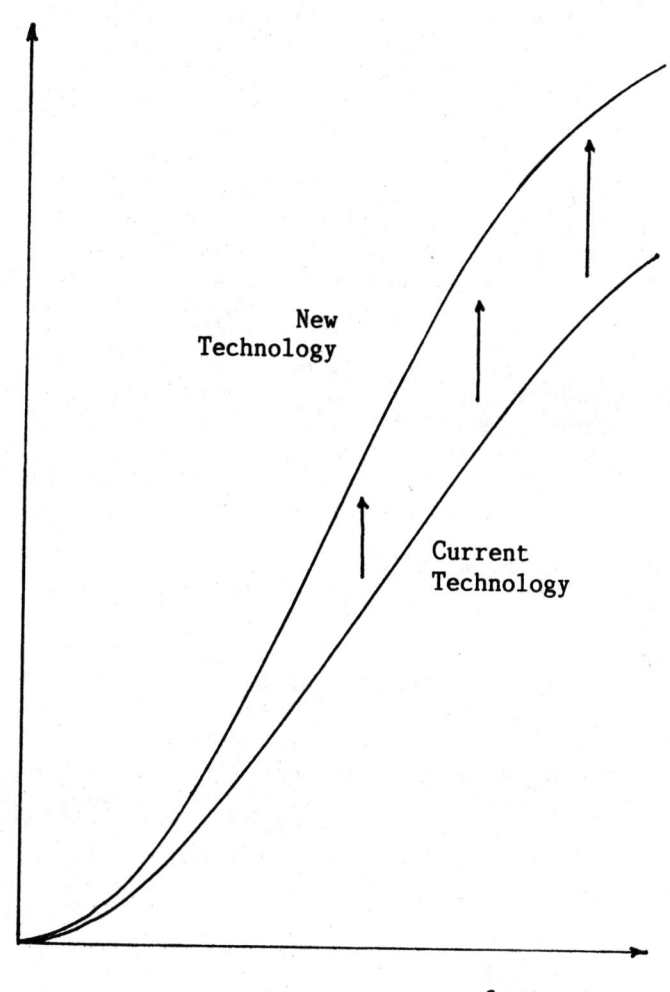

estimated a cross-section aggregate agricultural production function for the 15 Soviet republics. In her findings, the time trend coefficient has a value of 0.0002 and a t-statistic of 0.105 (Johnson and Brooks 1983; 147). Her results and estimates of this study both support the proposition that technical change in the Soviet Union and other socialist countries only has a minor role in agricultural growth.

In the beginning of Chapter II, it was stressed that change of output can come from two components: (a) alteration of the allocation of resources or factor inputs, and (b) achievement of technical change. Therefore, it is possible that a country may have had access to new technology, but the misallocation of resources may have overshadowed the contribution of the new technology so that the total factor productivity might not reflect the magnitude of technical change accurately. This appears to have happened in the nine socialist countries.

The interaction between technical change and misallocation of resources can be illustrated mathematically and graphically. Assuming a two-factor production function with output level at isoquant Q^1 and input level N^1 and K^1 for labor and capital respectively, the production function with technology F^1 can then be formulated as:

$$Q^1 = F^1(N^1, K^1) \tag{5.1}$$

Both the production function F^1 and the isocost for producing the quantity Q^1 are presented in Figure 5.2 at point A. Now, suppose a more efficient new technology F^2 is introduced so that more output can be produced with the same level of conventional inputs, which implies an inward shift of the isoquant curves while the isocost remains unchanged as long as input prices remains unchanged. Thus the producer can choose to produce the same amount of output Q^1 with less inputs required and hence smaller production cost, as shown in equation (5.2) and point B in Figure 5.2.

$$Q^1 = F^2(N^o, K^o) \tag{5.2}$$

On the other hand, with the more efficient new technology, the producer can choose to maintain the same level of inputs and production cost, thus producing more output, Q^2, as shown in equation (5.3) and at point C in Figure 5.2 which is still in competitive equilibrium.

$$Q^2 = F^2(N^1, K^1) \tag{5.3}$$

Figure 5.2: Technical Change and Misallocation of Resources

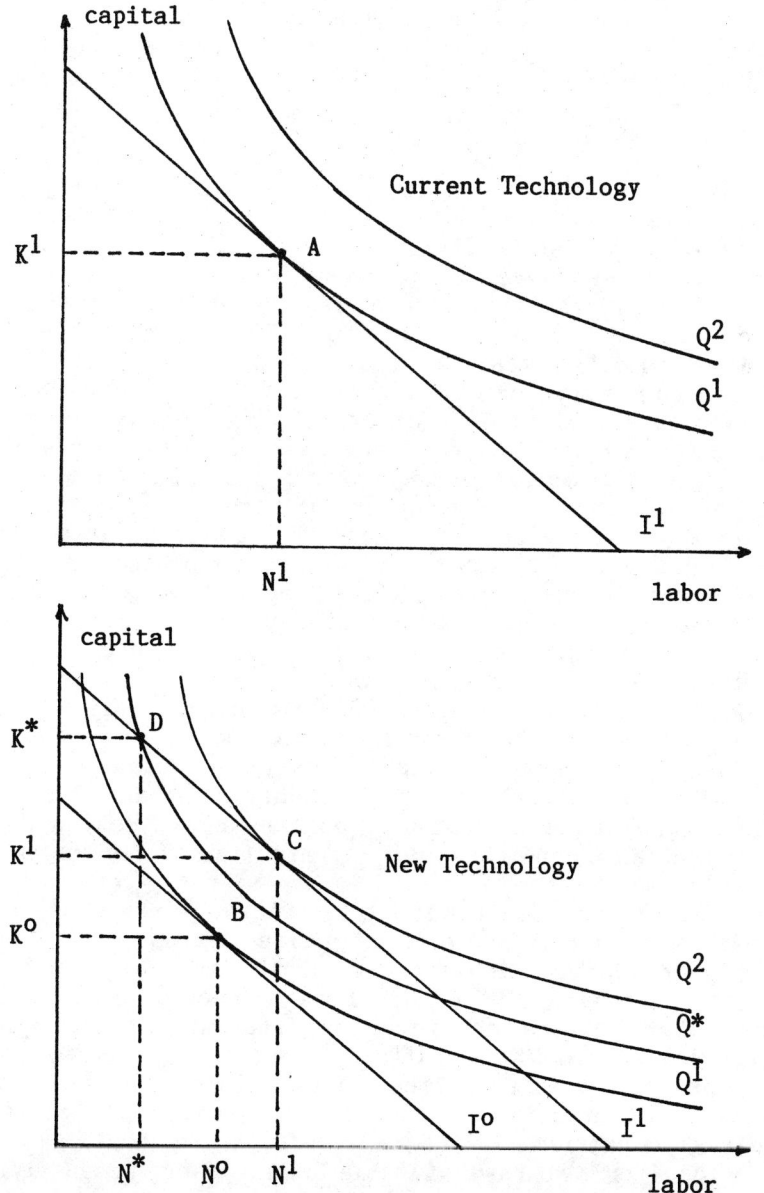

Now, suppose that a decision has been made to increase the level of output per labor by raising the level of capital and reducing the level of labor input. The new production point moves to point D, and output level becomes Q^*.

$$Q^* = F^2(N^*, K^*) \tag{5.4}$$

where $Q^* < Q^2$

In this case, even though the cost of production is the same between points C and D, the output level dropped from Q^2 to Q^* at point D. The loss due to this alteration of resources is the difference between Q^* and Q^2. Consequently, the gain from the new technology F^2 can be partially or totally taken away by the misallocation of resources. This kind of misallocation can easily occur in a state farm environment where the manager has little concern about minimizing the cost of production. The manager is more interested in fulfilling the administrative target or quota by maximizing the output level and/or the output per labor.

As mentioned in Chapter III, the estimated meta-production functions in Table 3.1 have positive and significant agricultural research coefficients. Since generating new technology is the major function of agricultural research, it can be concluded that new technology has been made available in these socialist countries. However, in order to determine the net gain from the new technology, the inequality between the gain (Q^2-Q^1) and the loss (Q^*-Q^2) needs to be examined. If the inequality is less than or equal to zero, it implies that the misallocation of resources wipes out all the benefit from technical change. If it is greater than zero, this means that a proportion of the contribution of technical change has been transmitted to agricultural growth.

The divergence between total factor productivity and partial productivity and the insignificant trend coefficients provides evidence that there is a misallocation of resources. On the other hand, the different magnitudes of divergences hinted that technical change makes different contributions to agricultural growth in different countries. In order to examine the different degrees of contribution by technical change, Table 5.1 was tabulated for the nine selected socialist countries.

The first two rows of Table 5.1 are labor productivity in 1960 and 1980, respectively. The difference between row 1 and row 2 is the gross growth caused by increases in inputs and/or technological advances during 1960-1980, shown in row

Table 5.1: Contribution of Technical Change in Agricultural Growth (1960-80)

	BUL	CZE	GDR	HUN	POL	ROM	YUG	USSR	PRC
(1)=Y/N, 1960	4.69	10.69	19.86	7.99	7.65	2.64	3.96	8.00	1.46
(2)=Y/N, 1980	16.46	27.12	37.19	27.44	11.61	6.28	9.65	15.14	2.39
(3)=(2)-(1)	11.77	16.43	17.33	19.45	3.96	3.64	5.69	7.14	.93
(4)=A(T), 1980	.79	.91	.95	.90	.50	.64	.79	.64	.53
(5)=(2)/(4)	20.84	29.80	39.15	30.49	23.22	9.81	12.22	23.66	4.51
(6)=(5)-(1)	16.15	19.11	19.29	22.50	15.57	7.17	8.26	15.66	3.05

GROWTH EXPLAINED BY:

INCREASED INPUT(%)

| (7)=(6)/(3)*100 | 137.17 | 116.33 | 111.29 | 115.68 | 393.18 | 197.05 | 145.08 | 219.28 | 327.90 |

TECHNICAL CHANGE(%)

| (8)=100.00-(7) | -37.17 | -16.33 | -11.29 | -15.68 | -293.18 | -97.05 | -45.08 | -119.28 | -227.90 |

3. Row 4 is the total factor productivity in 1980 (from Table 4.6). Hence, the "corrected" productivity in 1980, net of technical change, can be obtained by dividing row 2 with row 4. The "corrected" productivity in row 5 minus row 1 is the adjusted growth from 1960-1980, net of technical change, as shown in row 6. Therefore, the growth that can be explained by the alteration of input level is the ratio of adjusted growth (row 6) to the gross growth (row 3). And the unexplained proportion of growth is naturally attributable to technical change, as shown in row 8.

Figures in the last row of Table 5.1 suggest that all countries exhibited no gain from technical change, which implies that agricultural growth must have come from increased use of factor inputs. This means that despite the fact that the production function in these countries may have shifted upward over the past 20 years, the production point moved away from the expansion path in a way that may have counteracted the benefit of technical change. Figures in Table 5.1 also shown that Czechoslovakia, East Germany, and Hungary have smaller negative values which indicates that misallocation of resources was less serious in these countries.

5.3 Accounting for Sources of Productivity Growth

All the evidence presented so far points to the fact that the achievement of agricultural growth in the nine socialist countries came with a high cost. Labor and land productivity have substantially increased, but technical change plays only a small role in this process. Much of the growth resulted from moving along the production function rather than from a upward shift of the production function. The use of factor inputs is increasing at a much larger rate than the growth of output. The purpose of this section is to segregate the effects of individual factors on productivity and to examine the sources of productivity changes.

5.3.1 Sources of Labor Productivity Change

As stated earlier, the primary interest in estimating production coefficients is to use them to accounting for changes in labor and land productivity in the socialist countries between 1960 and 1980. The results obtained from estimating a pooled time series cross-country production function can be interpreted as the metaproduction function for these socialist countries. The sum of the estimated coefficients indicates that it is reasonable to assume a linearly homogeneous production function. In combination with the Euler theorem, this implies that the percentage differences in output per labor over time can be expressed as the sum of percentage differences in conventional and non-conventional inputs per labor, weighted by their respective production elasticities as shown in equation (5.5). Since agricultural research should be considered one of the sources of productivity change, it should be included in the growth accounting procedure. Hence, the estimated production elasticities in R7 in Table 3.1 are used in the following sections. A similar relation can also be established for land productivity.

$$\frac{\Delta(Y/N)}{(Y/N)_0} = 0.043 \frac{\Delta(L/N)}{(L/N)_0} + 0.212 \frac{\Delta(F/N)}{(F/N)_0} + 0.135 \frac{\Delta(M/N)}{(M/N)_0}$$
$$+ 0.368 \frac{\Delta(S/N)}{(S/N)_0} + 0.07 \frac{\Delta(R/N)}{(R/N)_0} + \text{unexplained}$$
(5.5)

In Table 5.2, figures in the "percent" columns represent the percentage change in agricultural labor productivity from 1960 to 1980. For example, the percent change in labor productivity is computed from the change in labor productivity during the period 1960-1980 divided by labor productivity in 1980. Other entries in the "percent" columns account for the percentage change of factor/labor ratios during the same period. The "index" columns account for the percentage of change in productivity that can be explained by the respective factor inputs, with the first row being set to 100. For example, the change in labor productivity between 1960 and 1980 in Bulgaria was 71.50 percent of the 1980 productivity level. Of this 71.50 percent, 26.12 (or 37 percent of 71.50) was attributable to the changes in resource endowments in Bulgaria.

The "index" columns are constructed for the purpose of comparison. As shown in the "index" columns, 20 to 40 percent (depending on the individual country) of the change in labor productivity in the USSR and East European countries can be explained by the change in resource endowment during the period 1960-1980. This indicates that the increase in land/labor ratio and the livestock/labor ratio in these countries accounts for approximately a quarter of the increase in labor productivity. The negative percentage for China is due to a decrease in the land/labor ratio and livestock/labor ratio.

Interestingly enough, the total change in fertilizer and machinery explained between 43-87 percent of the increase in labor productivity. This could have an important policy

Table 5.2: Accounting for Changes in Agricultural Labor Productivity Among Socialist Countries (1960 vs 1980)

COUNTRY	BULGARIA		CZECHOSLAVAKIA		E. GERMANY		HUNGARY		POLAND	
	percent	index	percent	index	percent	index	percent	index	percent	index
Changes in Labor Productivity (%)	71.50	100	60.58	100	46.61	100	70.88	100	34.11	100
Resource Endowment	26.12	37	18.67	31	17.20	37	21.26	30	13.59	40
Land	2.54	4	1.58	3	1.31	3	1.83	3	.55	2
Livestock	23.58	33	17.09	28	15.88	34	19.43	27	13.04	38
Technical Inputs	31.35	44	28.20	47	21.70	47	30.24	43	29.81	87
Fertilizer	19.42	27	17.51	29	12.68	27	19.88	28	17.31	51
Machinery	11.93	17	10.69	18	9.02	19	10.36	15	12.51	37
Agri. Research	6.19	9	5.66	9	5.66	12	5.99	8	5.66	17
Explained Total	63.66	89	52.53	87	44.55	96	57.48	81	49.06	144
Unexplained Total	7.85	11	8.05	13	2.06	4	13.39	19	-14.95	-44

Table 5.2 (continued)

COUNTRY	ROMANIA		YUGOSLAVIA		USSR		CHINA	
	percent	index	percent	index	percent	index	percent	index
Changes in Labor Productivity (%)	57.89	100	58.96	100	47.16	100	38.91	100
Resource Endowment	16.38	28	11.60	20	13.59	29	-4.73	-12
Land	.76	1	1.24	2	.54	1	-2.26	-6
Livestock	15.62	27	10.36	18	13.05	28	-2.47	-6
Technical Inputs	30.18	52	29.86	51	28.03	59	31.57	81
Fertilizer	20.10	35	17.12	29	19.68	42	19.42	50
Machinery	10.08	17	12.75	22	8.34	18	12.15	31
Agri. Research	5.96	10	4.43	8	4.67	10	6.16	16
Explained Total	52.52	91	45.90	78	46.28	98	33.00	85
Unexplained Total	5.37	9	13.06	22	.87	2	5.90	15

implication. It suggests that industrial inputs have been the major source of labor productivity growth in socialist countries - particularly the sizeable contribution from fertilizer.

The changes in the ratio of agricultural research to labor explained on the average 11 percent of the increase of labor productivity. Although agricultural research in Poland and China explained more than 15 percent of the changes, this was still quite low. Another study showed that human capital accounted for 35 percent of the differences in labor productivity between a group of developing and developed countries (Hayami and Ruttan 1971; 97).

Several generalizations are worth mentioning here. In all of the countries, fertilizer is the single most important source of change in labor productivity. On the other hand, resource endowment is not as important as might have been expected. Changes in the livestock/labor ratio accounted for almost a quarter of the change in labor productivity. The importance of land is evenly distributed among countries except China, whose land/labor ratio has been decreasing rather than increasing. Machinery is another important source for productivity change. Its effect is as large as 37 percent which, in some cases, is larger than the effect of livestock. Following machinery, agricultural research is another important source of change in labor productivity. This is especially true in Poland and China, but somewhat less so in other socialist countries. This suggests that other socialist countries are capable of increasing their labor productivity by expanding the capacity of their agricultural research and capturing more benefit from new technologies.

Altogether, the five factor/labor ratios explained 80 percent or more of the changes in labor productivity. In the case of Poland, one might interpret this exceptional case as indicating that all labor productivity changes are explained by the changes of the six factor/labor ratios. Hence, none of the change is unexplained.

The unexplained portion may be caused by other factors such as investment in infrastructure, climate condition, or shifts in policy. Another possible explanation for the unexplained portion is the change in managerial scheme. Collectivization is a distinct feature of socialist agriculture. One of its objectives is to mobilize rural labor to perform non-farm tasks collectively, such as building roads, schools, and dams. Such kinds of non-farm activities constrain the farmers' ability to engage in agricultural production. Although this policy prevailed in these socialist countries in the 1960s, it was less popular in the 1970s. Consequently, labor productivity might have increased due to these shifts in the managerial scheme, which are not explained by the changes in conventional inputs.

5.3.2 Sources of Land Productivity Change

The growth accounting for changes in land productivity from 1960-1980 is presented in Table 5.3. In general, except for China, the percentage change in land productivity was less than that for labor productivity, and was less than 50 percent of the current productivity level. Moreover, the labor/land ratios in East European countries and the Soviet Union sizably declined. This contributed negatively to the changes of land productivity. For example, the negative figure in the labor factor for Bulgaria can be explained as follows: had the labor/land ratio remained unchanged in that period, Bulgaria would have had another 24.72 percent increase in their land productivity.

The reason for the positive labor percentage in China is obvious. Unlike all East European countries and the Soviet Union which had a sizeable decrease in the number of agricultural laborers, the Chinese had a positive growth in agricultural labor. This, combined with other factors, made the percentage change in China's land productivity the largest of the nine socialist countries.

Again, as in the case of changes in labor productivity, the increase in fertilizer/land ratio was also the single most important source for the changes in land productivity for all nine countries. The livestock/land ratios in Bulgaria, Hungary, Czechoslovakia, and Yugoslavia showed a surprisingly small rate of change and a small contribution to the change in land productivity. In contrast, agricultural research was important in the explanation of changes in land productivity. It explained as much as 22 percent of the land productivity changes in East Germany and Poland.

Two more observations can be made from Table 5.3. Agricultural research in East European countries and the Soviet Union was, in general, a more important source for the changes of land productivity than for changes in labor productivity. The reverse holds true for China. But agricultural research still had a relatively lower effect in the socialist countries than in non-socialist countries. The negative percentage in the unexplained row for Poland supports the notion that a large share of the productivity growth, both in land and labor, can be explained by the change in conventional inputs and agricultural research.

Table 5.3: Accounting for Changes in Agricultural Land Productivity Among Socialist Countries (1960 vs 1980)

COUNTRY	BULGARIA		CZECHOSLAVAKIA		E. GERMANY		HUNGARY		POLAND	
	percent	index	percent	index	percent	index	percent	index	percent	index
Changes in Land Productivity (%)	30.54	100	37.75	100	23.18	100	49.30	100	24.50	100
Resource Endowment	-20.14	-66	-4.28	-11	-.84	-4	-6.18	-13	7.07	29
Labor	-24.72	-81	-9.96	-26	-7.55	-33	-12.74	-26	-2.51	-10
Livestock	4.58	15	5.68	15	6.70	29	6.56	13	9.58	39
Technical Inputs	26.53	87	24.43	65	15.99	69	26.93	55	29.10	119
Fertilizer	16.86	55	15.37	41	8.94	39	18.89	38	16.74	68
Machinery	9.68	32	9.06	24	7.05	30	8.03	16	12.36	50
Agri. Research	5.02	16	4.88	13	5.07	22	5.23	11	5.47	22
Explained Total	11.41	37	25.03	66	20.22	87	25.98	53	41.64	170
Unexplained Total	19.13	63	12.72	34	2.96	13	23.32	47	-17.14	-70

Table 5.3 (continued)

COUNTRY	ROMANIA		YUGOSLAVIA		USSR		CHINA	
	percent	index	percent	index	percent	index	percent	index
Changes in Land Productivity (%)	48.83	100	42.34	100	39.64	100	59.95	100
Resource Endowment	7.36	15	-7.31	-17	7.23	18	16.98	28
Labor	-3.70	-8	-6.96	-16	-2.45	-6	5.92	10
Livestock	11.06	23	-.34	-1	9.68	24	11.05	18
Technical Inputs	29.21	60	27.91	66	27.08	68	32.65	54
Fertilizer	19.86	41	15.46	37	19.47	49	20.03	33
Machinery	9.34	19	12.44	29	7.61	19	12.61	21
Agri. Research	5.73	12	3.39	8	4.34	11	6.45	11
Explained Total	42.30	87	23.99	57	38.64	97	56.08	94
Unexplained Total	6.53	13	18.35	43	1.00	3	3.87	6

Before closing this section, the question of the sensitivity of this accounting procedure merits attention. The above analyses are for the period 1960-1980, but only the data of 1960 and 1980 were used in the accounting. Hence, it only accounts for the discrete changes between these two years while changes occurring during that time are not accounted for. This implies an accounting bias problem for those countries that experienced sharp decreases or sharp increases in productivity in either 1960 or 1980. Data for China and Poland for example, is sensitive to this accounting procedure. As pointed out in earlier chapters, 1960 was one of the worst years for Chinese agriculture. Consequently, the percentage change in labor productivity and land productivity between 1960 and 1980 is overestimated. On the other hand, Poland had a substantial decrease in agricultural growth in 1980. Therefore, the percentage change of productivity for Poland between 1960 and 1980 is underestimated. These two examples make it clear that the growth accounting procedure is quite sensitive to the years of comparison. In the event that drastic changes occurred, the interpretation of the results should be done cautiously.

Another sensitive area of the growth accounting procedure is estimating the value of factor shares. In these analyses, the production elasticities of the estimated metaproduction function were used for factor shares. It is assumed that all countries have the same set of factor shares for the entire period 1960-1980. Since the values of factor shares have a large effect on the calculation of percentage change, it is possible to underestimate or overestimate the importance of certain factors in the accounting procedure. For instance, the small value of the factor share assigned to land (0.043) may be the reason why changes in land/labor ratio explained only a small proportion of changes in labor productivity.

5.4 Intercountry Comparisons of Productivity Differences

The tables and figures presented in this and the previous chapter highlighted the differences in agricultural productivity between socialist countries. The differences in labor and land productivity among these countries are indeed great. Measured in wheat units, agricultural output per labor ranged from 1.46 (China) to 19.86 (E.Germany) in 1960 and from 2.39 (China) to 37.19 (E.Germany) in 1980. The agricultural output per hectare, measured in wheat units, ranged from 0.38 (USSR) to 3.79 (East Germany) in 1960 and 0.63 (USSR) to 4.94 (East Germany) in 1980.

Table 5.4: Intercounty Productivity Series, 1960 and 1980

	LABOR PRODUCTIVITY		LAND PRODUCTIVITY	
SOCIALIST COUNTRIES	1960	1980	1960	1980
BULGARIA(BUL)	4.69	16.46	1.92	2.76
CZECHOSLOVAKIA(CZE)	10.69	27.12	2.35	3.77
EAST GERMANY(GDR)	19.86	37.19	3.79	4.94
HUNGARY(HUN)	7.99	27.44	2.07	4.08
POLAND(POL)	7.65	11.61	1.99	2.64
ROMANIA(ROM)	2.64	6.28	1.23	2.41
YUGOSLAVIA(YUG)	3.96	9.65	1.27	2.20
SOVIET UNION(USSR)	8.00	15.14	0.38	0.63
CHINA(PRC)	1.46	2.39	0.88	2.20
NON-SOCIALIST COUNTRIES				
ARGENTINA(AR)	34.93	63.78	0.30	0.44
AUSTRALIA(AU)	103.84	256.23	0.09	0.15
AUSTRIA(AS)	30.48	90.55	2.32	3.49
CANADA(CA)	66.12	193.60	0.58	0.85
DENMARK(DE)	46.38	131.25	4.60	5.58
EGYPT(EG)	4.41	4.63	6.90	9.18
FINLAND(FI)	30.46	104.16	2.02	3.34
FRANCE(FR)	32.37	101.79	2.49	4.09
WEST GERMANY(WG)	37.15	113.67	4.00	5.99
GREECE(GR)	9.09	25.75	1.22	2.21
INDIA(IN)	2.15	3.11	1.06	1.58
ITALY(IT)	14.52	47.96	3.40	4.97
JAPAN(JA)	10.29	27.84	8.71	12.23
MEXICO(ME)	5.15	7.49	0.27	0.52
NEW ZEALAND(NZ)	140.55	234.96	1.21	1.71
PHILIPPINES(PH)	3.29	5.87	2.11	3.47
PORTGUAL(PO)	7.14	18.68	1.70	1.98
SWEDEN(SW)	42.98	122.73	2.33	3.20
SWITZERLAND(SI)	29.18	77.64	3.38	4.53
SYRIA(SY)	7.23	10.00	0.31	0.65
TAIWAN,CHINA(TA)	7.14	12.37	10.34	18.65
TURKEY(TU)	6.07	12.72	0.59	1.09
UNITED KINGDOM(UK)	47.02	116.26	1.94	3.09
UNITED STATES(US)	93.81	285.06	0.80	1.16

Figure 5.3: Intercountry Comparison of Productivity Trends

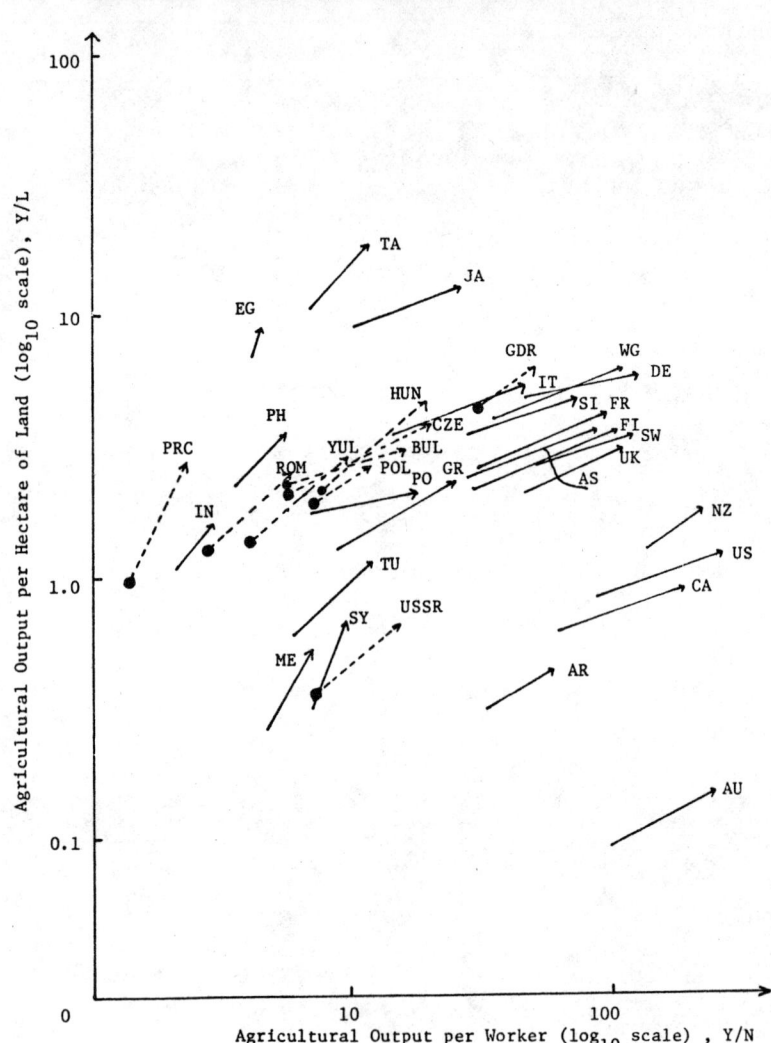

The differences in agricultural productivity among non-socialist countries are even greater. In 1980, labor productivity ranged from 3.11 (India) to 285.06 (USA), and land productivity ranged from 0.15 (Australia) to 12.23 (Japan). The differences of such a comparison can be observed in Table 5.4 and Figure 5.3 where the agricultural labor and agricultural land productivity for the nine socialist countries, together with 24 non-socialist countries, are plotted on one graph.[2]

As shown in Figure 5.3, the pattern of agricultural productivity growth in the nine socialist countries also diverges to three different paths that are similar to those observed by Hayami and Ruttan (1971; 69). Extended outward from the origin, the three paths can be classified as: (a) the path characterized by the group of countries with the new continents including New Zealand, Australia, Canada, and the U.S.A., where favorable man/land ratios prevail; (b) the path characterized by Asian countries where unfavorable man/land ratios prevail, including such countries as Japan and China; and (c) the path characterized by European countries, both in the East and the West, where relative factor endowments are between the (a) and (b) groups.

These growth patterns indicate the different processes of agricultural growth under alternative man/land ratios common in both socialist and non-socialist countries. The relative availability of resources in the agricultural sector not only determines the growth pattern, it is also the source of differences in land and labor productivity between socialist and non-socialist countries.

Besides examining the sources of change in labor and land productivity in the nine socialist countries, it is also interesting to examine the sources of differences in productivity between socialist and non-socialist countries as of 1980. The U.S. was chosen for the labor productivity comparison because it has achieved exceptionally high levels of labor productivity; Japan was chosen for the land productivity comparison because it has achieved exceptionally high levels of land productivity.[3]

5.4.1 Sources of Labor Productivity Differences

The results of comparisons of labor productivity between the socialist countries and the U.S. as of 1980 are summarized in Table 5.5. As shown in the first row, labor productivity is substantially higher in U.S. agriculture. More than one-third of the difference can be explained by differences in resource endowment, and another one-third can

Table 5.5: Accounting for Agricultural Labor Productivity Differences, Socialist vs USA, 1980

COUNTRY	BULGARIA			CZECHOSLAVAKIA			E. GERMANY			HUNGARY			POLAND		
	percent	index	percent	index	percent	index	percent	index	percent	index	percent	index	percent	index	percent index
Difference in labor productivity (%)	92.39	100		87.47	100		82.82	100		87.32	100		94.63	100
Resource endowment	38.08	41		36.34	42		34.30	41		37.83	43		38.10	40
Land	4.16	5		4.13	5		4.13	5		4.15	5		4.20	4
Livestock	33.92	37		32.21	37		30.17	36		33.69	39		33.90	36
Technical inputs	32.65	35		30.06	34		29.68	36		31.08	36		32.62	34
Fertilizer	19.16	21		16.58	19		16.20	20		17.59	20		19.13	20
Machinery	13.49	15		13.48	15		13.48	16		13.49	15		13.49	14
Agri. Research	5.45	6		-1.14	-1		3.03	4		4.51	5		4.97	5
Explained total	76.18	82		65.27	75		67.01	81		73.43	84		75.68	80
Unexplained total	16.21	18		22.20	25		15.80	19		13.89	16		18.95	20

Table 5.5 (continued)

COUNTRY	ROMANIA			YUGOSLAVIA			USSR			CHINA		
	percent	index	percent	index	percent	index	percent	index	percent	index	percent	index
Difference in labor productivity (%)	97.10	100		95.54	100		93.00	100		98.89	100	
Resource endowment	39.72	41		39.24	41		36.63	39		40.61	41	
Land	4.24	4		4.20	4		3.75	4		4.28	4	
Livestock	35.48	37		35.04	37		32.88	35		36.33	37	
Technical inputs	34.15	35		34.04	36		32.80	35		34.17	35	
Fertilizer	20.66	21		20.56	22		19.31	21		20.67	21	
Machinery	13.50	14		13.49	14		13.49	15		13.50	14	
Agri. Research	5.93	6		5.97	6		4.93	5		6.90	7	
Explained total	79.80	82		79.26	83		74.35	80		81.68	83	
Unexplained total	17.30	18		16.29	17		18.65	20		17.21	17	

103

be explained by differences in technical inputs. Differences in agricultural research explain less than 10 percent of the difference in labor productivity. This is quite low relative to the estimates of Hayami and Ruttan (1971; 91) whose comparisons between a group of developing countries and developed countries showed that human capital accounted for 35 percent of the differences in labor productivity.

The small effect of agricultural research in the explanation of the labor productivity difference between the U.S. and socialist countries indicates that merely expanding the capacity (scientist manyears) of agricultural research in socialist countries may not be sufficient to reduce the labor productivity gap between socialist countries and the U.S. It appears that the rigid structure of the research system may have diffused the effort and effect of agricultural research in socialist countries. Second, it indicates that the contribution of agricultural research to labor productivity in these socialist countries is as important as in the U.S., at least in a normality sense. Further discussion of the role of research in socialist agriculture will be presented later in this chapter.

5.4.2 Sources of Land Productivity Differences

Similar analysis can also be conducted about land productivity. Table 5.6 summarizes the results of comparing land productivity between the socialist countries and Japan as of 1980. The difference in the livestock/land ratio is the most important source of explanation for the differences in land productivity; while labor, machinery and fertilizer have the same degree of importance. The agricultural research ratio is not as important as other factors in the explanation of differences of land productivity between the socialist countries and Japan - it explained less than 10 percent of the differences.

For the majority of these countries, except China, more than 80 percent of the differences in land productivity can be explained by the differences in resource endowments, technical inputs, and agricultural research. Differences in these three categories explained only 70 percent of the land productivity differences between Japan and China. This suggests that there are more than factor/land ratios involved in the explanation of differences in land productivity between these two countries.

It is important to note that special attention is needed for the interpretation of agricultural research as the source of productivity changes over time within individual countries and productivity differences among socialist countries and non-socialist countries. The agricultural research variable used in this study is a physical count of the number of scientists involved in agricultural research, measured in scientist manyears. The variable represents, to a certain degree, the country's capacity for performing research in the agricultural sector. It does not, however, depict the quality of research or the effectiveness of the research and extension system.

Agricultural research requires more than intellectual ability. Results must be drawn from the collaborated efforts of experimentation and trial and error. The advancement of facilities is equally important; agricultural scientists need to be supported with adequate and appropriate equipment. Countries that are in early stages of development, or in an unstable stage, may have to suffer the consequences of lack of appropriate instruments. China, for instance, is committed to modernizing its agricultural sector before the turn of this century, but the ten years of turbulence in 1966-1976 slowed down the research effort substantially. Therefore, merely counting the scientist manyears does not reflect the actual research performance and capacity. The quality and productivity of the research system needs to be taken into consideration in comparisons of cross-country productivity.

In recent history, the Soviet Union also had an unpleasant period of agricultural development. The direction of research was controlled and misled by the Soviet agricultural scientist Lysenko. The quality of research was largely damaged by the so-called "legacy of Lysenko" which overshadowed the Russian research community in the 1940s and the 1950s (Joravsky 1972). Although Lysenko stepped down in 1964, his influence could still be felt years later. The Lysenko fiasco has no doubt detracted ability to generate new agricultural technology in both the Soviet Union and East European countries. At the same time, agricultural production can only benefit from the results of research, not the capacity of research. Therefore, even though the investment in research was not small and the potential of agricultural research was large, it did not act as an important factor in the growth in productivity in these socialist countries. Consequently, even though the difference in research capacity between the U.S. and the socialist countries is not large and agricultural research is not a major source of the differences in productivity, agricultural research quality may be indeed an important explanation for the differences in productivity between these countries.

Table 5.6: Accounting for Agricultural Land Productivity Differences, Socialist vs Japan, 1980

COUNTRY	BULGARIA		CZECHOSLAVAKIA		E. GERMANY		HUNGARY		POLAND	
	percent	index	percent	index	percent	index	percent	index	percent	index
Difference in land productivity (%)	77.42	100	69.14	100	59.61	100	66.60	100	78.39	100
Resource endowment	35.46	46	30.67	44	22.71	38	36.40	55	28.71	37
Labor	14.81	19	15.22	22	15.31	26	15.08	23	13.96	18
Livestock	20.65	27	15.45	22	7.40	12	21.32	32	14.75	19
Technical inputs	27.28	35	20.74	30	20.29	34	23.05	35	24.45	31
Fertilizer	13.80	18	7.28	11	6.83	11	9.56	14	10.99	14
Machinery	13.48	17	13.47	19	13.46	23	13.49	20	13.46	17
Agri. Research	6.62	9	5.34	8	6.23	10	6.46	10	6.32	8
Explained total	69.36	90	56.75	82	49.23	83	65.91	99	59.48	76
Unexplained total	8.06	10	12.39	18	10.39	17	.70	1	18.91	24

Table 5.6 (continued)

COUNTRY	ROMANIA		YUGOSLAVIA		USSR		CHINA	
	percent	index	percent	index	percent	index	percent	index
Difference in land productivity (%)	80.31	100	82.03	100	94.84	100	81.96	100
Resource endowment	31.63	39	37.39	46	47.95	51	26.47	32
Labor	11.74	15	13.96	17	16.61	18	4.08	5
Livestock	19.89	25	23.43	29	31.34	33	22.39	27
Technical inputs	30.18	38	31.47	38	32.99	35	24.10	29
Fertilizer	16.69	21	18.02	22	19.49	21	10.61	13
Machinery	13.48	17	13.45	16	13.49	14	13.50	16
Agri. Research	6.40	8	6.66	8	6.87	7	6.87	8
Explained total	68.21	85	75.52	92	87.81	93	57.45	70
Unexplained total	12.11	15	6.51	8	7.03	7	24.51	30

5.5 Implications of Empirical Findings

The downward trends of total factor productivity in the nine socialist countries contrast with the upward trends in partial productivity. In addition, these analyses indicate that technical change makes little net contribution to the process of agricultural growth. This does not necessarily imply that there is no technological improvement in the agricultural sector. Instead, it is suspected that the benefit of technical change was wiped out by the losses due to misallocation of resources. This led to the employment of the growth accounting procedure in an attempt to segregate the role of technical change in growth from the effects of increased use of conventional inputs. This procedure also makes it possible to trace the effects of changes in factor/land and factor/labor ratios in productivity changes.

It is estimated that a large portion of the changes in labor productivity are attributable to the changes in fertilizer/labor and machinery/labor ratios. For the changes in land productivity, it is estimated that a substantial percentage of change can be explained by changes in fertilizer/land, machinery/land, and research/land ratios.

The comparisons were expanded to include non-socialist countries. It was illustrated graphically that three growth paths can be observed which are common to both socialist and non-socialist countries. Furthermore, the results of growth accounting revealed that agricultural research is not an important source for the large differences in productivity between socialist countries, the U.S., and Japan.

In summary of this chapter, it is important to emphasize the role of agricultural research in productivity growth. Although the capacity and investment in agricultural research in the socialist countries is not small, it takes an efficient system to transform the results achieved into benefit for the farmers. The research institutes in these countries may be capable of generating new technology, but unless the new technology is suitable and transferrable to the field, farmers cannot benefit from it. Given the rigid structure of collectivization, it may take more time and more resources for new technology to become effective. The whole issue, therefore, involves more than just the number of scientists or the productivity of the scientists. It relates to the quality, efficiency, and economic organization of the agricultural research and extension system.

Not until recently have the Chinese realized the importance of the effectiveness of their agricultural research and extension system. A commentary in the official newspaper, People's Daily, frankly pointed out this problem, where it read:

> The agricultural administration, agricultural research institutes, and agricultural universities and colleges - the 'Three Agri' are responsible for regulating the agricultural research, production, dissemination of research results, and education activities. They (the 'Three Agri') are the three important forces for the development of our agriculture. It is necessary to find out the way to put these forces together, to put them in the same direction, and to make them more useful for agricultural production.....In some places, because of the presence of independent and non-cooperating systems, there is lack of communication among institutes of production, research, and education. Consequently, it formed the so-called 'The Opposing Three Agri'. This results in wasting our research resource which is very scarce to begin with. The problem is common in many places. For instance, while farmers are desperately waiting for new technology, research results are not made available to the public; while the farmers are having unsolvable problems, research and education institutes are not able to provide solutions. Yet, they are duplicating research efforts. While there is a shortage of trained officials, agricultural universities and colleges are not operating to full capacity. These phenomena emerged because of the lack of cooperation among the 'Three Agri'....therefore, local officials and institutes should lead and assist the collaboration among the 'Three Agri'. This should be treated as an important event in the studies of agricultural economics (People's Daily, February 27, 1984).

Therefore, if anything should be done to increase the efficiency of socialist agriculture, it is the improvement of the quality and effectiveness of agricultural research and the establishment of better communication between the research community and the agricultural population. Merely increasing the number of research scientists is not enough to make agricultural research a more effective engine of agricultural growth.

Notes

1. Hohenberg, <u>Chemicals in Western Europe</u>, p.57, also cited in Hayami and Ruttan 1971, p. 56.

2. Data of agricultural productivity for the non-socialist countries was estimated by Hayami and Ruttan (Hayami and Ruttan, 1985; 457-465). They used only male labor in the calculation of labor productivity. Hence, the absolute values of labor productivity may vary between the two studies, but the directions and trends of changes should be essentially the same.

3. Data for the U.S. and Japan is derived from Hayami and Ruttan (Hayami and Ruttan, 1985; 466-491) with some adjustment of the labor variable so that both male and female labor is included in the comparisons.

6

Prospects for Socialist Agriculture

6.1 Introduction

The recent development of the agricultural sectors and the changes in the conditions of food supply and demand in socialist countries have drawn economists' attention. Up until now, most studies of socialist agriculture have focused on agrarian policy. A quantitative comparative analysis of the differences in agricultural productivity growth among socialist countries has not been available. It is the intention of this study to bridge this research gap. The objectives of this study are:

First, a metaproduction function was estimated for the nine socialist countries, including seven East European countries, the USSR, and China. The purposes of this estimation are (a) to use the estimated production elasticities as proxies for factor shares in the computation of productivity indices, and (b) to determine the significance of agricultural research in the production process.

Secondly, partial and total factor productivities were constructed and compared for socialist agriculture. The goal of this objective is to examine the trends of productivity changes in these socialist countries over the last 31 years in order to determine if there is a common pattern of productivity change and to investigate the causes of these changes.

Thirdly, the sources of agricultural productivity changes among socialist countries were pinpointed. The purpose of this exercise is to find out the contribution of technical change to agricultural growth in these countries. It was also intended to reveal the relative importance of each factor input in productivity change. With the analyses presented in Chapters I through V, these objectives have been achieved.

The findings and conclusions are summarized in this chapter, together with a discussion of some policy implications.

6.2 Summary and Empirical Findings

As a first step to summarizing the empirical findings of this study, recall the growth indices of agricultural production presented in Chapter I. These indices illustrated the different growth rates among the nine socialist countries. Although the growth patterns among countries of similar size are dissimilar, the overall average rate of growth in the agricultural sector of the nine socialist countries was 2.85 in 1950-1980 and 2.91 in 1960-1980, which is not low compared to the historical performance of other developed countries. The rest of this study focused on aspects of and implications behind these growth patterns.

The main emphasis and effort of this study centered on collecting data and constructing productivity indices for the nine socialist countries for the period 1950-1980. These indices were then used to identify productivity growth patterns and to account for the sources of productivity change.

In Chapter II the methodology and procedures used for the construction of productivity indices were discussed extensively. The theories of productivity were reviewed and the identification of the different effects of technical change and allocative efficiency were emphasized. In general, technical change can be referred to as a shifting of the production function, while allocation of resources can be referred to as the choices of input combinations along the production function. It is possible for a country to have technological advancement and, at the same time, to misallocate its resources to a greater degree, thereby negating the potential gains in efficiency. This is more likely to happen in economies where decision making is not based on economic rationale.

The problems and advantages of using the index approach and production function approach were extensively discussed in Chapter II. It was decided then, considering the crudeness of the data utilized, to employ the index number approach for the construction of total factor productivity.

Chapter III discussed the meaning of the aggregate agricultural production function and the concept of the metaproduction function. In the context of this study, a metaproduction function was defined as the envelope of all possible production frontiers of the nine socialist countries. The results of the estimation of the time series cross-country function were also presented in that chapter. Aspects of model specification, particularly the choice of variables, were looked at. Several statistical techniques, such as Ordinary Least Squares, Autoregression, Principal Components Regression, and Mixed Estimation Regression were tested. It was concluded that the results of the regressions using principal components and mixed estimation provided the best estimates.

Plausibility of the estimated production elasticities was checked with eight other previous studies. The estimates of this study are: 0.172 for labor, 0.043 for land, 0.212 for fertilizer, 0.135 for machinery, 0.368 for livestock, and 0.07 for agricultural research. These estimates are all within a reasonable range and most of them are at an acceptable level of significance.

The core of this study was Chapter IV, where the partial and total factor productivity indices were constructed. The growth patterns of labor and land productivity indicated that labor productivity in East European countries and the USSR grew faster than land productivity. The reverse holds true for China. In contrast, the total factor productivity constructed with an arithmetic and geometric approach displayed strong downward trends for a majority of the nine countries. Four of these countries (Czechoslovakia, East Germany, Hungary, and Romania) seemed to be able to re-attain a positive growth rate of total factor productivity in the 1970s. In any case, the divergences in growth trends within individual countries became very obvious when partial productivity was plotted with total factor productivity.

The hypothesis tests of whether agricultural growth resulted from new technology or from the increase of conventional inputs were investigated in Chapter V. After inspecting the coefficients of the time trend variables and tabulating the contribution of technical change to agricultural growth, the conclusion was that socialist agricultures benefitted very little from technical change during the period 1960-1980. The conjecture of this study is that much of the benefit from technical change was wiped out by misallocation of resources.

Accounting for the sources of differences in productivity growth within and among socialist countries was another objective of Chapter V. The accounting tables illustrated that the increase in fertilizer/labor (fertilizer/land) ratio was the single most important source of the change in labor productivity (land productivity). In the explanation of labor productivity change, livestock was the second most important source of change while agricultural research explained about 10 percent of the change. In the explanation of land productivity, the importance of livestock and machinery were about equivalent, while agricultural research explained an average of 15 percent of the changes. Overall, the factor/labor ratios and the factor/land ratios explained about 95 percent of the changes in labor productivity and at least 37 percent of changes in land productivity, depending on the individual country.

The identification of sources of productivity difference was extended to include non-socialist countries. In the comparison with the United States, resource endowment and technical inputs each explained about one-third of the differences in labor productivity between the U.S. and socialist countries as of 1980. And land and agricultural research variables each explained less than 10 percent of the differences. In the comparison with Japan - labor, livestock, fertilizer, and machinery variables each explained about 20 percent of the differences of land productivity between Japan and socialist countries as of 1980. Agricultural research variables explained about 10 percent of the differences between Japanese and socialist agricultural land productivity.

6.3 Policy Implications for Productivity Growth

Our research raises two questions: What are the prospects for socialist agriculture and what are the policies needed to achieve further growth in agricultural productivity? These two questions can be further synthesized into one single question: what can be done for the farmers in socialist countries?

The following discussions are derived from insights obtained in the analyses of Chapters III, IV, and V, which will be discussed in four sections. First, the divergent trends of partial and total factor productivity will be discussed. Secondly, the issue of centralization will be looked at. Thirdly, the policy implications of the importance of technical change and research in agricultural growth will be deliberated. Finally, the implication of productivity to future trade activities in the international market will be addressed.

The divergences between partial and total factor productivities in socialist agriculture imply that growth in labor and land productivity was achieved at the high cost of misallocation of resources. It is apparent that policy makers in socialist countries have special interest in the figures of total output and output per unit input. They tend not to pay (or even avoid paying) attention to the issue of productivity. This attitude may have contributed to the slow growth (or lack of growth) of productivity. In addition, the economic organization in these countries makes it difficult, if not impossible, to improve its performance. For instance, the rationing of tractors and fertilizer make it very difficult for farmers to allocate their resources optimally. Until the consequences and the cost of unbalanced growth can be felt by the public, it is unlikely that policies and priorities will be reset to change the situation. Perhaps Johnson has the best explanation for this tolerance of slow improvement of efficiency in Soviet agriculture, where he writes: "Per capita incomes in the Soviet Union are high enough so the economy can afford an inefficient, high-cost agriculture". (Johnson 1983; 139)

One of the many ways to improve the situation in socialist agriculture is to further deregulate the flow of production factors. This is a necessary condition in the framework of modern economics for ensuring the optimal use of agricultural resources. The recent development in China's agricultural policy supports the above proposition. Since 1978, China has shown flexibility in its agricultural policy and allowed dozens of different types of responsibility systems to emerge. Recent reports show that this flexibility has contributed to rapid growth in Chinese agriculture, both in terms of total production and productivity.

Since 1980, Chinese peasants have been allowed to shift from agricultural production to non-agricultural production and township enterprises. Allowing agricultural labor to move freely allows more unskilled Chinese peasants to leave agriculture, resulting in more land for the remaining peasants. This raises the total income of other peasants and hence encourages more skillful and capable labor to stay in the agricultural sector. More importantly, transfer of contracted land among peasants has been permitted, which in effect recreates a pseudo land market in rural China. Furthermore, when Chinese peasants are allowed to shift their operations from growing grains to growing other more profitable crops, they can effectively change the usage of land and maximize the return of their resources. The consequence is that resources are allocated more efficiently while the system is still within the framework of socialist agriculture. This may set an example for other socialist countries for improving the performance of their agricultural sector. Only some adjustments in resources management would need to be made through an appropriate incentive scheme, while the overall ideology and structure of the socialist economy largely remained intact.

In this report, special attention was given to the comparison of the more-centralized and less-centralized countries. The analyses presented in sections 3.4.4, 4.2, and 4.3 did not support the hypothesis that less-centralized agriculture is more efficient than more-centralized agriculture, or vice versa. Thus, these hypotheses are not conclusive. There are two plausible reasons underlying this inconclusive result: (a) the criterion by which the level of centralization was determined is ambiguous, and (b) the diversity of economic organization among countries may have confounded the test.

Among the less-centralized countries are Poland, Hungary, Romania, and Yugoslavia. Although peasants in these countries generally have less constraints on their decision making processes, a large part of the Romanian and Hungarian economies are centralized, including the agricultural sector. And while the agricultural sectors in Yugoslavia and Poland are less centralized than in East Germany, Bulgaria, Czechoslovakia, the USSR, and China, the industrial sector in Poland and Yugoslavia are not quite decentralized. In that respect, the term "less-centralized" is only an arbitrary and relative measure meant to reflect the fact that policy settings for these agricultural sectors contain less centrally-planned elements. Furthermore, the degree of decentralization in the agricultural economy varies within the less-centralized countries. The combination of these factors may result in there being an insignificant difference between centralized and less-centralized countries in productivity measures.

In fact, merely relaxing the constraints of central planning on the agricultural sector may not be good enough to ensure better performance. It takes the whole economy - agricultural and non-agricultural sectors - to work together to demonstrate its strength. The strong support from the industrial sector in East German agriculture is a good example. On the other hand, although only 31 percent of Poland's land in 1980 was socialized, the private farms in Poland were not allowed to expand to a more economical scale. Such rigid agricultural policies may have constrained growth in agricultural output and productivity. These examples illustrate that neither decentralization nor land ownership is the sole key issue in socialist agricultural development - an opinion which contrasts with other criticisms of socialist agriculture. Instead, it is flexibility in the policy setting and linkages between industry and agriculture that affect the growth patterns of productivity.

As other scholars have pointed out, centralized control over productive factors may not be the most critical factor for declining trends of productivity growth. The consensus is that the institutional arrangement of the farm economy in these socialist countries is even more critical. The fact that farm managers and peasants do not have the flexibility to react to the ever-changing economic conditions may have caused socialist agriculture to be less competitive than its counterpart in the capitalist economy. Insufficient information and the lack of incentives may also have caused the industrial sectors not to react to new demands from the agricultural sectors, which consequently slowed down the embodied technological improvement in socialist agriculture. Therefore, it is important that agricultural policies be flexible enough to provide appropriate signals for decision makers in the agricultural and industrial sectors. A possible remedy for this problem would be to establish a better information feedback network and to provide more economic incentives for industries to fulfill their obligations to the agricultural sector.

Many researchers have already observed that undesirable weather in the Soviet Union may not be the major factor that has caused the inefficiency in Soviet agriculture. They conclude that fertilizer shortages and planting practices may be more important factors in the sluggish productivity of Soviet agriculture. This conclusion illustrates the fact that technology is becoming a more influential factor in socialist agriculture. This leads to the consideration of another aspect of the socialist system: the role of the agricultural research system.

From the analyses in Chapter V, it was observed that technical change contributed very little to agricultural growth, and that the capacity of agricultural research is not an important source in explaining the difference in productivity between socialist and non-socialist countries. However, it is widely believed that research has contributed significantly to agricultural growth in other developed and developing countries.[1] Despite the fact that agricultural research in the USSR was seriously damaged by the "Legacy of Lysenko," and in China was stagnated by the "Cultural Revolution," the effect of agricultural research in these countries generally was still smaller than expected. The question was then raised of the efficiency of agricultural research and extension systems in the socialist world.

The analysis in Chapter V shows that socialist agriculture has not benefitted from the type of agricultural research that brought about the productivity revolution in non-socialist agriculture. A new technology generated from the research system cannot benefit society until it reaches the hands of end-users. There are several factors that may contribute to the slow rate of technology dissemination in socialist agriculture. First, it may be easy to control farmers in terms of what they can grow, but difficult to command them how to grow it. Peasants will take the risk of adopting a new technology only if they can benefit from it. Thus, one way to ensure growth in productivity is to let peasants realize the benefit of new technology, which means a direct link between productivity and peasants' income.

Secondly, the rigid structure of economic organization and the decision making process also increases the time and cost of the development of appropriate technologies. The situation gets worst when almost all research activities are organized by the public sector. Without the existence of private research there are considerably less sources of innovation. Since advanced basic knowledge is required to generate innovations, interdisciplinary research would be the most effective approach. However, the emergence of such a research system may not be possible when research is only conducted in the public sector. It is, therefore, important to develop a dual research system and to maintain an effective pattern of communication and collaboration between public and private sector research organizations.[2]

Thirdly, an efficient research and extension system needs to have some direct linkage between research scientists and end-users, who in the case of agricultural production are the farmers on the field. A fully operational research system might be able to generate new technologies, but these technologies may not be appropriate in the field. Very often, even when new technologies are available, they are not used in the field because peasants do not have the incentive to adopt the new technology. An innovation has value only if it is used by the peasants. The reason for this gap between innovation and implementation is that state farm managers are concerned more with total output rather than productivity. They have little incentive to use new technology unless the state commands them to do so. The irony is that no one knows better than the peasants working in the field what technologies are most appropriate for the local bioecology conditions.

Finally, unless farmers can secure the benefit of new technology, there is little incentive for them to adopt any new technology. Peasants have little incentive to improve the setting that limits their productivity unless there was a corresponding improvement in their living condition and status. It is important to provide appropriate signals and economic incentives for farmers to perceive and benefit from the advantages of technological advancement. It is equally important to ensure peasants that there are opportunities for them to move up the agricultural ladder, especially through productivity enhancement. The Chinese have recently formed a new agricultural ladder system (Wong 1985b) to allow capable peasants to move to family farms, and the less productive peasants to leave agriculture. This has brought new, dynamic elements to Chinese agriculture.

Socialist agriculture has also suffered from the lack of competition. The non-existence of labor and land markets may have caused the less-than-optimal use of resources. Insolation from the international market may have also caused production plans and commodity mixes to be less than optimal. The Hungarians have demonstrated that using a market price mechanism to establish a close link between the domestic market and the international market can actually move resources and production in a more rational direction. Also the open policy adopted by the Chinese in recent years has helped China to reverse its trade position from grain importer to grain exporter. However, this may only be temporary, as income elasticity causes domestic food consumption to catch up with production. When this occurs, China may once again need to import agricultural commodities.

Recent trade records show that socialist countries have a sizeable impact on the international food market. Any significant improvement in agricultural productivity and therefore agricultural production can have a direct effect on the world food market. Some economists think it is unrealistic to expect any effective change in the performance of socialist agriculture. Considering the historical records and recent changes in socialist agriculture, it is possible for China, the Soviet Union, and other socialist countries to achieve higher growth in aggregate agricultural production through improved seeding practices, the introduction of new technology in fertilizer and machinery use, the implementation of new incentive systems, or the appropriate reform of institutional arrangements. A five percent growth in agricultural production would be possible and this would change the trade position of these socialist countries substantially.

This study identified some inefficient aspects of socialist agriculture. At the same time, the sources of productivity growth and future growth were accounted for. It is the conclusion of this study that socialist agriculture can be improved within the existing system and framework of a centrally planned economy. There is a need, however, for some policy adjustments and institutional rearrangements to soften the rigid economy and agricultural system. In other words, the prospects for socialist agriculture rely on whether their systems have the flexibility to react to the ever-changing domestic economy and world economy; whether there is a market link between resources and commodities; whether there is effective communication among peasants, research scientists, and the authorities; whether there is a dynamic path in society that would allow peasants to move up and to move resources according to their scarcities; and whether there are enough incentives for the industrial sector to be more supportive of the growth of the agricultural sector.

6.4 Suggestions for Future Research

The Stalin-style central-command agricultural model dominated the development of socialist agriculture in the 1940s and 1950s. Not until his death did modification of the Stalin model occur. In the last two decades, several diversified styles of agricultural development models emerged in the nine socialist countries. This report only studied the consequence of these changes, not the causes of the diversity.

This report concentrated on the patterns and sources of productivity change in socialist agriculture. These analyses raised several questions. Why does it take so long for these countries to resolve their problems in the agricultural sector? Is the unbalanced growth in partial and total factor productivity their choice or is it an inherent problem of the system? Is the different economic organization the cause of the different growth patterns or the extension of it?

This study cannot answer all of these questions. It would take specialists that are familiar with the economic settings and political environment in these socialist countries to provide the answers, if there are any.

There are at least three areas that were not discussed in this study that are important in the literature of socialist agriculture. First, the technological divergence between the private agricultural sector and socialized agricultural sector in these countries has not been discussed. This would certainly be one of the most interesting comparisons to make in terms of productivity growth. But until more data can be obtained, study of the private sector in socialist agriculture is beyond the capacity of the western researcher.

The test of the induced innovation hypothesis is another research area that was only touched on in this study and which deserves to be analyzed more extensively. The direction of productivity arrows in Figure 5.3 illustrates the direction of technical change in socialist agriculture, but does not test the forces that direct the change. However, unless a different model can be set up, any test of induced innovation would require a substantial amount of information on price structure - information which has not yet been made completely available.

It would be good to see a more extensive comparison of economic efficiency between socialist and non-socialist agriculture. The study should go beyond productivity comparisons. It should be a comparison of production costs and performance of the agricultural sector. The effectiveness of agricultural research systems in socialist and non-socialist economies should also be compared extensively.

Notes

1. The results of a large number of studies of the contribution of research to agricultural productivity growth were assembled by Vernon Ruttan, <u>Agricultural Research Policy</u>, University of Minnesota Press, Minneapolis: 1982, page 242-243. Ruttan's report shows that most studies have concluded that the annual internal rates of return of agricultural research are above 20 percent and in many cases are above 75 percent.

2. My perspective on the role of agricultural research has benefitted from the work of Vernon Ruttan (1982; page 211).

Appendixes

Appendix A
Aggregate Agricultural Output Series

In this appendix, the sources and computation procedures for the aggregate agricultural output series are explained. Although data for aggregate agricultural output for the nine socialist countries was reported in individual countries' statistical yearbooks, it was not adopted in this study for three reasons.

First, most of the output data for the period from 1950 to 1960 was not reported. Hence, a different series had to be constructed to include missing data of the earlier years.

Secondly, almost all the data was reported in terms of individual countries' own monetary units. The only way the data could be used for comparative study would be to convert all reported values into one single universal monetary unit, such as the U.S. dollar. The foreign exchange rates for these countries, however, were arbitrarily determined by their government, thus causing some biases in the conversion process. Should their currencies be freely convertible in the international money market, this problem would be less serious.

Thirdly, only the total market value of output was reported, which was calculated based on prices set by individual countries. The price structures in these socialist countries differ so much that they should not be used for comparative purposes. This problem would not exist if the prices of agricultural commodities in these countries were determined by market forces which might direct their prices to be closer to international prices.

Considering these problems, an output series which did not depend on any price and monetary unit would be ideal. Hayami and Ruttan (1971; 308) suggested a method of constructing an aggregate agricultural output series that is close to ideal.

The Hayami-Ruttan method takes several steps in calculation which are as follows: (a) collect data on gross output of individual agricultural commodity; (b) deduct intermediate products from the gross output, such as seed, feed (including the imported feed), eggs for hatching, and milk for calf-rearing; (c) adjust the amount by the change of inventory to obtain the net production level of a specific year; (d) aggregate the net quantity by three sets of wheat-relative prices (see Table A.1); and (e) combine these three series into a single composite series by taking their geometrical means.

The underlying rationale for the above aggregation procedures was spelled out in the book by Hayami and Ruttan, where it read:

> The underlying assumptions of the above aggregations are: (a) there exist three types of relative price structures characteristics of the three stages of economic development, which may be called "advanced stage", "mid-way stage", and "initial stage"; (b) these three stages may be represented by the U.S.A., Japan, and India, respectively; and (c) any bias arising from aggregating commodities by the prices of one of these representative countries will be cancelled out by the determination of the geometrical means of three such series. Needless to say, it is arbitrary to assume three stages (why not four?) and to represent the three stages by the U.S.A., Japan, and India. The availability of data rather than theory led us to the selection of the above criteria for our analysis (Hayami and Ruttan 1971; 309).

Thus, denoting the gross output of the jth commodity in the ith country by Q_{ij}, the corresponding intermediate products to be deduced by D_{ij}; and the wheat-relative price of the U.S.A.; Japan, and India by W_{Uj}, W_{Jj}, and W_{Ij} respectively, then the composite series of aggregate agricultural output may be expressed by equation (A.1).

$$Y_i = (Y_{Ui} Y_{Ji} Y_{Ii})^{1/3} \tag{A.1}$$

where $Y_{Ui} = \sum_j W_{Uj}(Q_{ij} - D_{ij})$

$Y_{Ji} = \sum_j W_{Jj}(Q_{ij} - D_{ij})$

$Y_{Ii} = \sum_j W_{Ij}(Q_{ij} - D_{ij})$

Because the Hayami-Ruttan procedures require a large amount of data and computation cost, only the aggregate agricultural output series for 1976 (average of 1975-1977) were computed. Using the computed 1976 output level as the output in the base year, the output level for other years were then extended from the aggregate agricultural output indices that were presented in Table 1.2 of Chapter I. The expanded output series for all nine countries, measured in wheat units, are presented in Table A.2 of this appendix.

Growth indices for the Soviet Union and East European countries are USDA estimates. Indices for 1950-1967 were derived from Indices of Agricultural Production in Eastern Europe and The Soviet Union 1950-68. USDA, ERS Foreign 273, Washington D.C.: July 1969, page 1. Indices for 1970-1980 were derived from Agricultural Statistics of Eastern Europe and The Soviet Union, 1960-80. Washington D.C.: USDA, Economic Research Service, Statistical Bulletin 700. Growth indices for China were official figures published in the Annual Economic Report of China. Bejing:1981, page VI-10.

Data for the average of 1975-1977 for individual agricultural commodity, seed, feed, and change of inventory was collected from the Food Balance Sheets, United Nations, Food and Agriculture Organization, Rome: 1980, page 183 - 997. The price structures of U.S.A., Japan, and India were prepared and reported by Yujiro Hayami in An International Comparison of Agricultural Production and Productivities. Technical Bulletin 277-1971, Agricultural Experiment Station, University of Minnesota, St. Paul: 1971, Table A-1, page 20.

The amount of gross output net of intermediate products of 53 agricultural commodities for the nine countries are presented in Tables A.3 to A.11 of this appendix.

Table A.1: Weights for Aggregation, Wheat-Relative Prices Per Metric Ton, 1957-1962

COMMODITY	USA (WU)	JAPAN (WJ)	INDIA (WI)
Grains			
Wheat	1.00	1.00	1.00
Barely	0.61	1.00	0.69
Buckwheat	0.74	1.24	0.84
Maize	0.63	0.72	0.78
Millet	0.68	0.74	0.87
Oats	0.63	0.70	0.69
Rough Rice	1.58	1.61	0.94
Rye	0.58	0.77	0.69
Sorghum	0.55	0.81	0.81
Mixed grain	0.61	0.74	0.69
Starchy roots			
Cassava	0.16	0.11	0.58
Potatoes	0.57	0.27	0.58
Sweet potatoes	0.81	0.22	0.58
Sugar			
Beets, not processed	0.19	0.15	0.15
Cane, not processed	0.12	0.18	0.10
Pulses and oil crops			
Copra	0.84	0.48	3.10
Cottonseed	0.75	0.83	0.78
Groundnuts	3.39	2.55	1.21
Linseed	1.30	0.66	1.50
Olives	1.66	1.31	1.13
Palm kernels	1.13	0.76	3.10
Pulses (all)	2.12	1.94	0.84
Rapeseed	0.87	1.45	1.91
Sesame seed	4.56	3.98	2.07
Soybeans	1.16	1.50	1.22
Sunflower seed	2.50	1.17	1.11
Nuts, Unshelled	13.14	2.31	5.24
Vegetables, all	0.83	0.42	1.31

Table A.1: (continued)

COMMODITY	USA (WU)	JAPAN (WJ)	INDIA (WI)
Fruits			
Bananas	0.65	1.52	0.63
Citrus	0.98	1.15	1.40
Dates	2.05	0.55	3.33
Other (fresh)	1.27	0.94	1.79
Unspecified	1.13	1.05	1.79
Livestock products			
Beef and veal	12.36	9.99	5.00
Mutton and lamb	12.58	5.03	5.00
Pork	9.51	7.36	5.00
Poultry	6.47	5.15	2.98
Eggs	7.35	5.12	5.24
Milk	1.36	0.76	1.21
Fibers			
Abaca	5.77	3.88	4.12
Cotton	10.30	6.06	2.17
Flax	5.50	3.37	6.27
Hemp	6.94	6.29	1.70
Henequen	2.54	2.30	2.41
Jute	3.11	2.30	1.93
Silk, cocoon basis	17.32	12.86	18.88
Sisal	2.54	2.30	2.41
Wool, greasy basis	14.44	13.52	14.58
Miscellaneous			
Cocoa	8.27	6.30	6.16
Coffee	10.84	7.82	8.21
Rubber	9.33	6.74	7.14
Tea	15.70	3.44	8.88
Tobacco	19.47	8.56	4.63

Note: All prices are farm-gate values and 1 metric ton of wheat in native currencies were: 67.6 dollars in the U.S.A., 36072 yen in Japan, and 46.4 rupees in India.
Source: Yujiro Hayami and associates, An International Comparison of Agricultural Production and Productivites, Agricultural Experiment Station Technical Bulletin 277-2971, University of Minnesota, St. Paul: 1971, page 20.

Table A.2: Aggregate Agricultural Output in Thousand Wheat Units

YEAR	BUL	CZE	GDR	HUN	POL	ROM	YUG	USSR	PRC
1950	6742	14770	16853	11087	32966	10392	9454	169237	216961
1951	9461	14770	20029	13601	29303	13975	14181	153008	238128
1952	7177	14602	21006	9461	29303	12542	8319	173873	275170
1953	9026	16280	21006	12418	30117	15229	14748	171555	283108
1954	7503	14770	21983	11383	32966	14154	12101	176192	293692
1955	8482	16112	20273	13601	32152	17200	15883	197056	314859
1956	7830	17287	20761	12270	36629	13438	12668	220239	330734
1957	9352	16448	21494	14488	37036	17200	18908	210966	341317
1958	9243	15944	22227	13601	37850	14333	15504	241104	351901
1959	11092	15777	21006	15966	37443	18634	21177	229513	304275
1960	10875	16784	24425	14783	40699	17917	18908	231831	264587
1961	10440	16280	18563	14044	45176	18634	18152	245741	259295
1962	10875	15777	21494	14783	40699	17200	18908	248059	275170
1963	10983	17455	21494	15227	43955	17917	20231	234149	306921
1964	12506	17791	22715	15670	45176	18813	21744	278197	346609
1965	13049	15273	23937	16114	45990	20604	20042	264287	375714
1966	15333	17958	23937	17149	48025	23650	24202	310653	407464
1967	15007	18294	26379	17444	50467	23292	23446	303699	415402
1968	13919	19301	26135	17444	52502	22754	22689	317608	404818
1969	14463	19637	24181	18627	50060	23471	24958	306017	410110
1970	14572	19805	25158	17592	50874	20425	22879	345428	457736
1971	15007	20979	24914	20253	49246	25263	25337	343110	470965
1972	16529	21819	27600	21731	53723	28488	24958	326882	468319
1973	15768	23161	27600	22323	57386	26696	26093	394113	508007
1974	14681	24168	30287	23801	57793	27413	29874	368611	529174
1975	15986	22994	28577	23505	56572	27950	29496	329200	555633
1976	17073	22490	27356	22914	58200	35117	31198	389476	568862
1977	15768	24336	29554	25131	53723	34042	32711	377884	576800
1978	16529	25679	31020	26018	58607	34579	30631	414977	629717
1979	17834	23833	31020	24688	56979	36013	31387	370930	685280
1980	17073	25847	31020	27053	50060	36013	31387	382521	703801

Table A.3: Aggregate Agricultural Output (75-77 Average) For Bulgaria

OUTPUT(000 METRIC TONS)		YU	YJ	YI
1	WHEAT	2393.00	2393.00	2393.00	2393.00
2	BARLEY	111.00	67.71	111.00	76.59
3	BUCKWHEAT	0	0	0	0
4	MAIZE	106.00	66.78	76.32	82.68
5	MILLET	0	0	0	0
6	OATS	25.00	15.75	17.50	17.25
7	RICE	55.00	86.90	88.55	51.70
8	RYE	10.00	5.80	7.70	6.90
9	SORGHUM	0	0	0	0
10	MIX GRAIN	0	0	0	0
11	CASSAVA	0	0	0	0
12	POTATOES	223.00	127.11	60.21	129.34
13	SWEET POT.	0	0	0	0
14	SUGAR BEET	1918.00	364.42	287.70	287.70
15	SUGAR CANE	0	0	0	0
16	COPRA	0	0	0	0
17	COTTONSEED	12.00	9.00	9.96	9.36
18	GROUNDNUT	3.00	10.17	7.65	3.63
19	LINSEED	2.00	2.60	1.32	3.00
20	OLIVES	0	0	0	0
21	PALM KER.	0	0	0	0
22	PULSES	52.00	110.24	100.88	43.68
23	RAPESEED	0	0	0	0
24	SESAMESEED	0	0	0	0
25	SOYBEAN	67.00	77.72	100.50	81.74
26	SUNFLOSEED	369.00	922.50	431.73	409.59
27	NUTS	29.00	381.06	66.99	151.96
28	BANANAS	0	0	0	0
29	CITRUS	0	0	0	0
30	DATES	0	0	0	0
31	OTHER	2173.00	2759.71	2042.62	3889.67
32	UNSPECIFY	0	0	0	0
33	VEGETABLE	1945.00	1614.35	816.90	2547.95
34	BEEF	100.00	1236.00	999.00	500.00
35	MUTTON	81.00	1018.98	407.43	405.00
36	PORK	293.00	2786.43	2156.48	1465.00
37	POULTRY	131.00	847.57	674.65	390.38
38	EGGS	95.00	698.25	486.40	497.80
39	MILK	1320.00	1795.20	1003.20	1597.20
40	ABACA	0	0	0	0
41	COTTON	8.00	82.40	48.48	17.36
42	FLAX	3.00	16.50	10.11	18.81
43	HEMP	6.00	41.64	37.74	10.20
44	HENEQUEN	0	0	0	0
45	JUTE	0	0	0	0
46	SILK	.23	3.98	2.96	4.34
47	SISAL	0	0	0	0
48	WOOL	34.15	493.13	461.71	497.91
49	COCOA	0	0	0	0
50	COFFEE	0	0	0	0
51	RUBBER	0	0	0	0
52	TEA	0	0	0	0
53	TOBACCO	165.00	3212.55	1412.40	763.95
SUM			21247.45	14321.09	16353.69

Table A.4: Aggregate Agricultural Output (75-77 Average) For Czechoslavakia

OUTPUT(000 METRIC TONS)		YU	YJ	YI
1	WHEAT	1420.00	1420.00	1420.00	1420.00
2	BARLEY	786.00	479.46	786.00	542.34
3	BUCKWHEAT	0	0	0	0
4	MAIZE	-353.00	-222.39	-254.16	-275.34
5	MILLET	0	0	0	0
6	OATS	-20.00	-12.60	-14.00	-13.80
7	RICE	0	0	0	0
8	RYE	384.00	222.72	295.68	264.96
9	SORGHUM	0	0	0	0
10	MIX GRAIN	5.00	3.05	3.70	3.45
11	CASSAVA	0	0	0	0
12	POTATOES	1958.00	1116.06	528.66	1135.64
13	SWEET POT.	0	0	0	0
14	SUGAR BEET	7013.00	1332.47	1051.95	1051.95
15	SUGAR CANE	0	0	0	0
16	COPRA	0	0	0	0
17	COTTONSEED	0	0	0	0
18	GROUNDNUT	0	0	0	0
19	LINSEED	9.00	11.70	5.94	13.50
20	OLIVES	0	0	0	0
21	PALM KER.	0	0	0	0
22	PULSES	11.00	23.32	21.34	9.24
23	RAPESEED	127.00	110.49	184.15	242.57
24	SESAMESEED	0	0	0	0
25	SOYBEAN	15.00	17.40	22.50	18.30
26	SUNFLOSEED	8.00	20.00	9.36	8.88
27	NUTS	14.00	183.96	32.34	73.36
28	BANANAS	0	0	0	0
29	CITRUS	0	0	0	0
30	DATES	0	0	0	0
31	OTHER	655.00	831.85	615.70	1172.45
32	UNSPECIFY	0	0	0	0
33	VEGETABLE	931.00	772.73	391.02	1219.61
34	BEEF	385.00	4758.60	3846.15	1925.00
35	MUTTON	1.00	12.58	5.03	5.00
36	PORK	714.00	6790.14	5255.04	3570.00
37	POULTRY	159.00	1028.73	818.85	473.82
38	EGGS	220.00	1617.00	1126.40	1152.80
39	MILK	5097.00	6931.92	3873.72	6167.37
40	ABACA	0	0	0	0
41	COTTON	0	0	0	0
42	FLAX	15.00	82.50	50.55	94.05
43	HEMP	2.00	13.88	12.58	3.40
44	HENEQUEN	0	0	0	0
45	JUTE	0	0	0	0
46	SILK	0	0	0	0
47	SISAL	0	0	0	0
48	WOOL	3.61	52.13	48.81	52.63
49	COCOA	0	0	0	0
50	COFFEE	0	0	0	0
51	RUBBER	0	0	0	0
52	TEA	0	0	0	0
53	TOBACCO	5.00	97.35	42.80	23.15
	SUM		27695.05	20180.11	20354.33

Table A.5: Aggregate Agricultural Output (75-77 Average) For East Germany

OUTPUT(000 METRIC TONS)	YU	YJ	YI
1 WHEAT	141.00	141.00	141.00	141.00
2 BARLEY	-115.00	-70.15	-115.00	-79.35
3 BUCKWHEAT	0	0	0	0
4 MAIZE	-1591.00	-1002.33	-1145.52	-1240.98
5 MILLET	0	0	0	0
6 OATS	24.00	15.12	16.80	16.56
7 RICE	0	0	0	0
8 RYE	718.00	416.44	552.86	495.42
9 SORGHUM	0	0	0	0
10 MIX GRAIN	2.00	1.22	1.48	1.38
11 CASSAVA	0	0	0	0
12 POTATOES	3024.00	1723.68	816.48	1753.92
13 SWEET POT.	0	0	0	0
14 SUGAR BEET	6699.00	1272.81	1004.85	1004.85
15 SUGAR CANE	0	0	0	0
16 COPRA	0	0	0	0
17 COTTONSEED	0	0	0	0
18 GROUNDNUT	0	0	0	0
19 LINSEED	1.00	1.30	.66	1.50
20 OLIVES	0	0	0	0
21 PALM KER.	0	0	0	0
22 PULSES	11.00	23.32	21.34	9.24
23 RAPESEED	327.00	284.49	474.15	624.57
24 SESAMESEED	0	0	0	0
25 SOYBEAN	35.00	40.60	52.50	42.70
26 SUNFLOSEED	0	0	0	0
27 NUTS	1.00	13.14	2.31	5.24
28 BANANAS	0	0	0	0
29 CITRUS	0	0	0	0
30 DATES	0	0	0	0
31 OTHER	616.00	782.32	579.04	1102.64
32 UNSPECIFY	0	0	0	0
33 VEGETABLE	895.00	742.85	375.90	1172.45
34 BEEF	421.00	5203.56	4205.79	2105.00
35 MUTTON	17.00	213.86	85.51	85.00
36 PORK	1152.00	10955.52	8478.72	5760.00
37 POULTRY	133.00	860.51	684.95	396.34
38 EGGS	277.00	2035.95	1418.24	1451.48
39 MILK	7968.00	10836.48	6055.68	9641.28
40 ABACA	0	0	0	0
41 COTTON	0	0	0	0
42 FLAX	1.00	5.50	3.37	6.27
43 HEMP	0	0	0	0
44 HENEQUEN	0	0	0	0
45 JUTE	0	0	0	0
46 SILK	.00	.03	.03	.04
47 SISAL	0	0	0	0
48 WOOL	10.09	145.70	136.42	147.11
49 COCOA	0	0	0	0
50 COFFEE	0	0	0	0
51 RUBBER	0	0	0	0
52 TEA	0	0	0	0
53 TOBACCO	5.00	97.35	42.80	23.15
SUM		34740.27	23890.35	24666.81

Table A.6: Aggregate Agricultural Output (75-77 Average) For Hungary

OUTPUT(000 METRIC TONS)	YU	YJ	YI
1 WHEAT	2974.00	2974.00	2974.00	2974.00
2 BARLEY	18.00	10.98	18.00	12.42
3 BUCKWHEAT	0	0	0	0
4 MAIZE	614.00	386.82	442.08	478.92
5 MILLET	4.00	2.72	2.96	3.48
6 OATS	-31.00	-19.53	-21.70	-21.39
7 RICE	45.00	71.10	72.45	42.30
8 RYE	10.00	5.80	7.70	6.90
9 SORGHUM	10.00	5.50	8.10	8.10
10 MIX GRAIN	0	0	0	0
11 CASSAVA	0	0	0	0
12 POTATOES	772.00	440.04	208.44	447.76
13 SWEET POT.	0	0	0	0
14 SUGAR BEET	3970.00	754.30	595.50	595.50
15 SUGAR CANE	0	0	0	0
16 COPRA	0	0	0	0
17 COTTONSEED	0	0	0	0
18 GROUNDNUT	0	0	0	0
19 LINSEED	17.00	22.10	11.22	25.50
20 OLIVES	0	0	0	0
21 PALM KER.	0	0	0	0
22 PULSES	80.00	169.60	155.20	67.20
23 RAPESEED	65.00	56.55	94.25	124.15
24 SESAMESEED	0	0	0	0
25 SOYBEAN	29.00	33.64	43.50	35.38
26 SUNFLOSEED	158.00	395.00	184.86	175.38
27 NUTS	26.00	341.64	60.06	136.24
28 BANANAS	0	0	0	0
29 CITRUS	0	0	0	0
30 DATES	0	0	0	0
31 OTHER	2284.00	2900.68	2146.96	4088.36
32 UNSPECIFY	0	0	0	0
33 VEGETABLE	2125.00	1763.75	892.50	2783.75
34 BEEF	187.00	2311.32	1868.13	935.00
35 MUTTON	17.00	213.86	85.51	85.00
36 PORK	833.00	7921.83	6130.88	4165.00
37 POULTRY	301.00	1947.47	1550.15	896.98
38 EGGS	202.00	1484.70	1034.24	1058.48
39 MILK	1848.00	2513.28	1404.48	2236.08
40 ABACA	0	0	0	0
41 COTTON	0	0	0	0
42 FLAX	6.00	33.00	20.22	37.62
43 HEMP	13.00	90.22	81.77	22.10
44 HENEQUEN	0	0	0	0
45 JUTE	0	0	0	0
46 SILK	0	0	0	0
47 SISAL	0	0	0	0
48 WOOL	8.65	124.91	116.95	126.12
49 COCOA	0	0	0	0
50 COFFEE	0	0	0	0
51 RUBBER	0	0	0	0
52 TEA	0	0	0	0
53 TOBACCO	19.00	369.93	162.64	87.97
SUM		27325.21	20351.05	21634.30

Table A.7: Aggregate Agricultural Output (75-77 Average) For Poland

OUTPUT(000 METRIC TONS)	YU	YJ	YI
1 WHEAT	1997.00	1997.00	1997.00	1997.00
2 BARLEY	-324.00	-197.64	-324.00	-223.56
3 BUCKWHEAT	3.00	2.22	3.72	2.52
4 MAIZE	-1579.00	-994.77	-1136.88	-1231.62
5 MILLET	0	0	0	0
6 OATS	141.00	88.83	98.70	97.29
7 RICE	0	0	0	0
8 RYE	1805.00	1046.90	1389.85	1245.45
9 SORGHUM	-524.00	-288.20	-424.44	-424.44
10 MIX GRAIN	48.00	29.28	35.52	33.12
11 CASSAVA	0	0	0	0
12 POTATOES	13655.00	7783.35	3686.85	7919.90
13 SWEET POT.	0	0	0	0
14 SUGAR BEET	15582.00	2960.58	2337.30	2337.30
15 SUGAR CANE	0	0	0	0
16 COPRA	0	0	0	0
17 COTTONSEED	0	0	0	0
18 GROUNDNUT	0	0	0	0
19 LINSEED	42.00	54.60	27.72	63.00
20 OLIVES	0	0	0	0
21 PALM KER.	0	0	0	0
22 PULSES	38.00	80.56	73.72	31.92
23 RAPESEED	798.00	694.26	1157.10	1524.18
24 SESAMESEED	0	0	0	0
25 SOYBEAN	0	0	0	0
26 SUNFLOSEED	0	0	0	0
27 NUTS	0	0	0	0
28 BANANAS	0	0	0	0
29 CITRUS	0	0	0	0
30 DATES	0	0	0	0
31 OTHER	1626.00	2065.02	1528.44	2910.54
32 UNSPECIFY	0	0	0	0
33 VEGETABLE	3888.00	3227.04	1632.96	5093.28
34 BEEF	765.00	9455.40	7642.35	3825.00
35 MUTTON	20.00	251.60	100.60	100.00
36 PORK	1624.00	15444.24	11952.64	8120.00
37 POULTRY	268.00	1733.96	1380.20	798.64
38 EGGS	458.00	3366.30	2344.96	2399.92
39 MILK	15351.00	20877.36	11666.76	18574.71
40 ABACA	0	0	0	0
41 COTTON	0	0	0	0
42 FLAX	55.00	302.50	185.35	344.85
43 HEMP	10.00	69.40	62.90	17.00
44 HENEQUEN	0	0	0	0
45 JUTE	0	0	0	0
46 SILK	.01	.10	.08	.11
47 SISAL	0	0	0	0
48 WOOL	10.34	149.31	139.80	150.76
49 COCOA	0	0	0	0
50 COFFEE	0	0	0	0
51 RUBBER	0	0	0	0
52 TEA	0	0	0	0
53 TOBACCO	109.00	2122.23	933.04	504.67
SUM		72321.43	48492.23	56211.54

Table A.8: Aggregate Agricultural Output (75-77 Average) For Romania

OUTPUT(000 METRIC TONS)		YU	YJ	YI
1	WHEAT	4556.00	4556.00	4556.00	4556.00
2	BARLEY	107.00	65.27	107.00	73.83
3	BUCKWHEAT	0	0	0	0
4	MAIZE	3762.00	2370.06	2708.64	2934.36
5	MILLET	0	0	0	0
6	OATS	-15.00	-9.45	-10.50	-10.35
7	RICE	47.00	74.26	75.67	44.18
8	RYE	13.00	7.54	10.01	8.97
9	SORGHUM	0	0	0	0
10	MIX GRAIN	0	0	0	0
11	CASSAVA	0	0	0	0
12	POTATOES	2373.00	1352.61	640.71	1376.34
13	SWEET POT.	0	0	0	0
14	SUGAR BEET	6022.00	1144.18	903.30	903.30
15	SUGAR CANE	0	0	0	0
16	COPRA	0	0	0	0
17	COTTONSEED	3.00	2.25	2.49	2.34
18	GROUNDNUT	0	0	0	0
19	LINSEED	44.00	57.20	29.04	66.00
20	OLIVES	0	0	0	0
21	PALM KER.	0	0	0	0
22	PULSES	88.00	186.56	170.72	73.92
23	RAPESEED	14.00	12.18	20.30	26.74
24	SESAMESEED	0	0	0	0
25	SOYBEAN	119.00	138.04	178.50	145.18
26	SUNFLOSEED	763.00	1907.50	892.71	846.93
27	NUTS	29.00	381.06	66.99	151.96
28	BANANAS	0	0	0	0
29	CITRUS	0	0	0	0
30	DATES	0	0	0	0
31	OTHER	2661.00	3379.47	2501.34	4763.19
32	UNSPECIFY	0	0	0	0
33	VEGETABLE	3753.00	3114.99	1576.26	4916.43
34	BEEF	288.00	3559.68	2877.12	1440.00
35	MUTTON	91.00	1144.78	457.73	455.00
36	PORK	757.00	7199.07	5571.52	3785.00
37	POULTRY	296.00	1915.12	1524.40	882.08
38	EGGS	271.00	1991.85	1387.52	1420.04
39	MILK	3791.00	5155.76	2881.16	4587.11
40	ABACA	0	0	0	0
41	COTTON	2.00	20.60	12.12	4.34
42	FLAX	35.00	192.50	117.95	219.45
43	HEMP	26.00	180.44	163.54	44.20
44	HENEQUEN	0	0	0	0
45	JUTE	0	0	0	0
46	SILK	.13	2.25	1.67	2.45
47	SISAL	0	0	0	0
48	WOOL	32.25	465.69	436.02	470.20
49	COCOA	0	0	0	0
50	COFFEE	0	0	0	0
51	RUBBER	0	0	0	0
52	TEA	0	0	0	0
53	TOBACCO	50.00	973.50	428.00	231.50
	SUM		41540.96	30287.93	34420.70

Table A.9: Aggregate Agricultural Output (75-77 Average) For Yugoslavia

OUTPUT(000 METRIC TONS)		YU	YJ	YI
1	WHEAT	4477.00	4477.00	4477.00	4477.00
2	BARLEY	157.00	95.77	157.00	108.33
3	BUCKWHEAT	-1.00	-.74	-1.24	-.84
4	MAIZE	2747.00	1730.61	1977.84	2142.66
5	MILLET	0	0	0	0
6	OATS	27.00	17.01	18.90	18.63
7	RICE	31.00	48.98	49.91	29.14
8	RYE	0	0	0	0
9	SORGHUM	3.00	1.65	2.43	2.43
10	MIX GRAIN	0	0	0	0
11	CASSAVA	0	0	0	0
12	POTATOES	1685.00	960.45	454.95	977.30
13	SWEET POT.	0	0	0	0
14	SUGAR BEET	4428.00	841.32	664.20	664.20
15	SUGAR CANE	0	0	0	0
16	COPRA	0	0	0	0
17	COTTONSEED	4.00	3.00	3.32	3.12
18	GROUNDNUT	0	0	0	0
19	LINSEED	0	0	0	0
20	OLIVES	17.00	28.22	22.27	19.21
21	PALM KER.	0	0	0	0
22	PULSES	153.00	324.36	296.82	128.52
23	RAPESEED	25.00	21.75	36.25	47.75
24	SESAMESEED	0	0	0	0
25	SOYBEAN	47.00	54.52	70.50	57.34
26	SUNFLOSEED	355.00	887.50	415.35	394.05
27	NUTS	35.00	459.90	80.85	183.40
28	BANANAS	0	0	0	0
29	CITRUS	0	0	0	0
30	DATES	0	0	0	0
31	OTHER	2785.00	3536.95	2617.90	4985.15
32	UNSPECIFY	0	0	0	0
33	VEGETABLE	3651.00	3030.33	1533.42	4782.81
34	BEEF	330.00	4078.80	3296.70	1650.00
35	MUTTON	59.00	742.22	296.77	295.00
36	PORK	669.00	6362.19	4923.84	3345.00
37	POULTRY	201.00	1300.47	1035.15	598.98
38	EGGS	177.00	1300.95	906.24	927.48
39	MILK	3630.00	4936.80	2758.80	4392.30
40	ABACA	0	0	0	0
41	COTTON	2.00	20.60	12.12	4.34
42	FLAX	.50	2.75	1.69	3.14
43	HEMP	8.00	55.52	50.32	13.60
44	HENEQUEN	0	0	0	0
45	JUTE	0	0	0	0
46	SILK	.01	.21	.15	.23
47	SISAL	0	0	0	0
48	WOOL	10.00	144.40	135.20	145.80
49	COCOA	0	0	0	0
50	COFFEE	0	0	0	0
51	RUBBER	0	0	0	0
52	TEA	0	0	0	0
53	TOBACCO	68.00	1323.96	582.08	314.84
SUM			36787.45	26876.73	30710.90

Table A.10: Aggregate Agricultural Output (75-77 Average) For USSR

	OUTPUT(000 METRIC TONS)		YU	YJ	YI
1	WHEAT	42953.00	42953.00	42953.00	42953.00
2	BARLEY	5120.00	3123.20	5120.00	3532.80
3	BUCKWHEAT	281.00	207.94	348.44	236.04
4	MAIZE	-4265.00	-2686.95	-3070.80	-3326.70
5	MILLET	909.00	618.12	672.66	790.83
6	OATS	2593.00	1633.59	1815.10	1789.17
7	RICE	1952.00	3084.16	3142.72	1834.88
8	RYE	7679.00	4453.82	5912.83	5298.51
9	SORGHUM	13.00	7.15	10.53	10.53
10	MIX GRAIN	68.00	41.48	50.32	46.92
11	CASSAVA	0	0	0	0
12	POTATOES	40578.00	23129.46	10956.06	23535.24
13	SWEET POT.	0	0	0	0
14	SUGAR BEET	78165.00	14851.35	11724.75	11724.75
15	SUGAR CANE	0	0	0	0
16	COPRA	0	0	0	0
17	COTTONSEED	4704.00	3528.00	3904.32	3669.12
18	GROUNDNUT	1.00	3.39	2.55	1.21
19	LINSEED	224.00	291.20	147.84	336.00
20	OLIVES	0	0	0	0
21	PALM KER.	0	0	0	0
22	PULSES	1405.00	2978.60	2725.70	1180.20
23	RAPESEED	15.00	13.05	21.75	28.65
24	SESAMESEED	0	0	0	0
25	SOYBEAN	345.00	400.20	517.50	420.90
26	SUNFLOSEED	4981.00	12452.50	5827.77	5528.91
27	NUTS	206.00	2706.84	475.86	1079.44
28	BANANAS	0	0	0	0
29	CITRUS	0	0	0	0
30	DATES	0	0	0	0
31	OTHER	14970.00	19011.90	14071.80	26796.30
32	UNSPECIFY	0	0	0	0
33	VEGETABLE	26838.00	22275.54	11271.96	35157.78
34	BEEF	6529.00	80698.44	65224.71	32645.00
35	MUTTON	936.00	11774.88	4708.08	4680.00
36	PORK	4957.00	47141.07	36483.52	24785.00
37	POULTRY	1579.00	10216.13	8131.85	4705.42
38	EGGS	3105.00	22821.75	15897.60	16270.20
39	MILK	81167.00	110387.12	61686.92	98212.07
40	ABACA	0	0	0	0
41	COTTON	2651.00	27305.30	16065.06	5752.67
42	FLAX	506.00	2783.00	1705.22	3172.62
43	HEMP	58.00	402.52	364.82	98.60
44	HENEQUEN	0	0	0	0
45	JUTE	48.00	149.28	110.40	92.64
46	SILK	3.46	59.93	44.50	65.32
47	SISAL	0	0	0	0
48	WOOL	452.50	6534.10	6117.80	6597.45
49	COCOA	0	0	0	0
50	COFFEE	0	0	0	0
51	RUBBER	0	0	0	0
52	TEA	92.00	1444.40	316.48	816.96
53	TOBACCO	308.00	5996.76	2636.48	1426.04
	SUM		482792.22	338096.10	361944.47

Table A.11: Aggregate Agricultural Output (75-77 Average) For China

OUTPUT(000 METRIC TONS)	YU	YJ	YI
1 WHEAT	42285.00	42285.00	42285.00	42285.00
2 BARLEY	10159.00	6196.99	10159.00	7009.71
3 BUCKWHEAT	2873.00	2126.02	3562.52	2413.32
4 MAIZE	21896.00	13794.48	15765.12	17078.88
5 MILLET	8441.00	5739.88	6246.34	7343.67
6 OATS	672.00	423.36	470.40	463.68
7 RICE	117893.00	186270.94	189807.73	110819.42
8 RYE	1521.00	882.18	1171.17	1049.49
9 SORGHUM	8763.00	4819.65	7098.03	7098.03
10 MIX GRAIN	0	0	0	0
11 CASSAVA	1625.00	260.00	178.75	942.50
12 POTATOES	8925.00	5087.25	2409.75	5176.50
13 SWEET POT.	71017.00	57523.77	15623.74	41189.86
14 SUGAR BEET	2492.00	473.48	373.80	373.80
15 SUGAR CANE	19584.00	2350.08	3525.12	1958.40
16 COPRA	0	0	0	0
17 COTTONSEED	4084.00	3063.00	3389.72	3185.52
18 GROUNDNUT	2559.00	8675.01	6525.45	3096.39
19 LINSEED	33.00	42.90	21.78	49.50
20 OLIVES	1.00	1.66	1.31	1.13
21 PALM KER.	0	0	0	0
22 PULSES	10974.00	23264.88	21289.56	9218.16
23 RAPESEED	1361.00	1184.07	1973.45	2599.51
24 SESAMESEED	358.00	1632.48	1424.84	741.06
25 SOYBEAN	10301.00	11949.16	15451.50	12567.22
26 SUNFLOSEED	105.00	262.50	122.85	116.55
27 NUTS	286.00	3758.04	660.66	1498.64
28 BANANAS	220.00	143.00	334.40	138.60
29 CITRUS	5.00	4.90	5.75	7.00
30 DATES	83.00	170.15	45.65	276.39
31 OTHER	5307.00	6739.89	4988.58	9499.53
32 UNSPECIFY	0	0	0	0
33 VEGETABLE	67032.00	55636.56	28153.44	87811.92
34 BEEF	2087.00	25795.32	20849.13	10435.00
35 MUTTON	621.00	7812.18	3123.63	3105.00
36 PORK	10250.00	97477.50	75440.00	51250.00
37 POULTRY	3267.00	21137.49	16825.05	9735.66
38 EGGS	3512.00	25813.20	17981.44	18402.88
39 MILK	4101.00	5577.36	3116.76	4962.21
40 ABACA	0	0	0	0
41 COTTON	2363.00	24338.90	14319.78	5127.71
42 FLAX	1.00	5.50	3.37	6.27
43 HEMP	23.00	159.62	144.67	39.10
44 HENEQUEN	0	0	0	0
45 JUTE	1430.00	4447.30	3289.00	2759.90
46 SILK	15.61	270.37	200.74	294.72
47 SISAL	10.00	25.40	23.00	24.10
48 WOOL	61.33	885.61	829.18	894.19
49 COCOA	0	0	0	0
50 COFFEE	5.00	54.20	39.10	41.05
51 RUBBER	26.00	242.58	175.24	185.64
52 TEA	326.00	5118.20	1121.44	2894.88
53 TOBACCO	991.00	19294.77	8482.96	4588.33
SUM		683216.77	549029.91	490756.02

Appendix B
Time Series
Cross-Country Data

The theme of this study is to perform a comparative analysis of agricultural productivity growth. Thus, all data used in this study must be compatible or at least close to compatible. Although most countries included in this study published their own statistical yearbooks, the data reported was neither compatible cross-country nor consistent over time. Therefore, secondary sources of data that are more compatible and consistent were used in this study. These data was derived by international organizations such as the International Labor Organization, the Food and Agriculture Organization, the United States Department of Agriculture, and other international research institutes. When necessary, official statistical yearbooks were used to fill in the missing values and to make some adjustments. When sources of information were exhausted, the technique of regression of linear interpolations was used to estimate the missing observations.

All the data used in the analysis in Chapters III and IV is presented in Tables B.1 to B.9. The numbers of livestock that were used in the calculation of livestock units are presented in Tables B.10 to B.18. Following the Hayami-Ruttan notation, definitions and sources of the input variables are as follows.

Definitions

LABOR: Agricultural labor defined as economically active population including all working farmers, their wives working in agriculture, helping members, and hired labor, measured in full-time manyears.

LAND: Agricultural land defined as the total area of arable land, permanent crop land, permanent pasture and meadows, measured in hectares.

FERT: Chemical fertilizer defined as the gross weight of total consumption of nitrogenous, phosphate, and potash ($N_2 + P_2O_5 + K_2O$), measured in metric tons.

MACH: Agricultural machinery defined as the total number of wheel and crawler tractors (excluding the garden tractors) used in agriculture. Most East European countries used to report their tractor numbers in terms of 15 horsepower units. In order to be consistent with the assumption that large tractors are 30 h.p. and small tractors are 5 h.p., the figures of 15 h.p. units are converted into 30 h.p. units as presented in Tables B.1 to B.9. When information about 15 h.p. units was not available, the number of tractors was used instead. The regression analysis in Chapter III used the calculated total horsepower of large and small tractors. Since the number of small tractors is not available, the same number as large tractors is assumed.

HORSE: Working animals defined as the total number of horses. The assumption is that each horse can provide service equivalents to one tractor horsepower.

LVSK: Livestock measured in livestock units, defined as the aggregate unit of various animals, weighted by the FAO conversion factors. Conversion factors are: camels 1.1; buffalo, horse, and mules 1.0; cattle and asses 0.8; pigs 0.2; sheep and goats 0.1; and poultry 0.01. (See Tables B.10 to B.18 for individual livestock numbers.)

ARABLE: Agricultural arable land defined as total area of arable land and land under permanent crops. It is a subset of the variable LAND. Arable land refers to land under temporary crops (double-cropped areas are counted only once), temporary meadows for mowing or pasture, land under market and kitchen gardens (including cultivation under glass), and land temporarily fallow or lying idle. Land under permanent crops refers to land cultivated with crops which occupy the land for long periods and need not be replanted after each harvest, such as cocoa, coffee, and rubber. It includes land under shrubs, fruit trees, nut trees and vines, but excludes land under trees grown for wood or timber.

POPUL: Rural population defined as all persons actively engaged in agriculture and their non-working dependents.

SCHOOL: School enrollment ratio defined as the number of students enrolled in the first and second levels of the population of potential enrollment.

RE: Agricultural research defined as the manpower involved in agricultural research, measured in scientist manyears.

Sources

Labor

Bulgaria: Figures 1950-1964 were derived from Gregor Lazarick, "Bulgarian Agricultural Production, Output, Expense, Gross and Net Product, and Productivity at 1968 Prices, 1939, and 1948-1970". Research Project on National Income in East Central Europe, Occasional Paper OP-39, New York: 1973, p. 20. Figures for 1965-1980 were derived from OP-71 (1982), p. 29.

Czechoslovakia: Figures for 1950-1958 were derived from James Ypsilantis, "The Labor Force of Czechoslovakia," Department of Commerce, International Population Statistics Report, Series P-90, No. 13, Washington D.C.: 1960. Figures for 1959-1964 were derived from Yearbook of Labor Statistics, International Labor Office, Geneva, various issues. Figures for 1965-1980 were derived from OP-71 (1982), p. 29.

East Germany: Figures for 1950-1964 were derived from Ronald Francisco, "The Future of East German Agriculture: the Feasibility of the 1976-1980 Plan". The Future of Agriculture in the Soviet Union and Eastern Europe. Laird (et al), Westview Press, Boulder, Colorado: 1977, p. 188. Figures for 1965-1980 were derived from OP-71 (1982), page 29.

Hungary: Figures for 1950-1961 were derived from Samuel Baum, "The Labor Force of Hungary", U.S. Department of Commerce, International Population Statistics, series P-90, No. 18, Washington D.C.: 1962, p. 13. Figures for 1962-1964 were derived from Yearbook of Labor Statistics, ILO, Geneva, various issues. Figures for 1965-1980 were derived from OP-71 (1982), p. 29.

Poland: Figures for 1950-1964 were derived from OP-37 (1972), p.18. Figures for 1965-1980 were derived from OP-71 (1982), p.29.

Romania: Figure for 1950 was derived from Directia Centrala de Statistica, Anuarul Statistic al Republic Socialiste Romania 1981, Table 115, p. 255. Figures for 1951-1958 were derived from Samuel Baum, "The Labor Force of Romania," U.S. Department of Commerce, International Population Statistics Reports, series P-90, No. 14, Washington D.C.: 1961. Figures for 1960, 1965, 1970, and 1975-1980 were derived from Production Yearbook, FAO, Rome, various issues. Figures for 1959, 1961-1964, 1966-1969, 1971-1974 were interpolated.

Yugoslavia: Figures for 1950-1952, and 1954-1960 were derived from OP-31 (1970), p. 26. Figures for 1953, and 1961 were derived from Statisticki Godisnjak Jugoslavije, Beograd: 1981, Table 104.9, p. 115. Figures for 1962-1964 were interpolated. Figures for 1965-1980 were derived from OP-71 (1982), p.29.

USSR: Figure for 1950 was derived from Roy Laird, Handbook of Soviet Social Science Data, Ellen Mickiewicz (ed), The Free Press, New York: 1973, p. 75. Figures for 1951-1958 were interpolated. Figures for 1959-1980 were derived from Yearbook of Labor Statistics, ILO, Geneva, various issues.

China: Figures for 1950-1979 were derived from Anthony Tang and Bruce Stone, Food Production in the PRC, International Food Policy Research Institute, Research Report No. 15, Washington D.C.: May 1980, Table 11, p. 43. Figure for 1980 was derived from Statistical Yearbook for China 1981, Beijing: 1982.

Land

Figures for 1950-1980 for the East European countries (except Yugoslavia) and USSR were derived from USDA, Agricultural Statistics of Eastern Europe and The Soviet Union 1950-70, ERS 349, Washington D.C.: 1973, p. 9-16, and USDA, Agricultural Statistics of Eastern Europe and The Soviet Union 1960-80, ERS 700, Washington D.C.: 1983, page 8-15.

Figures for Yugoslavia for all years were derived from FAO, Production Yearbook, Rome, various issues.

Figures for China for 1950, 1951, 1954, 1964, and 1970-1980 were derived from FAO, Production Yearbook, Rome, various issues. Figures for 1952, and 1955-1963 were interpolated. Figures for 1953, 1955, 1956, and 1965-1969 were derived, with some adjustment, from Anthony Tang and Bruce Stone, Food Production in the PRC, IFPRI, Research Report No. 15, Washington D.C.: May 1980.

Fertilizer

Most figures (with few exceptions as shown below) were derived from FAO, Fertilizer Yearbook, Rome, various issues.

Figures for 1950-1955 for Bulgaria were derived from OP-39, page 47.

Figures for 1950, 1960, and 1975-1979 for Romania were derived from Directia Centrala de Statistica, Anuarul Statistic al Republic Socialiste Romania 1981, p. 45. Figures for 1951-1953 were derived from OP-38 (1973), page 46.

Figures for 1952-1956 for China were derived from FAO estimates adjusted with Anthony Tang and Bruce Stone, Food Production in the PRC, IFPRI, 1982, p. 40. Figures for 1957-1979 were derived from China Agricultural Yearbook, Zhongguo Nongye Nianjian Publishing Company, Beijing: 1980, p. 40. Figure for 1980 was derived from Statistical Yearbook of China 1981, Beijing: 1982.

Machinery

Figures for 1950-1980 for Bulgaria, Czechoslovakia, Hungary, Poland, and Yugoslavia were derived from USDA, Agricultural Statistics of Eastern Europe and The Soviet Union 1950-70, ERS 349, Washington D.C.: 1973, p. 23, and USDA, Agricultural Statistics of Eastern Europe and The Soviet Union 1960-80, ERS 700, Washington D.C.: 1983, page 24.

Figures for East Germany for 1950, 1953, 1955, and 1957 were derived from Statistisches Jahrbuch ddr, East Berlin: 1981, p. 26. Figures for 1952, 1954, 1956, 1958, and 1959 were derived from FAO, Production Yearbook, Rome, various issues. Figures for 1960-1980 were derived from USDA, Agricultural Statistics of Eastern Europe and The Soviet Union 1960-80, ERS 700, Washington D.C.: 1983, p. 24.

Figures for Romania for all years were derived from FAO, Production Yearbook, Rome, various issues.

Figures for the USSR for 1950, and 1953-1955 were derived from Central Statistical Administration, The USSR Economy, A Statistical Abstract, London: Lawrence & Wishart Ltd. 1957, p. 144. Figures for 1951, and 1952 were interpolated. Figures for 1956-1959 were derived from FAO, Production Yearbook, Rome, various issues. Figures for 1960-1980 were derived from USDA, Agricultural Statistics of Eastern Europe and The Soviet Union 1960-80, ERS 700, Washington D.C.: 1983, p. 24.

Figures for China for 1950-1970 were derived from China Agricultural Yearbook, Zhongguo Nongyu Nianjian Publishing Company, Beijing: 1980, p. 39. Figures for 1966-1969 were adjusted with Anthony Tang's estimate (Tang and Stone 1980; p. 65). Figure for 1980 was derived from Statistical Yearbook of China 1981, Beijing: 1982, p. 171.

Livestock & Horses

Figures for all years for all countries were derived from FAO, Production Yearbook, Rome, various issues.

Arable Land

Figures for East European countries and the USSR for all years were derived from USDA, Agricultural Statistics of Eastern Europe and The Soviet Union 1950-70, ERS 349, Washington D.C.: 1973, p. 9-16, and USDA, Agricultural Statistics of Eastern Europe and The Soviet Union 1960-80, ERS 700, Washington D.C.: 1983, p. 8-15, except for figures for Poland for 1951, 1952, and 1954 and for the USSR for 1950-1953, 1956, and 1957 were interpolated.

Figures for China for all years were derived from FAO, Production Yearbook, Rome, various issues.

Population

Figures for Bulgaria, Czechoslovakia, East Germany, Poland, Romania, Yugoslavia, USSR for 1950-1980 were derived from FAO, Production Yearbook, Rome, various issues. Except figures for the USSR for 1959 were derived from Paul Shaup, The East European and Soviet Data Handbook, Columbia University Press, New York: 1981, p. 395.

Figures for Hungary were derived from Statisztikai Evkonyv 1978, Kozpontic Statisztikai Hiratal, Budapest.

Figures for China were mostly derived from Anthony Tang and Bruce Stone, Food Production in the PRC, IFPRI, Washington D.C.: 1980. Figures for 1952, 1957, 1965, 1975, and 1979 were derived from Annual Economic Report of China, Beijing: 1981, p. VI-3. Figures for 1950-1951 were interpolated backwards assuming rural population increased 6,637,000 per year.

School

Figures for all countries were derived from UNESCO, Statistics of Educational Attainment and Illiteracy, 1945-1979, Paris: 1977, and UNESCO, Statistical Yearbook, Paris, various issues.

Research

Figures for all countries were derived from James Boyce and Robert Evenson, Agricultural Research and Extension Programs, Agricultural Development Council, New York, page 22, 30, and supplemented with Ann Judd, James Boyce, and Robert Evenson, "Investment in Agricultural Supply," Mimeograph, Economic Growth Center, Yale University: 1983, p. 51, 61.

Table B.1: Aggregate Agricultural Output and Input Table for Bulgaria (1950-80)

YEAR	OUTPUT 1000 W.U.	LABOR 1000 MAN-YR	LAND 1000 HA	FERT 1000 MT	MACH 1000 30HP/U	HORSE 1000 HEAD	LVSK 1000 UNIT	ARABLE 1000 HA	POPUL 1000 PERSON	SCHOOL 1000 RATIO	RE 1000 SMY
1950	6742	2777	5721	12	5	471	3529	4564	0	63	0
1951	9461	2674	5673	16	6	471	3529	4559	0	0	0
1952	7177	2605	5649	20	6	471	3529	4546	0	0	0
1953	9026	2613	5641	22	7	471	3529	4542	0	0	0
1954	7503	2586	5645	30	8	467	3461	4556	0	0	0
1955	8482	2615	5592	35	9	468	3454	4545	4198	72	0
1956	7830	2653	5598	49	12	472	3477	4549	0	0	0
1957	9352	2602	5543	71	14	460	3404	4531	0	0	0
1958	9243	2668	5509	79	14	431	3417	4516	0	63	0
1959	11092	2533	5630	202	17	382	3379	4623	0	0	250
1960	10875	2318	5672	156	20	334	3337	4624	3823	82	0
1961	10440	2305	5673	144	22	312	3604	4619	0	0	0
1962	10875	2149	5685	151	24	301	3748	4538	0	0	300
1963	10983	2082	5693	175	28	277	3624	4531	0	89	0
1964	12506	2019	5772	284	31	256	3548	4574	0	91	0
1965	13049	1770	5792	361	33	249	3644	4563	4227	97	350
1966	15333	1713	5802	477	36	240	3550	4564	0	100	0
1967	15007	1687	5863	607	38	229	3480	4554	0	100	0
1968	13919	1605	5881	742	42	224	3425	4558	0	89	650
1969	14463	1524	6022	692	45	199	3322	4555	0	94	0
1970	14572	1461	6010	639	47	182	3219	4527	3957	98	981
1971	15007	1400	6009	636	50	169	3355	4516	0	98	0
1972	16529	1370	6022	646	55	159	3527	4510	0	94	0
1973	15768	1315	5982	633	61	148	3511	4502	0	94	960
1974	14681	1270	5988	567	67	142	3486	4488	0	94	0
1975	15986	1188	5951	679	69	137	3752	4339	3466	96	0
1976	17073	1129	6198	658	72	133	3989	4327	3358	94	0
1977	15768	1084	6206	742	75	128	3925	4313	3252	96	0
1978	16529	1056	6215	738	76	126	3987	4292	3143	95	966
1979	17834	1056	6206	820	77	124	4074	4258	3035	94	0
1980	17073	1037	6185	830	77	120	4156	4176	2947	94	0

149

Table B.2: Aggregate Agricultural Output and Input Table for Czechoslavakia (1950-80)

YEAR	OUTPUT 1000 W.U.	LABOR 1000 MAN-YR	LAND 1000 HA	FERT 1000 MT	MACH 1000 30HP/U	HORSE 1000 HEAD	LVSK 1000 UNIT	ARABLE 1000 HA	POPUL 1000 PERSON	SCHOOL 1000 RATIO	RE 1000 SMY
1950	14770	2063	7506	100	15	635	4865	5411	0	76	0
1951	14770	1927	7474	100	13	623	5084	5412	0	0	0
1952	14602	1855	7455	100	15	611	5302	5430	0	0	0
1953	16280	1862	7215	100	16	599	5521	5261	0	0	0
1954	14770	1903	7294	137	18	544	5032	5359	0	0	0
1955	16112	1938	7414	140	21	543	5129	5458	2416	79	0
1956	17287	1898	7377	395	24	543	5288	5409	0	0	0
1957	16448	1827	7336	420	27	542	5321	5392	0	0	0
1958	15944	1775	7389	514	31	517	5268	5448	0	0	0
1959	15777	1725	7328	497	37	456	5250	5438	0	0	1470
1960	16784	1570	7147	496	47	389	5368	5427	3495	85	0
1961	16280	1480	7277	554	58	330	5425	5419	0	0	0
1962	15777	1439	7237	575	69	292	5490	5412	0	0	1770
1963	17455	1422	7213	673	81	254	5418	5413	0	87	0
1964	17791	1392	6819	820	83	227	5377	5401	0	85	0
1965	15273	1259	7160	896	90	204	5367	5387	3026	77	2070
1966	17958	1254	7144	928	127	188	5186	5373	0	79	0
1967	18294	1223	7132	945	131	177	5203	5362	0	78	0
1968	19301	1204	7117	1119	133	166	5252	5353	0	77	4015
1969	19637	1189	7103	1188	134	156	5020	5342	0	77	0
1970	19805	1178	7093	1282	136	144	4993	5334	2429	75	0
1971	20979	1161	7077	1373	138	135	5174	5329	0	77	3150
1972	21819	1089	7071	1417	139	118	5269	5323	0	77	0
1973	23161	1056	7060	1406	141	101	5379	5311	0	76	0
1974	24168	1048	7042	1549	142	84	5480	5290	0	77	4100
1975	22994	1024	7004	1684	142	71	5543	5256	1961	77	0
1976	22490	1003	6990	1676	141	62	5522	5258	1871	77	0
1977	24336	980	6976	1634	140	57	5659	5259	1790	78	0
1978	25679	962	6952	1749	140	53	5939	5246	1724	78	4654
1979	23833	955	6924	1745	138	49	6323	5214	1650	77	0
1980	25847	953	6851	1730	137	47	6085	5169	1571	77	0

Table B.3: Aggregate Agricultural Output and Input Table for East Germany (1950-80)

YEAR	OUTPUT 1000 W.U.	LABOR 1000 MAN-YR	LAND 1000 HA	FERT 1000 MT	MACH 1000 30HP/U	HORSE 1000 HEAD	LVSK 1000 UNIT	ARABLE 1000 HA	POPUL 1000 PERSON	SCHOOL 1000 RATIO	RE 1000 SMY
1950	16853	1483	6528	650	36	695	4661	5235	0	84	0
1951	20029	1483	6548	707	40	723	5213	5261	0	0	0
1952	21006	1498	6526	648	44	741	5662	5255	0	0	0
1953	21006	1488	6511	708	47	749	6230	5253	0	0	0
1954	21983	1523	6497	733	52	727	5899	5235	0	0	0
1955	20273	1583	6482	770	55	695	5903	5218	3488	79	0
1956	20761	1514	6474	869	58	669	5996	5206	0	0	0
1957	21494	1461	6466	901	65	624	5790	5184	0	69	0
1958	22227	1461	6448	953	66	624	5825	5148	0	0	0
1959	21006	1376	6448	952	69	607	5994	5089	0	0	0
1960	24425	1230	6440	971	71	560	6441	5067	3026	84	0
1961	18563	1199	6478	959	90	447	6465	5013	0	0	0
1962	21494	1199	6459	1024	100	403	6412	4969	0	78	0
1963	21494	1198	6440	1114	111	369	6160	4930	0	79	0
1964	22715	1205	6463	1277	118	341	6516	4932	0	95	0
1965	23937	1132	6442	1313	125	306	6419	4921	2601	96	0
1966	23937	1102	6438	1350	133	272	6465	4898	0	92	0
1967	26379	1081	6430	1354	139	250	6639	4893	0	90	0
1968	26135	1026	6310	1485	144	219	6671	4863	0	101	0
1969	24181	986	6286	1500	146	188	6714	4840	0	93	0
1970	25158	956	6286	1535	149	148	6737	4817	2214	94	0
1971	24914	931	6287	1601	149	140	6709	4824	0	95	0
1972	27600	893	6292	1618	146	106	6946	4843	0	94	0
1973	27600	875	6287	1755	143	94	7082	4858	0	94	0
1974	30287	860	6290	1840	142	82	7277	4890	1880	93	0
1975	28577	852	6295	1826	140	76	7515	4936	1817	94	0
1976	27356	836	6293	1804	138	70	7462	4998	1757	93	0
1977	29554	831	6291	1670	137	68	7380	5029	1707	96	0
1978	31020	834	6282	1670	140	66	7536	5039	1654	95	0
1979	31020	833	6280	1639	143	66	7573	5041	1600	95	0
1980	31020	834	6283	1638	145	66	7684	5027			

Table B.4: Aggregate Agricultural Output and Input Table for Hungary (1950-80)

YEAR	OUTPUT 1000 W.U.	LABOR 1000 MAN-YR	LAND 1000 HA	FERT 1000 MT	MACH 1000 30HP/U	HORSE 1000 HEAD	LVSK 1000 UNIT	ARABLE 1000 HA	POPUL 1000 PERSON	SCHOOL 1000 RATIO	RE 1000 SMY
1950	11087	2105	7376	11	7	610	3859	5901	5400	77	0
1951	13601	2082	7348	12	7	634	3224	5893	0	0	0
1952	9461	2053	7338	12	7	657	3529	5896	0	0	0
1953	12418	1934	7277	40	7	681	3835	5856	0	0	0
1954	11383	1910	7277	40	9	683	3637	5836	0	0	0
1955	13601	1952	7246	54	12	711	3991	5775	0	74	0
1956	12270	1991	7214	50	13	729	4098	5764	0	0	0
1957	14488	2032	7201	73	14	720	3721	5760	0	0	0
1958	13601	2005	7195	95	14	724	3793	5754	0	74	0
1959	15966	1928	7186	130	18	717	4037	5751	0	74	400
1960	14783	1850	7141	164	24	628	3778	5703	5547	84	0
1961	14044	1675	7083	200	27	463	3742	5624	0	0	0
1962	14783	1663	7012	268	31	374	3803	5622	0	0	500
1963	15227	1586	6985	340	36	334	3613	5626	0	81	0
1964	15670	1527	6979	343	42	323	3899	5638	0	80	0
1965	16114	1266	6953	357	46	321	4095	5649	0	87	1500
1966	17149	1252	6927	387	49	295	3847	5642	0	79	0
1967	17444	1238	6914	514	49	287	3972	5626	0	78	0
1968	17444	1228	6903	629	50	274	4148	5613	0	76	1560
1969	18627	1210	6888	699	52	249	3721	5604	0	85	0
1970	17592	1180	6875	837	57	231	3866	5594	5211	82	0
1971	20253	1154	6855	954	59	219	4194	5578	5163	83	1420
1972	21731	1126	6846	1017	59	204	4041	5565	5129	84	0
1973	22323	1086	6835	1202	59	189	3941	5555	5102	84	0
1974	23801	1051	6782	1336	60	172	4028	5503	5072	85	1500
1975	23505	1024	6770	1518	62	163	4187	5495	5058	76	0
1976	22914	998	6757	1388	64	156	3812	5471	5029	77	0
1977	25131	983	6729	1511	58	147	4073	5422	5002	78	0
1978	26018	978	6698	1539	56	144	4150	5388	4974	79	1471
1979	24688	984	6651	1502	55	134	4228	5356	4941	79	0
1980	27053	986	6626	1399	55	126	4266	5332	4900	79	0

Table B.5: Aggregate Agricultural Output and Input Table for Poland (1950-80)

YEAR	OUTPUT 1000 W.J.	LABOR 1000 MAN-YR	LAND 1000 HA	FERT 1000 MT	MACH 1000 30HP/U	HORSE 1000 HEAD	LVSK 1000 UNIT	ARABLE 1000 HA	POPUL 1000 PERSON	SCHOOL 1000 RATIO	RE 1000 SMY
1950	32966	5420	20440	385	13	2677	11018	16223	0	70	0
1951	29303	5411	20415	389	17	2797	11314	16223	0	0	0
1952	29303	5402	20415	444	20	2759	11489	16223	0	0	0
1953	30117	5393	20403	451	23	2720	11663	16223	0	0	0
1954	32966	5384	20403	503	26	2650	12018	16223	0	0	0
1955	32152	5375	20403	575	30	2560	12422	16223	11244	68	0
1956	36629	5364	20403	634	32	2547	12897	16224	0	0	0
1957	37036	5352	20403	696	35	2623	13061	16223	0	0	0
1958	37850	5341	20403	651	37	2732	13107	16223	0	0	0
1959	37443	5329	20403	745	36	2839	13260	16223	0	86	1240
1960	40699	5318	20403	795	39	2805	13846	16223	11103	85	0
1961	45176	5343	20322	893	45	2731	14374	16176	0	0	0
1962	40699	5346	20262	918	51	2657	14615	16068	0	0	2170
1963	43955	5356	20184	987	59	2620	14328	15971	0	90	0
1964	45176	5383	20130	1107	65	2593	14699	15942	0	90	0
1965	45990	5289	19946	1303	73	2554	14918	15682	13742	82	3210
1966	48025	5271	19947	1582	81	2590	15414	15682	0	92	0
1967	50467	5248	19819	1829	92	2643	15893	15518	0	93	0
1968	52502	5231	19777	2141	102	2673	15975	15494	0	93	4100
1969	50060	5226	19557	2416	114	2633	16171	15333	0	78	0
1970	50874	5210	19543	2572	140	2585	15782	15326	12688	87	0
1971	49246	5198	19508	2888	160	2570	15357	15277	0	83	4700
1972	53723	5158	19371	3047	182	2422	16872	15147	0	69	0
1973	57386	5170	19326	3343	209	2373	17896	15107	0	82	0
1974	57793	5198	19258	3460	240	2312	18940	15078	0	82	5150
1975	56572	4860	19209	3671	264	2237	19056	15084	11757	82	0
1976	58200	4765	19151	3586	289	2151	18502	15038	11578	83	0
1977	53723	4670	19111	3606	322	2062	18886	15018	11395	90	0
1978	58607	4574	19060	3567	355	1891	17918	15989	11204	91	5259
1979	56979	4422	18991	3260	396	1856	17712	14931	10994	91	0
1980	50060	4310	18947	3510	429	1780	17381	14901	10801	91	0

Table B.6: Aggregate Agricultural Output and Input Table for Romania (1950-80)

YEAR	OUTPUT 1000 W.U.	LABOR 1000 MAN-YR	LAND 1000 HA	FERT 1000 MT	MACH 1000 30HP/U	HORSE 1000 HEAD	LVSK 1000 UNIT	ARABLE 1000 HA	POPUL 1000 PERSON	SCHOOL 1000 RATIO	RE 1000 SMY
1950	10392	6209	14324	6	14	1079	7105	9789	0	47	0
1951	13975	6107	14297	2	12	1079	7105	9785	0	0	0
1952	12542	6152	14321	3	9	1079	7105	9874	0	0	0
1953	15229	6153	14171	3	10	1073	7060	9851	0	0	0
1954	14154	6187	14145	4	25	1067	7058	9968	0	0	0
1955	17200	6626	14112	4	30	1120	7236	10058	9307	50	0
1956	13438	6369	14168	9	32	1150	7577	10092	0	0	0
1957	17200	6466	14281	12	38	1230	7573	10125	0	0	0
1958	14333	6552	14423	40	33	1309	7068	10196	0	0	0
1959	18634	6598	14546	61	37	1223	7096	10328	0	69	650
1960	17917	6776	14547	75	44	1110	7157	10346	11861	71	0
1961	18634	6544	14601	91	52	1010	7159	10393	0	0	0
1962	17200	6517	14688	102	58	1013	7541	10491	0	0	850
1963	17917	6490	14724	188	65	780	7047	10475	0	82	0
1964	18813	6463	14742	188	75	709	7132	10496	0	87	0
1965	20604	6553	14791	266	81	689	7543	10475	11454	82	1285
1966	23650	6410	14835	336	91	689	7598	10502	0	82	0
1967	23292	6383	14838	441	93	705	7974	10526	0	83	0
1968	22754	6356	14972	485	96	715	8211	10560	0	85	1900
1969	23471	6329	14968	538	102	703	8046	10544	0	94	0
1970	20425	6354	14930	594	107	686	7978	10512	11341	87	0
1971	25263	6275	14935	633	114	665	8175	10506	0	88	2500
1972	28488	6249	14943	639	116	654	8770	10488	0	88	0
1973	26696	6222	14904	854	117	631	9216	10426	0	86	0
1974	27413	6195	14929	921	117	610	9343	10469	0	91	3200
1975	27950	6126	14946	929	120	557	9241	10500	10967	93	0
1976	35117	6068	14955	1005	128	562	9516	10518	10882	95	0
1977	34042	6004	14960	1025	139	576	10162	10534	10784	95	0
1978	34579	5926	14904	1111	139	550	9946	10542	10704	94	3698
1979	36013	5848	14967	1217	140	570	10516	10481	10607	94	0
1980	36013	5735	14963	1223	147	566	10525	10497	10484	94	0

153

154

Table B.7: Aggregate Agricultural Output and Input Table for Yugoslavia (1950-80)

YEAR	OUTPUT 1000 W.U.	LABOR 1000 MAN-YR	LAND 1000 HA	FERT 1000 MT	MACH 1000 30HP/U	HORSE 1000 HEAD	LVSK 1000 UNIT	ARABLE 1000 HA	POPUL 1000 PERSON	SCHOOL 1000 RATIO	RE 1000 SMY
1950	9454	5520	13793	17	8	1097	7621	7839	0	55	0
1951	14181	5467	13900	25	9	1095	7124	7792	0	0	0
1952	8319	5413	13998	24	10	1102	7277	7820	0	0	0
1953	14748	5360	14251	24	10	1126	7645	7944	0	0	0
1954	12101	5277	14533	56	9	1193	7813	8077	0	0	0
1955	15883	5193	14752	82	10	1242	8098	8192	0	58	0
1956	12668	5110	14933	124	15	1296	8005	8263	0	0	0
1957	18908	5026	14920	165	21	1307	7549	8290	0	0	0
1958	15504	4943	14967	219	27	1296	7586	8327	0	0	0
1959	21177	4859	14955	275	32	1274	8016	8345	10324	73	1080
1960	18908	4776	14923	233	34	1272	8375	8353	0	79	0
1961	18152	4692	14952	262	38	1220	8506	8382	0	0	0
1962	18908	4613	14863	325	40	1226	8549	8363	0	0	1100
1963	20231	4532	14763	444	43	1175	7943	8353	0	84	0
1964	21744	4452	14773	468	45	1140	7921	8343	0	85	0
1965	20042	4365	14756	455	45	1109	8105	8306	11040	78	1140
1966	24202	4288	14716	502	51	1131	8108	8266	0	77	0
1967	23446	4211	14687	516	47	1134	8362	8267	0	77	0
1968	22689	4134	14666	551	44	1126	8398	8246	0	77	1720
1969	24958	4057	14640	583	68	1109	7827	8237	0	77	0
1970	22879	3980	14626	631	67	1076	7651	8205	10145	77	0
1971	25337	3903	14520	669	97	1230	8104	8173	0	79	1890
1972	24958	3825	14490	716	121	1015	7793	8130	0	80	0
1973	26093	3748	14435	706	135	964	7921	8091	0	81	0
1974	29874	3673	14421	674	195	945	8426	8065	0	82	1970
1975	29496	3600	14388	720	226	922	8683	8034	9284	84	0
1976	31198	3528	14321	738	261	864	8256	8005	9111	85	0
1977	32711	3457	14274	802	297	812	8269	7948	8914	86	0
1978	30631	3388	14281	855	342	759	8367	7927	8748	87	2006
1979	31387	3320	14241	870	385	701	8128	7848	8562	88	0
1980	31387	3254	14284	824	416	617	7942	7833	8348	88	0

Table B.8: Aggregate Agricultural Output and Input Table for USSR (1950-80)

YEAR	OUTPUT 1000 W.U.	LABOR 1000 MAN-YR	LAND 1000 HA	FERT 1000 MT	MACH 1000 30HP/U	HORSE 1000 HEAD	LVSK 1000 UNIT	ARABLE 1000 HA	POPUL 1000 PERSON	SCHOOL 1000 RATIO	RE 1000 SMY
1950	169237	30700	626300	1098	595	13705	77719	217362	0	83	0
1951	153008	30873	625200	1147	645	13705	78679	218301	0	0	0
1952	173873	30617	624200	1197	693	14700	82015	219240	0	0	0
1953	171555	30360	623100	1247	744	14700	81169	220179	0	0	0
1954	176192	30103	647800	1297	795	16200	94511	219700	0	0	0
1955	197056	29847	621000	1347	844	15400	96295	219000	0	0	0
1956	220239	29590	620000	1336	877	14200	97896	230286	0	0	0
1957	210966	29333	618900	1505	911	13000	100844	223936	0	0	0
1958	241104	29077	609100	1505	1001	11904	93124	223400	0	0	0
1959	229513	29940	608900	1593	1036	11500	98045	224400	0	79	12000
1960	231831	28970	608700	1541	1122	11000	101920	226100	81000	89	0
1961	245741	28250	609300	2404	1212	9900	102824	228500	90000	0	0
1962	248059	27770	609400	2749	1329	9400	109652	229800	0	0	20400
1963	234149	27320	609200	3230	1442	9100	114196	230000	0	97	0
1964	278197	27550	609100	4464	1539	8500	104839	229400	0	100	0
1965	264287	27760	609700	5677	1613	7900	106876	229350	77964	95	24450
1966	310653	27530	608900	6222	1660	7977	114125	229300	0	95	0
1967	303699	27250	608500	6922	1739	7990	117825	229250	0	95	0
1968	317608	27050	608300	7378	1821	8025	116941	229900	0	95	25600
1969	306017	26690	608100	8883	1908	8000	115770	233205	0	95	0
1970	345428	26440	606800	10312	1977	7522	115553	232809	62294	100	0
1971	343110	26260	607300	11346	2046	7400	121689	232609	0	94	29800
1972	326882	26200	607700	12360	2112	7320	125786	232431	0	94	0
1973	394113	26280	607900	13461	2180	7075	125925	232101	0	91	0
1974	368611	26290	607800	14740	2267	6848	128993	232704	0	91	33350
1975	329200	25940	604200	17243	2336	6749	132274	232207	52227	99	0
1976	389476	25880	605700	17732	2402	6415	129649	232306	50536	90	0
1977	377884	25650	606000	18026	2458	5996	129912	232404	48824	100	0
1978	414977	25650	606100	18412	2515	5822	134174	231761	47200	100	31394
1979	370930	25400	606000	17358	2540	5700	136498	231871	45570	100	0
1980	382521	25260	606300	18756	2562	5600	137727	231900	43602	100	0

155

Table B.9: Aggregate Agricultural Output and Input Table for China (1950-80)

YEAR	OUTPUT 1000 W.U.	LABOR 1000 MAN-YR	LAND 1000 HA	FERT 1000 MT	MACH 1000 30HP/U	HORSE 1000 HEAD	LVSK 1000 UNIT	ARABLE 1000 HA	POPUL 1000 PERSON	SCHOOL 1000 RATIO	RE 1000 SMY
1950	216961	166151	330055	81	1	2023	67593	106446	489916	20	0
1951	238128	167414	319379	110	1	3520	80221	107173	496553	0	0
1952	275170	168677	308703	295	1	5017	88015	107900	503190	0	0
1953	283108	169940	298027	473	2	6512	102685	108500	508011	0	0
1954	293692	171575	287350	646	3	6939	105050	109354	516464	0	0
1955	314859	174134	290209	973	5	7312	104908	110100	528001	35	0
1956	330734	176396	293067	1236	5	7411	105208	111800	539004	0	0
1957	341317	177267	295925	1794	11	7357	111665	111800	547040	0	0
1958	351901	178193	296211	2708	14	7302	117941	107800	552127	58	0
1959	304275	179688	295755	2533	26	7800	123610	107300	559830	0	1250
1960	264587	180925	299601	3164	33	7600	125646	107200	566091	0	0
1961	259295	182544	300110	2242	46	7600	136947	107100	572424	0	0
1962	275170	185017	301761	3105	52	7600	148239	107000	580786	0	4000
1963	306921	188107	305104	4483	54	7600	150444	107000	591101	0	0
1964	346609	192005	308714	5363	59	7600	152152	119900	603359	0	0
1965	375714	196471	308500	8812	66	7600	154062	120800	623680	0	8000
1966	407464	201265	309300	12582	73	7600	155268	121800	630246	0	0
1967	415402	205476	312100	13628	83	7500	163087	108900	641517	0	0
1968	404818	210076	322900	10129	97	7400	164078	102900	653483	0	11000
1969	410110	214946	311400	13611	106	7400	165028	124800	666033	0	0
1970	457736	220702	310484	15351	117	7300	166354	125800	681448	66	0
1971	470965	226582	310927	18142	126	7200	167199	127000	697127	0	13500
1972	468319	232388	310721	20931	150	7100	169449	107300	712420	0	0
1973	508007	238274	320449	25553	190	7000	170834	101200	727995	0	0
1974	529174	244111	312443	24051	234	7000	172374	130000	742956	0	16000
1975	555633	250010	312960	26579	280	7000	172881	130000	807990	92	0
1976	568862	255956	319516	28850	345	6900	174905	129000	821991	0	0
1977	576800	262052	310500	31920	397	6800	176901	100300	835112	98	0
1978	629717	265666	319487	43681	467	6700	182088	106500	838706	95	17000
1979	685280	271739	319624	52476	557	6600	185303	99600	842300	83	0
1980	703801	294004	319200	61321	667	6500	191341	99310	850000	83	0
					745			99200			

Table B.10: Livestock Numbers for Bulgaria (1000 heads)

YEAR	HORSE	MULE	ASS	CATTLE	BU'LO	CAMEL	PIG	SHEEP	GOAT	CHICKEN
1950	471	36	197	1687	277	0	1337	7759	688	12610
1951	471	36	197	1687	277	0	1337	7759	688	12610
1952	471	36	197	1687	277	0	1337	7759	688	12610
1953	471	36	197	1687	277	0	1337	7759	688	12610
1954	467	35	198	1591	259	0	1436	7867	668	12851
1955	468	35	199	1607	260	0	1316	7802	669	13611
1956	472	36	206	1602	254	0	1413	7829	652	13817
1957	460	37	231	1529	243	0	1468	7596	617	14117
1958	431	37	233	1442	231	0	1993	7742	620	14302
1959	382	36	244	1356	216	0	2052	8619	400	15236
1960	334	34	242	1284	174	0	2266	8769	273	21666
1961	312	33	257	1452	190	0	2553	9333	246	23366
1962	301	33	263	1582	201	0	2331	10161	265	22800
1963	277	32	263	1582	177	0	2066	10107	286	20969
1964	256	31	268	1494	147	0	2097	10308	353	21922
1965	249	31	276	1474	138	0	2607	10440	422	21883
1966	240	29	287	1450	127	0	2408	10312	436	20845
1967	229	30	291	1385	107	0	2276	9998	409	27726
1968	224	30	301	1363	99	0	2314	9905	384	24874
1969	199	30	300	1297	89	0	2140	9652	376	29590
1970	182	29	299	1255	77	0	1967	9223	350	33706
1971	169	30	305	1279	74	0	2369	9678	335	34000
1972	159	30	302	1379	74	0	2806	10127	318	31319
1973	148	30	307	1441	71	0	2598	9921	302	32187
1974	142	30	312	1454	67	0	2431	9765	286	34320
1975	137	30	317	1554	68	0	3422	9791	299	32694
1976	133	31	326	1656	69	0	3889	10014	321	35891
1977	128	31	320	1722	65	0	3456	9723	308	37329
1978	126	30	330	1736	61	0	3399	10144	326	39025
1979	124	31	334	1763	56	0	3772	10105	374	38331
1980	120	30	337	1787	52	0	3830	10536	433	39164

Table B.11: Livestock Numbers for Czechoslovakia
(1000 heads)

YEAR	HORSE	MULE	ASS	CATTLE	BU'LO	CAMEL	PIG	SHEEP	GOAT	CHICKEN
1950	635	0	0	4140	0	0	3242	480	982	12356
1951	623	0	0	4242	0	0	3801	647	965	14612
1952	611	0	0	4343	0	0	4359	814	949	16868
1953	599	0	0	4445	0	0	4918	982	932	19124
1954	544	0	0	4082	0	0	4174	1017	916	19408
1955	543	0	0	4041	0	0	4771	1017	899	20743
1956	543	0	0	4107	0	0	5285	1000	846	21736
1957	542	0	0	4134	0	0	5369	956	790	22365
1958	517	0	0	4091	0	0	5435	889	739	22848
1959	456	0	0	4183	0	0	5282	817	696	24017
1960	389	0	0	4303	0	0	5687	727	662	26062
1961	330	0	0	4387	0	0	5962	646	616	26718
1962	292	0	0	4518	0	0	5895	603	597	28507
1963	254	0	0	4507	0	0	5897	524	588	26736
1964	227	0	0	4480	0	0	5845	527	582	28591
1965	204	0	0	4436	0	0	6139	568	559	27416
1966	188	0	0	4389	0	0	5544	614	521	26408
1967	177	0	0	4462	0	0	5305	670	477	28026
1968	166	0	0	4437	0	0	5601	770	417	29728
1969	156	0	0	4249	0	0	5136	906	364	31060
1970	144	0	0	4223	0	0	5037	977	318	33392
1971	135	0	0	4288	0	0	5530	981	285	37570
1972	118	0	0	4349	0	0	5935	932	241	36701
1973	101	0	0	4466	0	0	6093	889	212	37672
1974	84	0	0	4556	0	0	6266	842	174	39676
1975	71	0	0	4566	0	0	6719	811	140	38017
1976	62	0	0	4555	0	0	6683	805	121	38720
1977	57	0	0	4654	0	0	6820	797	98	42559
1978	53	0	0	4758	0	0	7510	841	83	42986
1979	49	0	0	4887	0	0	7601	865	72	45191
1980	47	0	0	4915	0	0	7588	875	63	46473

Table B.12: Livestock Numbers for E. Germany (1000 heads)

YEAR	HORSE	MULE	ASS	CATTLE	BU'LO	CAMEL	PIG	SHEEP	GOAT	CHICKEN
1950	695	0	0	3311	0	0	4317	900	1644	19902
1951	723	0	0	3615	0	0	5705	1085	1610	18786
1952	741	0	0	3801	0	0	7068	1236	1429	20000
1953	749	0	0	3936	0	0	9100	1428	1327	23690
1954	727	0	0	3796	0	0	8208	1550	1136	22476
1955	695	0	0	3793	0	0	8367	1712	961	23300
1956	669	0	0	3760	0	0	9029	1807	860	24683
1957	624	0	0	3718	0	0	8326	1893	764	26091
1958	624	0	0	3744	0	0	8255	2019	693	28354
1959	607	0	0	4145	0	0	7504	2111	625	29689
1960	560	0	0	4465	0	0	8283	2115	547	38604
1961	447	0	0	4675	0	0	8316	2015	446	36910
1962	403	1	0	4548	0	0	8864	1930	446	35879
1963	369	1	0	4508	0	0	8045	1792	388	35626
1964	341	1	0	4614	0	0	9289	1899	397	39581
1965	306	1	0	4682	0	0	8759	1972	353	38210
1966	272	1	0	4762	0	0	8878	1963	302	37988
1967	250	1	0	4918	0	0	9312	1928	278	37070
1968	219	1	0	5019	0	0	9254	1818	236	37976
1969	188	1	0	5139	0	0	9132	1794	204	38802
1970	148	1	0	5217	0	0	9198	1696	158	38900
1971	140	1	0	5235	0	0	9049	1650	150	39000
1972	106	1	0	5293	0	0	9995	1607	113	43343
1973	94	1	0	5379	0	0	10361	1657	96	43657
1974	82	1	0	5482	0	0	10849	1742	78	45667
1975	76	1	0	5585	0	0	11519	1847	65	47529
1976	70	1	0	5532	0	0	11501	1883	53	47122
1977	68	1	0	5471	0	0	11291	1870	42	48445
1978	66	1	0	5549	0	0	11757	1927	34	48258
1979	66	1	0	5572	0	0	11734	1965	29	50240
1980	66	0	0	5596	0	0	12132	1979	25	51444

Table B.13: Livestock Numbers for Hungary (1000 heads)

YEAR	HORSE	MULE	ASS	CATTLE	BU'LO	CAMEL	PIG	SHEEP	GOAT	CHICKEN
1950	610	2	4	2050	0	0	6500	1344	201	14968
1951	634	2	4	1700	0	0	4500	1442	191	16105
1952	657	2	4	1968	0	0	4739	1539	181	17242
1953	681	2	4	2236	0	0	4977	1637	170	18379
1954	683	2	4	2075	0	0	4454	1869	160	19516
1955	711	2	4	2128	0	0	5818	1857	165	20653
1956	729	2	4	2170	0	0	6056	1930	155	20797
1957	720	2	4	1973	0	0	4996	1873	129	21790
1958	724	2	4	1937	0	0	5338	2050	119	22927
1959	717	2	4	2004	0	0	6225	2155	108	24064
1960	628	2	3	1971	0	0	5356	2381	72	25225
1961	463	1	3	1957	0	0	5921	2643	66	25473
1962	374	1	3	1987	0	0	6409	2850	65	26245
1963	334	1	3	1906	0	0	5428	3043	75	35345
1964	323	1	3	1883	0	0	6358	3305	86	45592
1965	321	1	3	1964	0	0	6963	3400	80	45863
1966	295	1	3	1973	0	0	5799	3270	74	47556
1967	287	1	3	2014	0	0	6005	3274	78	53378
1968	274	1	3	2096	0	0	6609	3311	79	53311
1969	249	1	3	2006	0	0	5334	3277	80	46096
1970	231	1	4	1933	0	0	5970	3024	80	57973
1971	219	1	4	1917	0	0	7510	2657	80	66148
1972	204	0	3	1901	0	0	7353	2271	36	61216
1973	189	0	3	1965	0	0	6980	2259	35	55219
1974	172	0	3	1930	0	0	8011	1813	35	52261
1975	163	0	4	2017	0	0	8293	2021	35	54329
1976	156	0	4	1904	0	0	6953	2039	15	53390
1977	147	0	4	1887	0	0	7854	2350	20	60498
1978	144	0	4	1949	0	0	7850	2619	10	61116
1979	134	0	4	1966	0	0	8011	2863	11	62857
1980	126	0	0	1925	0	0	8355	2927	15	63520

Table B.14: Livestock Numbers for Poland (1000 heads)

YEAR	HORSE	MULE	ASS	CATTLE	BU'LO	CAMEL	PIG	SHEEP	GOAT	CHICKEN
1950	2677	0	0	7200	0	0	9400	2068	654	42909
1951	2797	0	0	7163	0	0	9928	2194	617	52007
1952	2759	0	0	7274	0	0	9829	2762	580	61105
1953	2720	0	0	7385	0	0	9730	3330	543	70204
1954	2650	0	0	7687	0	0	9788	4170	506	79302
1955	2560	0	0	7912	0	0	10888	4243	469	88400
1956	2547	0	0	8353	0	0	11561	4223	432	89000
1957	2623	0	0	8265	0	0	12325	4040	315	92500
1958	2732	0	0	8210	0	0	11959	3882	278	99900
1959	2839	0	0	8353	0	0	11209	3778	279	109100
1960	2805	0	0	8695	0	0	12615	3661	273	116850
1961	2731	0	0	9168	0	0	13434	3494	266	124600
1962	2657	0	0	9589	0	0	13617	3251	251	121300
1963	2620	0	0	9841	0	0	11653	3056	239	117551
1964	2593	0	0	9940	0	0	12918	3022	222	124629
1965	2554	0	0	9947	0	0	13779	3061	205	132368
1966	2590	0	0	10391	0	0	14251	3164	194	132500
1967	2643	0	0	10768	0	0	14233	3321	181	143900
1968	2673	0	0	10940	0	0	13911	3328	163	141900
1969	2633	0	0	11049	0	0	14337	3329	139	148500
1970	2585	0	0	10844	0	0	13446	3199	127	150000
1971	2570	0	0	10213	0	0	13870	3200	124	151000
1972	2422	0	0	11453	0	0	17347	3110	104	149677
1973	2373	0	0	12192	0	0	19782	3050	109	149700
1974	2312	0	0	13023	0	0	21496	3023	79	160000
1975	2237	0	0	13254	0	0	21311	3175	72	162891
1976	2151	0	0	12879	0	0	18848	3430	63	192923
1977	2062	0	0	13019	0	0	20051	3934	54	200000
1978	1891	0	0	13115	0	0	21717	4248	44	76229
1979	1856	0	0	13036	0	0	21224	4221	35	75526
1980	1780	0	0	12649	0	0	21326	4207	30	79292

Table B.15: Livestock Numbers for Romania (1000 heads)

YEAR	HORSE	MULE	ASS	CATTLE	BU'LO	CAMEL	PIG	SHEEP	GOAT	CHICKEN
1950	1079	7	10	4696	80	0	3437	11683	574	26085
1951	1079	7	10	4696	80	0	3437	11683	574	26085
1952	1079	7	10	4696	80	0	3437	11683	574	26085
1953	1073	7	10	4674	80	0	3654	10914	580	27223
1954	1067	7	10	4652	80	0	4088	10145	587	28362
1955	1120	7	10	4630	80	0	4370	10882	593	29500
1956	1150	7	10	4800	80	0	4950	11120	598	33000
1957	1230	7	10	4635	80	0	5078	11287	556	34000
1958	1309	7	10	4470	80	0	3249	10374	513	35000
1959	1223	7	10	4394	80	0	4008	10662	446	35000
1960	1110	7	10	4450	80	0	4300	11200	415	37000
1961	1010	7	10	4530	80	0	4300	11500	404	38000
1962	1013	7	10	4707	83	0	4665	12285	562	44692
1963	780	7	10	4566	82	0	4518	12168	550	34150
1964	709	7	10	4637	81	0	4658	12400	619	38358
1965	689	7	10	4756	81	0	6034	12734	744	39910
1966	689	7	10	4935	80	0	5365	13125	800	40084
1967	705	7	10	5198	82	0	5400	14109	828	43960
1968	715	7	10	5332	80	0	5752	14380	732	47418
1969	703	7	10	5136	79	0	5853	14298	632	47618
1970	686	7	10	5035	76	0	5972	13836	565	53894
1971	665	7	10	5215	75	0	6358	13812	540	54164
1972	654	0	35	5324	204	0	7742	14071	563	61262
1973	631	0	36	5556	211	0	8785	14455	534	64496
1974	610	0	37	5679	218	0	8987	14302	499	66511
1975	557	0	37	5774	209	0	8566	13929	433	67672
1976	562	0	38	5912	214	0	8813	13865	445	78626
1977	576	0	37	6129	222	0	10193	14331	444	91503
1978	550	42	36	6085	221	0	9744	14463	404	80119
1979	570	92	35	6283	228	0	10337	15612	412	90225
1980	566	0	36	6285	228	0	10899	15820	375	87517

Table B.16: Livestock Numbers for Yugoslavia (1000 heads)

YEAR	HORSE	MULE	ASS	CATTLE	BU'LO	CAMEL	PIG	SHEEP	GOAT	CHICKEN
1950	1097	32	152	5236	65	0	4287	10042	786	17622
1951	1095	32	152	4729	60	0	3911	10273	728	14980
1952	1102	31	160	4821	64	0	3990	10518	818	16328
1953	1126	31	166	5007	71	0	4527	11404	623	17045
1954	1193	31	166	5097	71	0	4310	12112	420	19214
1955	1242	31	166	5290	71	0	4780	11979	218	21382
1956	1296	30	166	5206	67	0	4655	11360	218	22566
1957	1307	29	166	4947	67	0	3725	10622	218	22613
1958	1296	29	166	4863	59	0	4226	10626	218	24913
1959	1274	29	137	5038	51	0	5657	11249	216	24394
1960	1272	27	143	5297	49	0	6210	11449	214	26653
1961	1220	32	140	5702	59	0	5818	10823	213	25413
1962	1226	30	140	5884	57	0	5161	11143	212	24908
1963	1175	30	140	5335	59	0	5013	10055	211	26946
1964	1140	30	140	5094	61	0	6100	9707	200	29258
1965	1109	30	140	5219	55	0	6895	9433	190	28286
1966	1131	30	140	5584	59	0	5118	9868	185	28015
1967	1134	30	125	5710	63	0	5525	10329	180	31079
1968	1126	30	125	5693	44	0	5865	10345	175	31873
1969	1109	30	120	5261	44	0	5095	9730	165	33057
1970	1076	30	110	5029	46	0	5544	8974	160	36566
1971	1230	30	100	5138	54	0	6562	8703	158	40104
1972	1015	30	90	5148	66	0	6216	8326	150	40078
1973	964	30	90	5366	59	0	6342	7774	150	44286
1974	945	30	90	5681	62	0	7401	7852	150	49217
1975	922	50	90	5872	66	0	7683	8175	150	50591
1976	864	48	90	5755	66	0	6536	7831	150	49623
1977	812	41	90	5641	65	0	7326	7484	150	53779
1978	759	13	27	5550	75	0	8452	7514	125	60398
1979	701	14	28	5491	87	0	7747	7339	125	61513
1980	617	13	25	5436	64	0	7502	7354	125	63055

Table B.17: Livestock Numbers for USSR (1000 heads)

YEAR	HORSE	MULE	ASS	CATTLE	BU'LO	CAMEL	PIG	SHEEP	GOAT	CHICKEN
1950	13705	5	999	56000	392	471	27100	82200	16800	218000
1951	13705	5	999	57200	392	471	27100	82200	16800	218000
1952	14700	5	980	58800	392	448	26700	89200	18300	251100
1953	14700	5	961	56624	392	425	28506	94273	15657	284200
1954	16200	5	942	63036	392	402	47632	114877	21021	317300
1955	15400	5	923	64930	392	379	51080	117515	19271	350400
1956	14200	5	904	67068	392	356	52155	124982	17654	383500
1957	13000	5	885	70431	392	333	56482	129879	15774	416600
1958	11904	5	866	66766	392	310	44336	120200	9923	449700
1959	11500	5	847	70842	392	287	48680	129869	9306	482800
1960	11000	5	850	74155	392	278	53368	136084	7880	514300
1961	9900	5	850	75780	392	274	58674	133014	7290	515600
1962	9400	5	850	82077	392	270	66705	137465	7033	542600
1963	9100	5	850	86988	390	266	69964	139715	6695	550400
1964	8500	5	850	85448	390	263	40858	133909	5651	448900
1965	7900	5	850	86807	364	259	52843	125231	5443	456011
1966	7977	5	850	93028	408	255	59576	129764	5552	490508
1967	7990	3	695	97111	440	251	58028	135483	5559	516156
1968	8025	3	705	97167	473	256	50867	138461	5580	528352
1969	8000	3	687	95700	485	263	49000	140587	5554	546930
1970	7522	3	581	95162	461	244	56100	130665	5148	590339
1971	7400	3	560	99142	460	238	67362	137940	5360	600000
1972	7320	3	569	102434	442	236	71434	139916	5417	653913
1973	7075	3	551	104006	429	249	66593	139086	5604	671090
1974	6848	3	525	106266	433	245	70032	142634	5900	714674
1975	6749	3	501	109122	427	253	72273	145305	5927	754000
1976	6415	2	464	111034	418	247	57899	141436	5655	705504
1977	5996	2	444	110346	393	239	63055	139834	5539	747744
1978	5822	2	418	112690	383	230	70511	141025	5586	846400
1979	5700	2	410	114086	360	220	73484	142600	5504	909024
1980	5600	2	407	115100	350	210	73898	143599	5824	941664

Table B.18: Livestock Numbers for China (1000 heads)

YEAR	HORSE	MULE	ASS	CATTLE	BU'LO	CAMEL	PIG	SHEEP	GOAT	CHICKEN
1950	2023	1905	8561	18200	18095	0	90544	25615	13976	209335
1951	3520	1818	9779	25752	18095	0	90544	25615	54253	226748
1952	5017	1731	10997	33304	18095	0	90544	25615	46197	244161
1953	6512	1645	12215	40856	19227	0	96131	36881	38142	611573
1954	6939	1717	12700	43264	20359	0	101718	48147	33157	278986
1955	7312	1723	12402	44847	21104	0	87920	50406	33812	296399
1956	7411	1708	11796	45289	21312	0	84026	53400	38254	313812
1957	7357	1707	11330	44945	21242	0	115006	56200	44057	331225
1958	7302	1706	10864	44600	20992	0	145985	59000	49860	348638
1959	7800	1704	11090	45900	21600	0	160000	61000	51530	366051
1960	7600	1703	11093	44490	20940	0	180000	59000	52020	383463
1961	7600	1702	11097	52413	24377	0	185000	62000	52510	400876
1962	7600	1700	11100	60335	27814	0	190000	63200	53000	435702
1963	7600	1700	11100	61169	28013	0	195000	64500	54000	446595
1964	7600	1700	11100	62003	28212	0	198000	65800	54000	457760
1965	7600	1700	11100	62837	28410	0	202000	67100	54000	469204
1966	7600	1700	11100	62800	28608	0	206000	68400	55000	470000
1967	7500	1620	11500	62900	28800	15	210000	69700	55500	1111000
1968	7400	1620	11550	62950	29000	16	213000	70000	56000	1124000
1969	7400	1610	11600	63000	29200	16	215000	70300	56500	1144000
1970	7300	1600	11620	63100	29300	16	220000	70600	57000	1160000
1971	7200	1590	11650	63150	29400	17	223000	71000	57500	1170000
1972	7100	1580	11650	63295	29664	17	231079	71300	58170	1196702
1973	7000	1570	11600	63348	29750	17	235831	72000	58678	1230332
1974	7000	1570	11669	63487	29929	17	239193	72967	59236	1267211
1975	7000	1550	11590	64119	29923	999	232809	73500	60188	1281170
1976	6900	1540	11550	64629	30121	999	238315	74500	60691	1312005
1977	6800	1530	11550	65129	30321	999	243300	76000	62196	1332840
1978	6700	1520	11500	63854	30084	620	295540	90360	71201	755489
1979	6600	1510	11450	63978	30071	600	305612	94940	75198	798360
1980	6500	1500	11400	64681	30080	590	325123	102880	80448	838941

Appendix C
Principal Components
Regression

The technique of Regression on Principal Components (RPC) was used extensively in Chapter III for the estimation of metaproduction functions. There are three reasons for choosing principal components as the statistical solution to the multicollinearity problem: (a) it does not require dropping of variables from the data, (b) it has a sound statistical framework, and (c) the criteria for selecting the principal components are well defined; hence, no arbitrary bias. Thus, when every variable is important to the estimated function, principal components is a useful technique for dealing with the problem of multicollinearity.

Although in recent years this technique has received considerable attention, the theoretical framework of RPC has not been presented in detail. Most notably, the procedures used to compute the components were not illustrated clearly in regular econometric textbooks. On the other hand, some statistical references discuss the theory and property of principal components, but not its economic meaning. Therefore, step-by-step procedures for regressing principal components will be presented and explained here in the context of econometrics and statistics. For a more detailed discussion, readers are referred to Maddala (1977) and Kmenta (1971) for economic interpretation; Morrison (1976) for econometric explanation; and Greenberg and Webster (1983) for statistical illustration.

Explanation of Principal Components

Suppose the goal is to estimate a production function with three independent variables, X_1, X_2, and X_3. And suppose statistical analysis shows that the variables X_1 and X_2 are highly correlated such that the rank of matrix X is less than 3. A simple solution for this problem is to drop either X_1 or X_2. However, if these correlated variables have some special meaning or are crucial to the production function, neither of the correlated variables should be dropped. Then the technique of principal components can be used to reconstruct the variables according to the following procedures:

Step 1. Express the variables X_1, X_2, and X_3 in terms of principal components L_1, L_2, and L_3. Since each of the L's is a linear combination of the X's, all of the x-variables are included in the newly constructed principal components, L's.

Step 2. Select a subset of L's (or eliminate the least important L_j) such that the majority (i.e. 95%) of the variation is still retained in the subset.

Step 3. Use the selected principal components to do regression, then transform the estimated coefficients back to coefficients for X_1, X_2, and X_3 and compute their standard errors.

The above procedures can be illustrated more clearly by mathematics and graphics. Mathematically, to compute the first principal component, L_1, is to maximize the variance of the first linear combination of X's, subject to a normalization condition. The normalization condition is required because otherwise this variance of L_1 can be increased indefinitely. That is, to choose values for h_i such that the variance, $L_1'L_1$, is maximized, and subject to a normalization condition $H'H=1$, where $L_1 = h_1X_1 + h_2X_2 + h_3X_3$. Similar procedures can be used to compute the second principal component, L_2, except that L_2 must be orthogonal (uncorrelated) to L_1.

Choose k_i to maximize $L_2'L_2$

Subject to $K'K = 1$ (normalization)

and $H'K = 1$ (orthogonal)

where $L_2 = k_1X_1 + k_2X_2 + k_3X_3$

The orthogonal condition is crucial because it minimizes the correlation between the newly constructed principal components. To find out the value for h_i and k_i is not a simple task. Fortunately, it can be shown that the value for

h_i and k_i is the eigen vector of matrix X. This saves a lot of trouble in the computation of principal components.

Graphically, the transformation is to map every point from the X's plane to the L's plane as shown below:

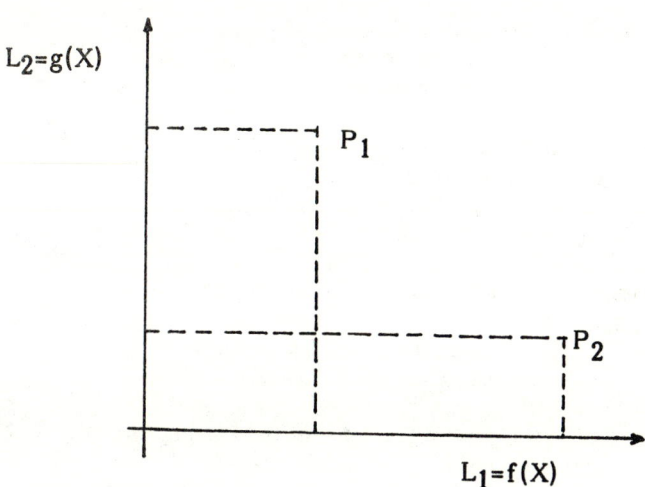

If the first and second principal components explain a large portion of the variation of the X's, then one can use only two principal components to represent three x-variables.

Since the calculated values for h_i and k_i are closely related to the scale of X's when the x-variables are not expressed by the same measuring unit, the x-variables should be normalized before any computation. For example, using the correlation matrix of X instead of the X matrix itself can normalize the data so that estimates are unit independent.

Procedures for Regression

Most standard econometric packages consist of the option for Regression on Principal Components, but intermediate steps are often omitted and overlooked by users. The procedures used to perform regression on principal components (expressed in matrix notation) follow.

Step 1: Compute the correlation matrix, R_X

$$R_X = (X-\overline{X})'(X-\overline{X}) / (N-1)(V_X)$$

where $\overline{X}$ is the mean of X
V_X is the variance of X

Step 2: Compute the eigen vector of R_x, which is the values for the parameter h's and k's.

$$(R_x - r*I) V = 0 \quad \text{or} \quad |R_x - r*I| = 0$$

where r = eigen value of R_x
I = identity matrix
V = eigen vector of R_x

Step 3: Compute principal components, PC, such that the variance equals to 1.

$$PC = (X - \bar{X}) * V * D_x / S_x$$

where S_x = standard deviation of R_x

D_x = diagonal matrix with $r^{-1/2}$ as its diagonal value

Step 4: Select a subset of principal components so that the majority of the variance can be explained. There are three criteria for deciding how many components should be included in the regression. The first is to look at the eigen values and exclude those that are zero or close to zero. The second is to look at the percentage variation that an eigen value can explain. And the third is to compute the cumulative percentage variation that a subset of principal components can explain.

Step 5: Do regression $Y-\bar{Y}$ on PC such as:

$$Y-\bar{Y} = a_0 + a_1 PC_1 + a_2 PC_2$$

Since PC_3 is excluded from the regression, this in turn restricts $a_3 = 0$. Thus, RPC is in fact a restricted regression.

Step 6: Transform the a_i to c_i

$$C = P * A \quad \text{where} \quad P = V * D_x$$

such that the centered regression can be established:

$$Y-\bar{Y} = c_1(X_1-\bar{X}_1)/S_{x1} + c_2(X_2-\bar{X}_2)/S_{x2} + ..$$

Step 7: Transform the centered equation back to the original X's

$$B_0 = Y - \sum (c_i * X_i / S_{xi})$$

$$B_i = c_i / S_{xi} \quad \text{for } i=1,2,3$$

The statistical package SHAZAM was used for the analysis in this study. The results from SHAZAM were double checked by a matrix manipulation program MATTER, using the above procedures. The results from SHAZAM and MATTER were essentially the same.

Appendix D
Trends of Yearly
Shift Factors

The total factor productivity indices computed in Chapter IV utilized Solow's geometric index approach. As pointed out in section 4.4, one of the favorable features of Solow's approach was that yearly shift factors of the productivity indices were actually estimated. The trends of these yearly shift factors reflect, in some degree, the patterns of technical change. Hence, the plots of yearly shift factors presented in this appendix reveal the movements of technological changes in the agricultural sectors of the nine socialist countries included in this study.

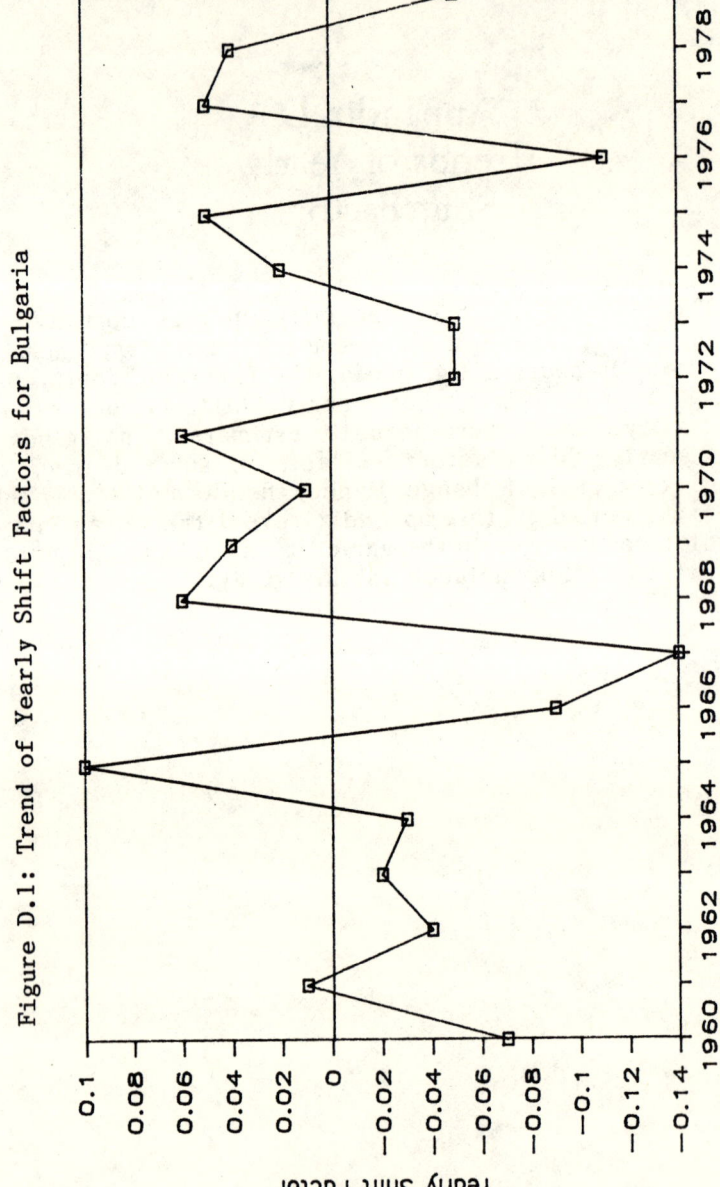

Figure D.1: Trend of Yearly Shift Factors for Bulgaria

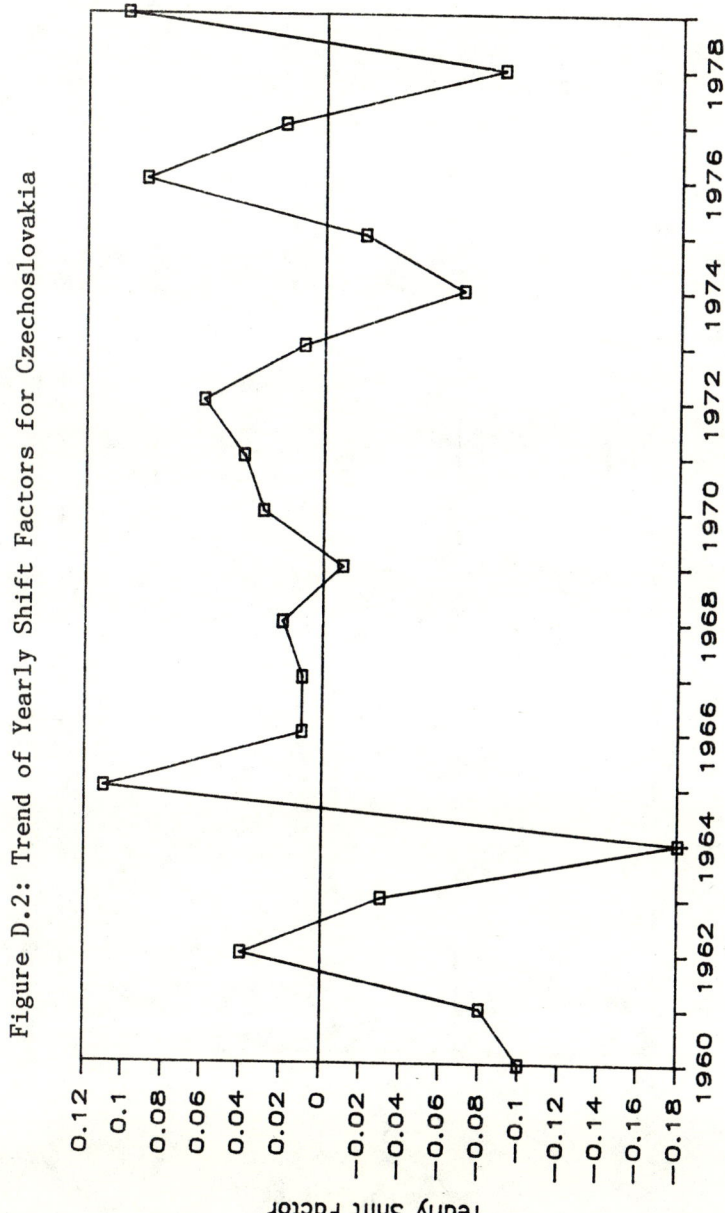

Figure D.2: Trend of Yearly Shift Factors for Czechoslovakia

Figure D.3: Trend of Yearly Shift Factors for East Germany

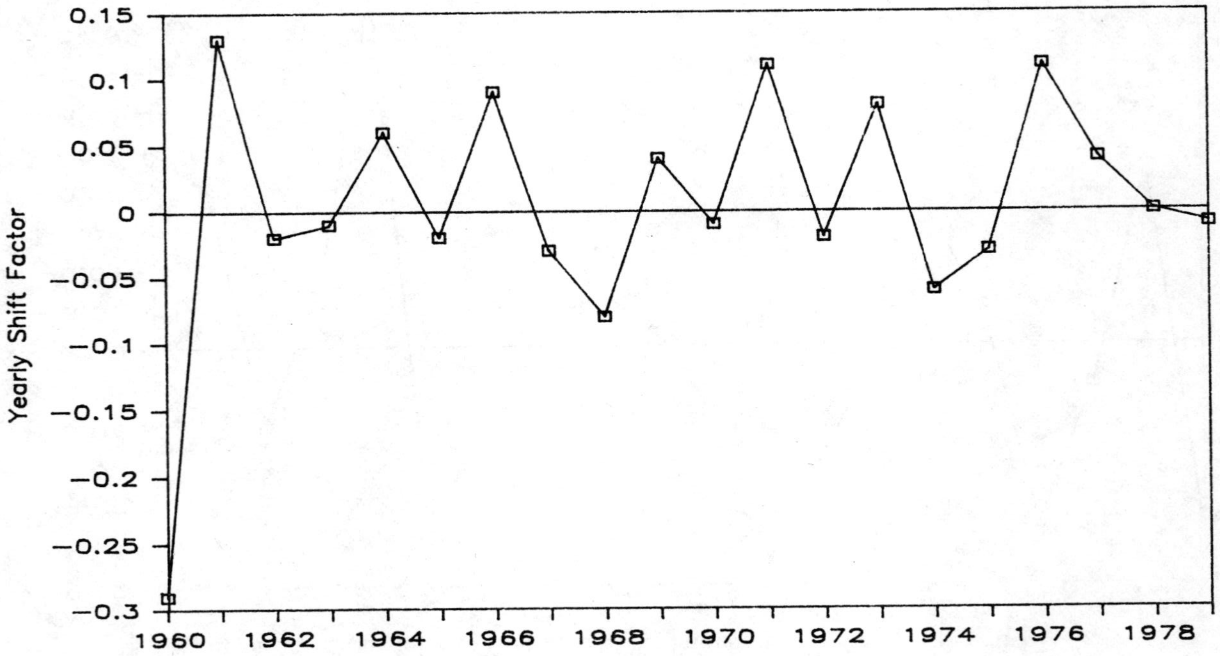

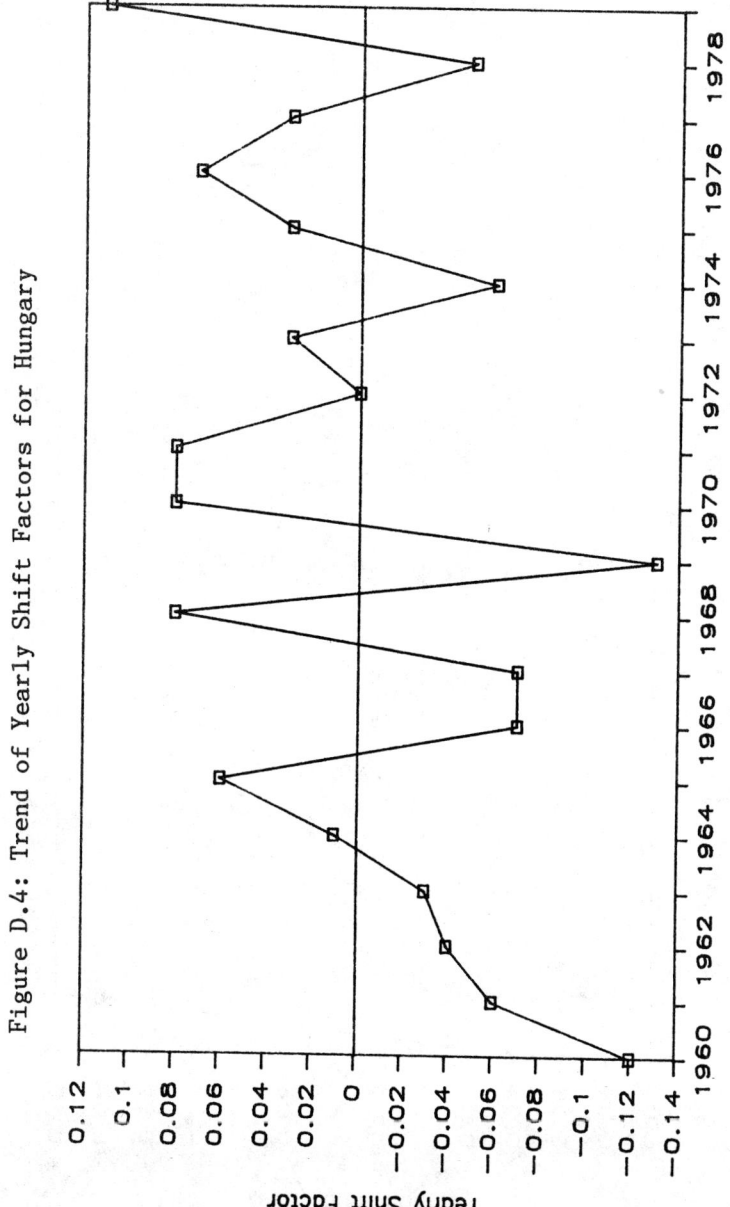

Figure D.4: Trend of Yearly Shift Factors for Hungary

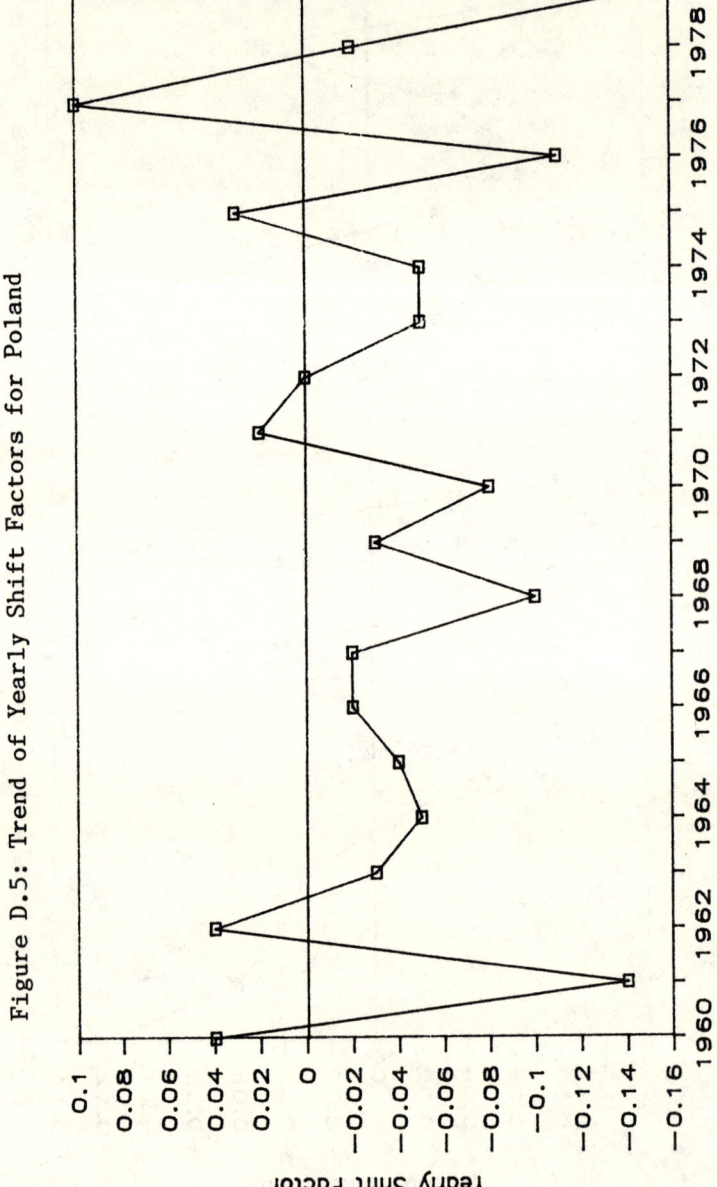

Figure D.5: Trend of Yearly Shift Factors for Poland

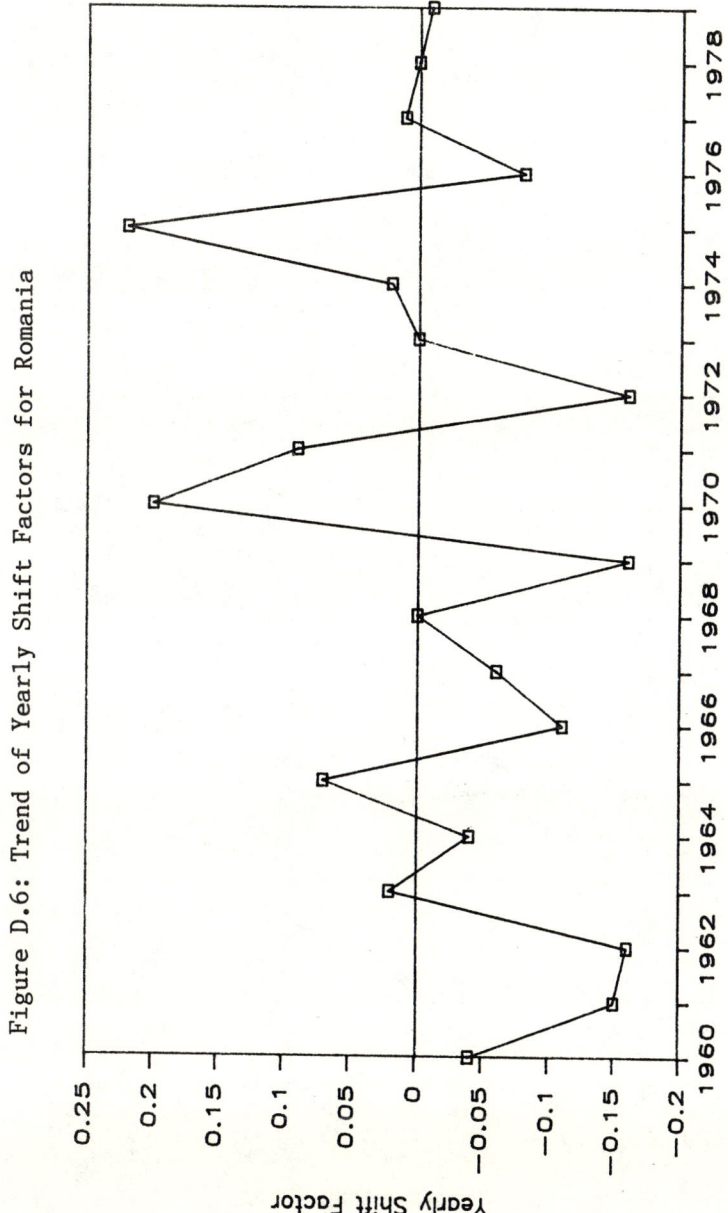

Figure D.6: Trend of Yearly Shift Factors for Romania

Figure D.7: Trend of Yearly Shift Factors for Yugoslavia

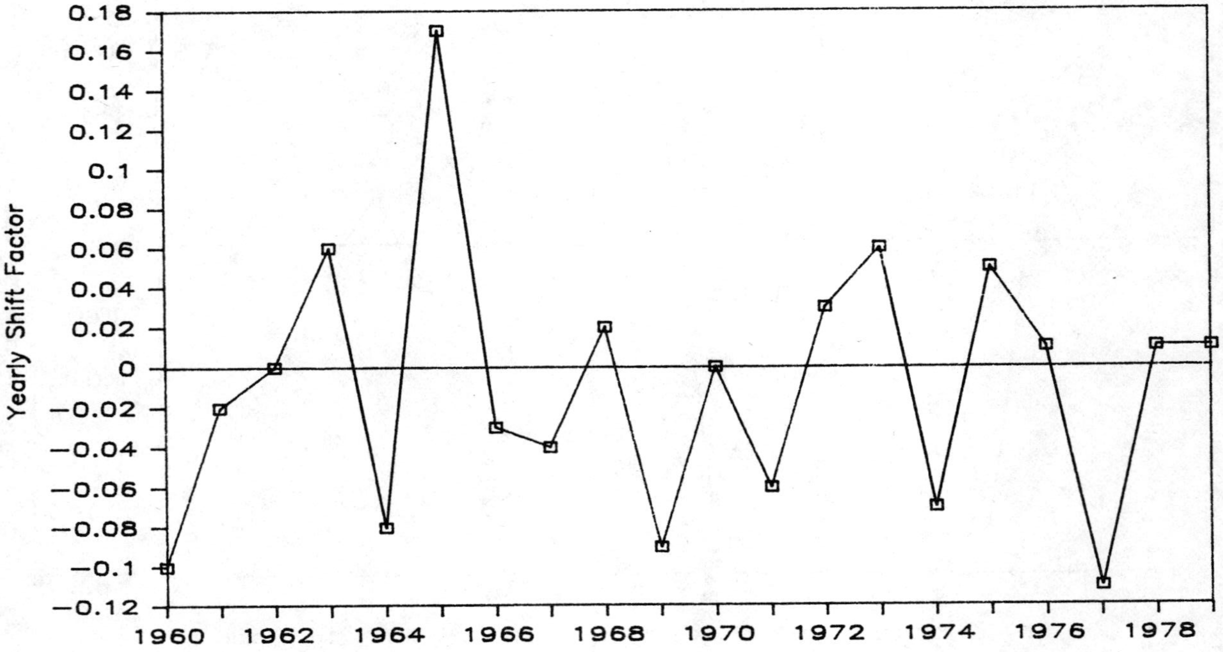

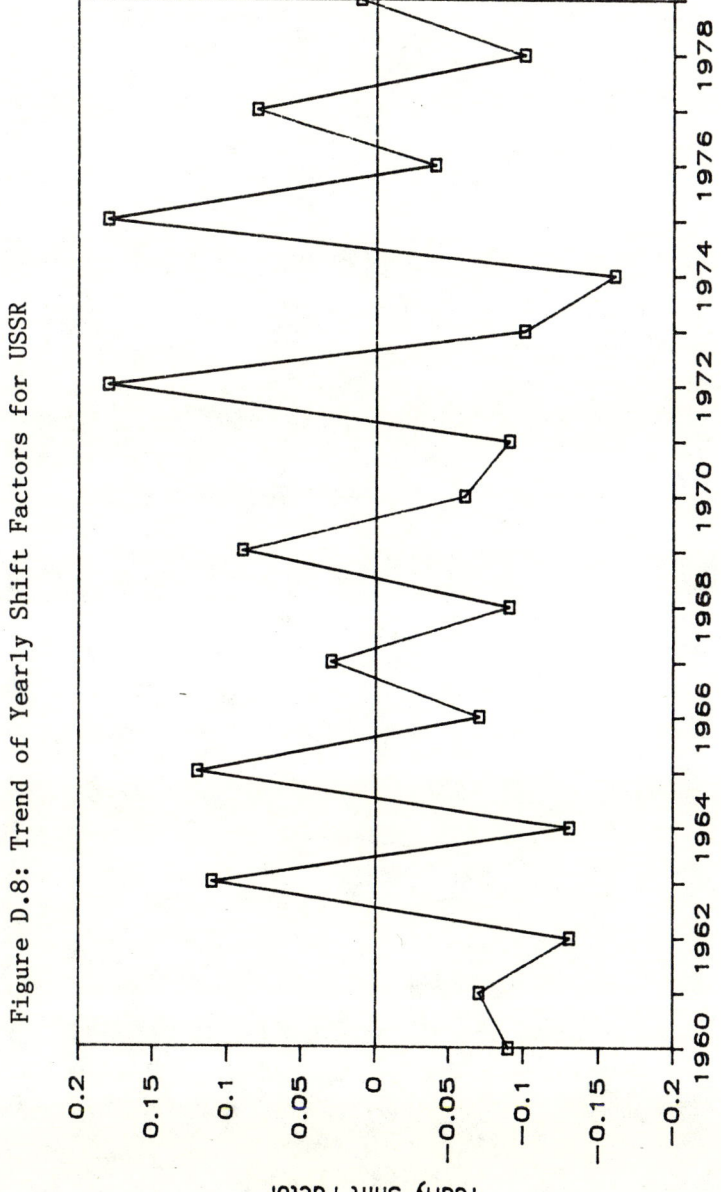

Figure D.8: Trend of Yearly Shift Factors for USSR

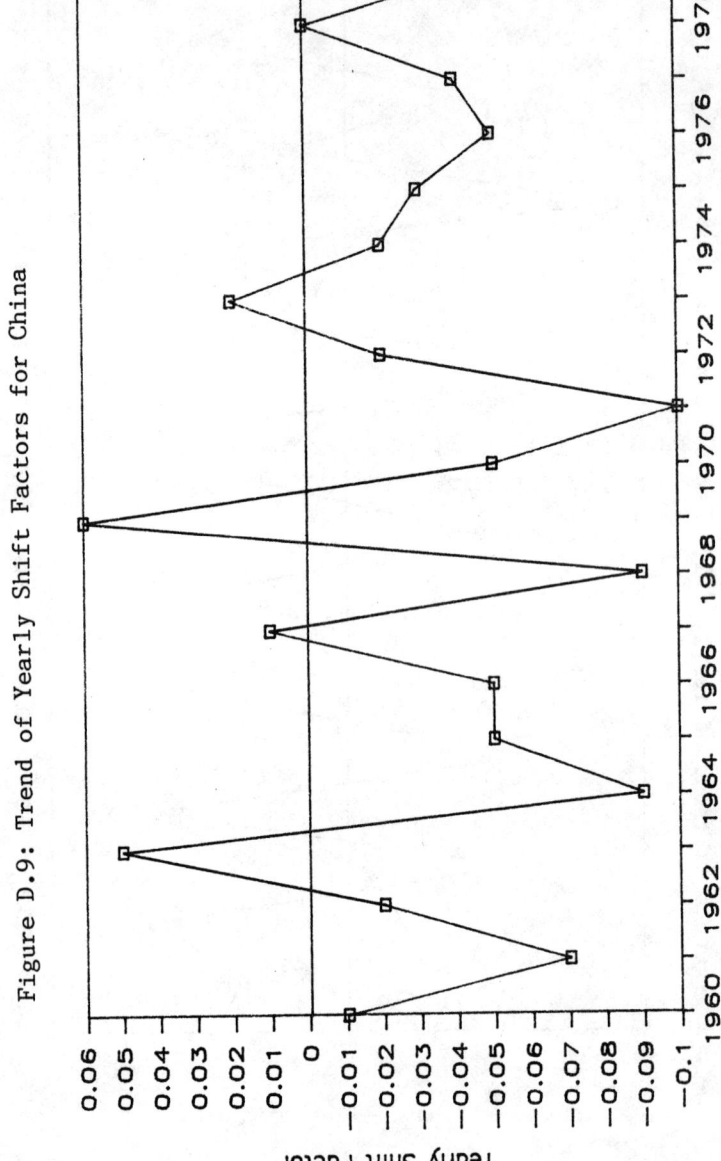

Figure D.9: Trend of Yearly Shift Factors for China

Bibliography

Alton, Thad P. (1981) "Production and Resource Allocation in Eastern Europe: Performance, Problems, and Prospects." East European Economic Assessment. Washington D.C.: Joint Economic Committee, US 97th Congress, 348-408.

Alton, Thad P., Elizabeth M. Bass, Joseph T. Bombelles, Gregor Lazarcik, and Wassyl Znayenlo. (1982) "Agricultural Output, Expenses and Depreciation, Gross Product and Net Product in Eastern Europe, 1965, 1970, and 1975-1981." Occasional Paper No. 71, Research Project on National Income in East Central Europe, New York: Columbia University.

Antle, John M. (1981) "Infrastructure and Aggregate Agricultural Productivity International Evidence." Department of Agricultural Economic, University of California, Davis.

Bergson, Abram. (1975) "Index Numbers and the Computation of Factor Productivity." The Review of Income and Wealth, 21 (3): 259-78.

Bergson, Abram. (1978) Productivity and the Social System - the USSR and the West. Cambridge: Harvard University Press, Massachusetts.

Bhattacharjee, Jyoti P. (1955) "Resource Use and Productivity in World Agriculture." Journal of Farm Economics. 37 (Feb.): 57-71.

Binswanger, Hans P. and Vernon W. Ruttan. (1978) Induced Innovation - Technology, Institutions and Development. Baltimore: The Johns Hopkins University Press.

Boyce, James K. and Robert E. Evenson. (1975) Agricultural Research and Extension Programs. New York: Agricultural Development Council, Inc.

Bredahl, Maury and Willis Peterson. (1976) "The Productivity and Allocation of Research: U.S. Agricultural Experiment Stations." *American Journal of Agricultural Economics,* 58 (Nov.): 684-692.

Bradley, M. and M.G. Clark. (1972) "Supervision and Efficiency in Socialized Agriculture." *Soviet Studies,* 23: 465-73.

Brooks, Karen M. (1983) "The Technical Efficiency of Soviet Agriculture," Chapter 9, *Prospects for Soviet Agriculture in the 1980s,* co-authored with D. Gale Johnson, Bloomington: Indiana University Press.

Chen, Edward K.Y. (1977) "Factor Inputs, Total Factor Productivity, and Economic Growth: The Asian Case." *Developing Economics,* 15 (June 3): 121-143.

Christensen, L.R. (1975) "Concepts and Measurement of Agricultural Productivity." *American Journal of Agricultural Economics,* 57: 910-15.

Chung Min Pang and A. John DeBoer. (1983) "Management Decentralization on China's State Farms." *American Journal of Agricultural Economics,* 65 (4): 657-666.

Clayton, Elizabeth. (1980) "Productivity in Soviet Agriculture." *Slavic Review,* 39:446-58.

Denny, M. and M. Fuss. (1983) "A General approach to Intertemporal and Interspatial Productivity Comparisons." *Journal of Econometrics,* 23 (Dec.): 315-330.

Diamond, Douglas B., Lee W. Bettis, and Robert E. Ramsson. (1983) "Agricultural Production." *The Soviet Economy Toward The Year 2000.* ed. Abram Bergson and Herbert S. Levine. London: George Allen and Unwin Ltd., 143-77.

Diamond, Douglas B. and Constance B. Krueger. (1973) "Recent Developments in Output and Productivity in Soviet Agriculture," U.S. Congress, *Soviet Economic Prospects for the Seventies,* Washington, D.C., p. 328-330.

Doan, thomas A. and Robert B. Litterman. (1981) *User's Manual RATS,* VAR Econometrics, Minneapolis.

Domar, Evsey. (1961) "On the Measurement of Technological Change." *The Economic Journal,* 71: 709-29.

Dung, Nguyen. (1979) "On Agricultural Productivity Differences Among Countries." *American Journal of Agricultural Economics,* 61(3): 565-570.

Du Runsheng. (1981) "Good Beginning for Reform of Rural Economic system," *Beijing Review,* 48 (Nov. 30): 15-20.

Ellman, Michael. (1981) "Agricultural Productivity Under Socialism." *World Development,* 9 (9/10): 979-89.

FAO. *Production Yearbook.* Rome: various issues.

Francisco, Ronald A., Betty A. Laird, and Roy D. Laird. ed et. (1979) *The Political Economy of Collectivized Agricultural, A Comparative Study of Communist and Non-Communist Systems.* New York: Pergmon Press.

Francisco, Ronald A., Betty A. Laird, and Roy D. Laird. ed et. (1980) *Agricultural Policies in the USSR and Eastern Europe.* Boulder: Westview Press, Colorado.

Gary, Kenneth R. (1979) "Soviet Agricultural Specialization and Efficiency." *Soviet Studies,* 31 (4): 542-58.

Greenberg, Edward and Charles Webster Jr. (1983) *Advanced Econometrics - A Bridge to the Literature.* New York: John Wiley and Sons.

Griliches, Zvi. (1957) "Specification Bias in Estimates of Production Functions." *Journal of Farm Economics* 39 (1): 8-20.

Griliches, Zvi. (1963) "Specification and Estimation of Agricultural Production Function." *Journal of Farm Economics,* 45 (2): 419-28.

Griliches, Zvi. (1964) "Research Expenditures, Education, and The Aggregate Agricultural Production Function." *The American Economic Review.* 54 (6): 961-74.

Griliches, Zvi. (1971) *Price Indexes and Quality Change.* Cambridge: Harvard University Press, Massachusetts.

Harvey, A.C. (1981) *The Econometric Analysis of Time Series,* New York: John Wiley & Sons Inc.

Hayami, Yujiro and associates. (1971) *An International Comparison of Agricultural Production and Productivity.* St. Paul: Agricultural Experiment Station, University of Minnesota, Technical Bulletin 277-1971.

Hayami, Yujiro. (1975) *A Century of Agricultural Growth in Japan.* Minneapolis: University of Minnesota Press.

Hayami, Yujiro and Vernon W. Ruttan. (1971) *Agricultural Development: An International Perspective.* Baltimore: The John Hopkins University Press.

Hayami, Yujiro and Vernon W. Ruttan. (1985) *Agricultural Development, An International Perspective.* Revised and Expanded Version, Baltimore: The John Hopkins University Press.

Hoerl, A.E. and R.W. Kennard. (1970) "Ridge Regression: Biased Estimation for Non-othogonal Problems." *Technometrics,* 12 (Feb.): 55-67.

Hulten, C.R. (1973) "Divisia Index Numbers." *Econometrica,* 41: 1017-25.

Johnson, D. Gale. (1982) "Agricultural in the Centrally Planned Economies." *American Journal of Agricultural Economics,* 64 (5): 845-53.

Johnson, D. Gale. (1983) "Agricultural Organization and Management." The Soviet Economy Toward the Year 2000. ed. Abram Bergson and Herbert S. Levine. London: George Allen and Unwin Ltd., 112-142.

Johnson, D. Gale and Karen M. Brooks. (1983) Prospects for Soviet Agriculture in the 1980s. Bloomington: Indiana University Press.

Johnson, Richard and Dean Wichern. (1982) Applied Multivariate Statistical Analysis. Englewood Cliffs: Prentice-Hall, New Jersey.

Johnston, J. (1972) Econometric Methods, 2nd edition. New York: McGraw-Hill Book Company.

Joravsky, David. (1970) The Lysenko Affair. Cambridge: Harvard University Press, Massachusetts.

Jorgenson, D.W. and Z. Griliches. (1971) "Divisia Index and Productivity Measurement." Review of Income and Wealth. 17: 227-29.

Judd, M. Ann, James K. Boyce, and Robert E. Evenson. (1982) "Investment in Agricultural Supply." Mimeographed, Boston: Economic Growth Center, Yale University.

Judge, George G., William E. Griffiths, and Tsoung-chao Lee. (1980) The Theory and Practice of Economics. New York: John Wiley and Sons, Inc.

Kawagoe, Toshihiko, Yujiro Hayami, and Vernon W. Ruttan. (1983) "Agricultural Productivity Differences Among Countries Revisited." Mimeographed.

Kendick, John W. (1973) Postwar Productivity Trends in the U.S., 1948-1968. New York: Columbia University Press.

Kleiman, Z., N. Halevi, and D. Levhari. (1966) "The Relationships Between Two Measures of Total Productivity." Review of Economic and Statistics, 48: 345-47.

Kmenta, Jan. (1971) Elements of Econometrics. New York: Macmillan Publishing Co., Inc.

Kozlowski, Z. (1975) "Agriculture and the Economic Growth of East European Socialist Countries." Agriculture in Development Theory. ed. Lloyd G. Reynolds. New Haven: Yale University Press, 411-450.

Kravis, Irving B., Alan Heston, and Robert Summers. (1982) World Product and Income, International Comparisons of Real Gross Product. Baltimore: The Johns Hopkins University Press.

Langham, Max R. and Ismet Ahmad. (1983) "Measuring Productivity in Economic Growth." American Journal of Agricultural Economics, 65 (2); 445-51.

Lave, Lester B. (1966) Technological Change: Its Conception and Measurement. New Jersey: Prentice-Hall.

Lazarcik, Gregor. (1973) "Bulgarian Agricultural Production, Output, Expenses, Gross and Net Product, and Productivity, at 1968 Prices, 1939, and 1950-1971." Occasional Paper No. 39, Research Project on National Income in East Central Europe, New York: Columbia University.

Lu, Yao-Chi. (1975) "Measuring Productivity Changes in U.S. Agriculture." Southern Journal of Agricultural Economics, December, 69-75.

Lu, Yao-Chi and L.B. Fletcher (1968) "A Generalization of the CES Production Function." Review of Economics and Statistics, 50 (4): 449-52.

Lu, Yao-Chi, Philip Cline, and Levoy Quance. (1979) Prospects for Productivity Growth in U.S. Agriculture. United States Department of Agriculture - Economics, Statistics, and Cooperatives Services, Agricultural Economic Report No. 435.

Maddala, G.S. (1977) Econometrics. New York: McGraw-Hill Book Company.

Millar, James R. (1970) "Soviet Rapid Development and The Agricultural Surplus Hypothesis." Soviet Studies, 22 (July): 77-93.

Mittelhammer, Ron C. and John L. Baritelle. (1977) "On Two Strategies for Selecting Principal Components in Regression Analysis." American Journal of Agricultural Economics, 59 (2) 336-43.

Morrison, Donald F. (1976) Multivariate Statistical Methods. New York: McGraw-Hill Book Company.

Mundlak, Yair. (1981) "On the Concept of Non-significant Functions and Its Relation to Regression Analysis." Journal of Econometrics, 16: 139-49.

Mundlak, Yair and Rene Hellinghausen. (1982) "The Intercountry Agricultural Production Function: Another View." American Journal of Agricultural Economics, 64 (4): 664-72.

Nadiri, M. Ishaq. (1970) "Some Approaches to the Theory and Measurement of Total Factor Productivity: A Survey." Journal of Economic Literature, 8 (Dec.): 1137-77.

Nerlove, Marc. (1965) Estimation and Identification of Cobb-Douglas Production Function, Chicago: Rand McNally & Company.

Nove, Alec. (1980) The Soviet Economic System. 2nd edition, London: George Allen & Unwin Ltd.

Nove, Alec. (1983) The Economics of Feasible Socialism, London: George Allen & Unwin Ltd.

Oi, Walter Y. and Elizabeth M. Clayton. (1968) "A Peasant's View of a Soviet Collective Farm." American Economic Review, 58 (1): 37-59.

Peng Xianchu. (1984) "Prosperity Under New Rural Policies." China Reconstructs, February 1984, 16-27.

Peterson, Willis, and Yujiro Hayami. (1977) "Technical Change in Agriculture." A Survey of Agricultural Economics Literature. Volume 1. ed. Lee R. Martin. Minneapolis: University of Minnesota Press, 497-540.

Rawski, Thomas. (1979) Economic Growth and Employment in China. New York: Oxford University Press.

Rawski, Thomas. (1982) "Agricultural Employment and Technology." The Chinese Agricultural Economy, ed et. Randolph Barker, Radha Sinha, and Beth Rose, Colorado: Westview Press, 121-36.

Richter, Marcel K. (1966) "Invariance Axioms and Economic Indexes." Econometrica, 34 (4): 739-755.

Ruttan, Vernon W. (1982) Agricultural Research Policy. Minneapolis: University of Minnesota Press.

Schrenk, Martin, Cyrus Ardalan, and Nawal Tataway. (1979) Yugoslavia: Self-management Socialism and the Challenges of Development. Baltimore: John Hopkins University Press.

Solow, Robert. (1957) "Technical Change and The Aggregate Production Function." Review of Economics and Statistics, 39 (Aug.): 312-22.

Star, Spencer. (1974) "Accounting for the Growth of Output." American Economic Review, 64: 123-35.

Tang, Anthony. (1984) An Analtycial and Empirical Investigation of Agriculture in Mainland China, 1952-1980. Taipei: Chung-Hua Institution for Economic Research.

Tang, Anthony and Bruce Stone. (1980) Food Production in PRC. Washington D.C.: International Food Policy Research Institute.

Theil, Henri. (1971) Principal of Econometrics. New York: Wiley.

Thirtle, Colin G. "Induced Innovation in US Agriculture." Ph.D. Dissertation, Columbia University.

Tsui, Chapman and Lung-Fai Wong. (1985) "Modernization and Income Inequality in Rural China." Part I in Ming Pao Yuekan, 230: 77-80, Part II in Ming Pao Yuekan, 231: 80-83. Hong Kong.

USDA. (1973) Agricultural Statistics of Eastern Europe and The Soviet Union 1950-70. Washington D.C.: USDA, Economic Research Service, Foreign 349.

USDA. (1980) <u>Measurement of US Agricultural Productivity - A Review of Current Statistics and Proposals for Change</u>. Washington D.C.: USDA, Economic, Statistics, and Cooperative Service, Technical Bulletin No. 1614.

USDA. (1981) <u>World Indices of Agricultural and Food Production</u>. Washington D.C.: Economic Research Service, Statistical Bulletin No. 669.

USDA. (1983) <u>Agricultural Statistics of Eastern Europe and The Soviet Union, 1960-80</u>. Washington D.C.: USDA, Economic Research Service, Statistical Bulletin Number 700.

Vais, Tibor. (1981) "Manpower Policy." <u>East European Economic Assessment</u>. Washington D.C.: Joint Economic Committee, U.S. 97th Congress, 229-258.

Wadekin, Karl-Eugen. (1982) <u>Agrarian Policies in Communist Europe</u>. New Jersey: Netherlands, Allanheld, Osmum & Company.

Watson, Andrew. (1983) "Agricultural Looks for 'Shoes that Fit': The Production Responsibility System and Its Implications." <u>World Development</u>, 11 (8): 705-30.

White, Kenneth. (1981) "User's Guide for SHAZAM, an Econometrics Computer Program." Department of Economics, University of British Columbia, Vancouver.

Wiens, Thomas B. (1982) "The Limits to Agricultural Intensification: The Suzhou Experience." <u>China Under the Four Modernization</u>, Part I. Washington D.C.: Joint Economic Committee, 97 US Congress, 462-74.

Wilczynski, J. (1982) <u>The Economics of Socialism</u>, 4th Edition. Boston: George Allen and Unwin Ltd.

Wizarat, Schahida. (1981) "Technological Change in Pakistan's Agriculture: 1953-54 to 1978-79." <u>The Pakistan Development Review</u>. 20 (4): 427-45.

Wong, Lung-Fai. (1982) "Supply-Siders, Reaganomics, and China's Supply-Side Economic Policy." <u>Ming Pao Yuekan</u>, 195: 40-43.

Wong, Lung-Fai. (1985a) <u>A Comparative Analysis of Agricultural Productivity Growth Among Socialist Countries</u>. Ph.D. Dissertation, University of Minnesota, Minneapolis.

Wong, Lung-Fai. (1985b) "The New Socialist Agricultural Ladder System in China: the Formation, Productivity Effect and Distributive Effect." Monograph, St. Paul.

Wong, Lung-Fai and Henry Hwang. (1980) "User's Guide for Utility Program PLOTLNE for Automatically Scaled Graphical Plotting of Continuous Lines." Staff Paper Series P80-23, Department of Agricultural and Applied Economics, University of Minnesota, St. Paul.

Wong, Lung-Fai and Chapman Tsui. (1983) "Agricultural Modernization and Rural Development in China." Ming Pao Yuekan, 215: 19-23.

Wong, Lung-Fai and Vernon W. Ruttan. (1983) "Sources of Differences in Agricultural Productivity Growth Among Socialist Countries." Paper presented at the 5th Annual Conference on Current Issues in Productivity, Rutgers University, Newark, New Jersey, Dec. 5th to 7th, 1983.

Wyzan, Michael. (1981) "Empirical Analysis of Soviet Agricultural Production and Policy." American Journal of Agricultural Economics, 63 (3): 425-83.

Yamada, Saburo. (1975) A Comparative Analysis of Asian Agricultural Productivities and Growth Patterns. Tokyo: Asian Productivity Organization, Productivity Series No. 10.

Yamada, Saburo and Vernon W. Ruttan. (1980) "International Comparisons of Productivity in Agriculture." New Developments in Productivity Measurement and Analysis. ed et. John W. Kendrick and Beatrice N. Vaccara. Chicago: The University of Chicago Press, 509-94.

Young, Brigitta. (1983) Prospects for Soviet Grain Production. Boulder, Colorado: Westview Press.

Index

Agricultural labor, 31
  coefficient, 38
  definition, 141
  in China, 56
  in USSR, 55
  income, 9
  mobility, 80
Agricultural ladder in
    China, 119
Agricultural land, 31
  definition, 142
  definition for USSR, 57
  reclamation, 31
Agricultural
    metaproduction
    function, 27
  definition, 29
Agricultural output,
  definition, 10
  growth, 11(table)
Agricultural planning, 5
Agricultural production,
  historical performance,
    112
Agricultural productivity,
  sources of growth, 90
Agricultural research, 31-
    33, 46
  coefficient, 36, 38
  in China, 94
  in Poland, 94
  in USSR, 105, 117

quality, 105
Analysis of Covariance, 24
Arithmetic index, 63(table)
  formula, 62
Asian country, 101
Australia, 101
Average cost, 9
Barzel, 22
Bettis, Lee W., 83
Bhattacharjee, Cjyoti P.,
    29, 43
Binswanger, Hans P., 29
Brooks, Karen M., 33, 44,
    55, 86
Bulgaria,
  agricultural growth, 10-13
  area, 7(table)
  labor productivity, 52-
    53(table)
  land productivity, 58-
    59(table)
  total factor productivity,
    63-67(table)
  population, 7(table)
  technical change,
    89(table)
  yearly shift factor,
    69(table)
Canada, 101
Capital, return on, 20
Centralized countries,
  definition, 41

191

production function,
  42(table)
Centrally Planned
  Economy (CPE), 6
Chemical inputs, 31
China
  agricultural growth, 10-13
  area, 7(table)
  labor productivity, 52-53(table)
  land productivity, 58-59(table)
  total factor productivity, 63-67(table)
  population, 7(table)
  technical change, 89(table)
  yearly shift factor, 69(table)
  <u>See also</u> Cultural Revolution, commune
Clayton, Elizabeth, 33, 44
Climate, 46
Cobb-Douglas production function, 22, 24, 30, 31
Collective farm, 5
  definition, 8
Commune, in China, 8
Competitive equilibrium, 18
Constant Elasticity of Substitution (CES), 24, 30
Constant rate of return, 21
Conversion procedures, 10
Correlation coefficient matrix, 35
Cultural Revolution in China, 12, 117
Czechoslovakia,
  agricultural growth, 10-13
  area, 7(table)
  labor productivity, 52-53(table)
  land productivity, 58-59(table)

total factor productivity, 63-67(table)
population, 7(table)
technical change, 89(table)
yearly shift factor, 69(table)
Diamond, Douglas B., 64, 83
Divisia index, 22, 23
Domestic economy, 120
Domestic market, 119
East European countries,
  agricultural growth, 10-13
  area, 7(table)
  labor productivity, 52-53(table)
  land productivity, 58-59(table)
  total factor productivity, 63-67(table)
  population, 7(table)
  technical change, 89(table)
  yearly shift factor, 69(table)
East Germany,
  agricultural growth, 10-13
  area, 7(table)
  labor productivity, 52-53(table)
  land productivity, 58-59(table)
  total factor productivity, 63-67(table)
  population, 7(table)
  technical change, 89(table)
  yearly shift factor, 69(table)
Economic efficiency, 18
  definition, 16
Economic reform,
  in East European, 10, 66
  in USSR, 10
Economic rent, 9
Education, 31
Ellman, Michael, 5
Euler's theorem, 19, 21

Evenson, Robert, 28, 44, 147
Exchange rate, 19
Factor share, 62
Farm size,
   in USSR, 6
   in Yugoslavia, 6
   in Poland, 6
Farrell, 24
Fertilizer, 83, 94
   definition, 142
Fisher, Irving, 22
Fletcher, 30
Food and Agriculture Organization (FAO), 127
Garden plot in China, 6
Generalized Power function, 24
Geometric index, 67(table)
   formula, 65
Griliches, Zvi, 24
Growth indices,
   agricultural output, 10
Hayami, Yujiro, 19, 28, 38, 29, 43, 61, 10, 127
Hellinghausen, Rene, 28, 44
Hicks' neutral, 18
Homogeneous translog function, 22
Hulter, C.R., 23
Human capital, 31
   improvement, 16
Hungary,
   agricultural growth, 10-13
   area, 7(table)
   labor productivity, 52-53(table)
   land productivity, 58-59(table)
   total factor productivity, 63-67(table)
   population, 7(table)
   technical change, 89(table)
   yearly shift factor, 69(table)
Incentive system, 5, 119

Income, agricultural labor, 9
Industrial input, 94
Industrial sector, 120
Innovation possibility curve, 29
Input, conventional, 19
Institutional innovation, 16
International market, 83, 114, 119
Irrigation, 83
Isocost, 18, 86
Isoquant, 18, 86
   map, 16
Japan, 101
Johansen, 24
Johnson, D. Gale, 5, 55, 115
Joravsky, David, 105
Kendrick, John W., 16, 20
Kislav, 28, 44
Labor productivity,
   definition, 50
   indices, 52-53(table)
   source of growth, socialist countries, 92-93(table)
   source of difference, socialist vs non-socialist countries, 102-103(table)
Land productivity,
   definition, 57
   indices, 58-59(table)
   sources of growth, socialist countries, 96-97(table)
   source of difference, socialist vs non-socialist countries, 106-107(table)
Laspeyres index, 22
Lave, Laster B., 19, 20
Leontief's input-output model, 24
Less-centralized countries, definition, 41

Linear Elasticity of
    Substitution function,
    30
Livestock,
    coefficient, 31, 36
    conversion factor, 142
    numbers in socialist
        countries, 157-
        165(table)
Lu, Yao-Chi, 24, 30
Lysenko Affair, 105, 117
Machinery, 31
    definition, 142
Managerial skill, 19
Marginal cost, 9, 18
Marginal product, 18
Market, open, 10
Misallocation of resources,
    86
Mixed Estimation, 33, 38
Multicollinearity, 33
Multiple cropping, in
    China, 60
Mundlak, Yair, 28, 44
National income
    accounting, 20
Neutral technical change,
    assumption, 68
New Zealand, 101
Nguyen, 28, 43
Ordinary Least Squares
    (OLS), 32, 33
Opportunity cost, 9
Paasche index, 22
Partial productivity index,
    49
    definition, 50
People's Daily, 109
Peterson, Willis, 19, 61
Physical capital,
    accumulation, 16
Planning. See agricultural
    planning.
Poland,
    agricultural growth, 10-13
    area, 7(table)
    labor productivity, 52-
        53(table)
    land productivity, 58-
        59(table)
    total factor productivity,
        63-67(table)
    population, 7(table)
    technical change, 89(table)
    yearly shift factor,
        69(table)
Population, world, 5
    in socialist countries,
        7(table)
Price,
    determination of, 9
    mechanism of, 5
    of land, 9
    procurement, 10
    structure of, 9
    wheat unit, 128-129(table)
Principal Component
    Regression, 33, 35, 38,
    167
Private farm,
    in Yugoslavia, 8
    in Poland, 8
Private research, 118
Private sector, 5
Production cost, 9, 86
Production elasticity, 44
Production function, 19
Productivity,
    definition, 16
    function, 39
Quota,
    administrative, 88
    procurement, 10
Ramsson, Robert E., 83
Rawski, Thomas, 51, 60,
    64
Resource endowment, 31,
    94
Responsibility system in
    China, 115
Richter, Marcel K., 23
Ridge Regression, 33, 35

Romania,
  agricultural growth, 10-13
  area, 7(table)
  labor productivity, 52-53(table)
  land productivity, 58-59(table)
  total factor productivity, 63-67(table)
  population, 7(table)
  technical change, 89(table)
  yearly shift factor, 69(table)
Ruttan, Vernon W., 28, 29, 38, 43, 101
SHAZAM, 171
Socialist ideology, 8
Socialized agricultural land, 7(table)
  in Poland, 6
  in Yugoslavia, 6
  in USSR, 6
Soil quality, 46
Solow, Robert, 21, 22, 68
Soviet Union,
  agricultural growth, 10-13
  area, 7(table)
  labor productivity, 52-53(table)
  land productivity, 58-59(table)
  total factor productivity, 63-67(table)
  population, 7(table)
  production function, 44
  technical change, 89(table)
  yearly shift factor, 69(table)
Stalin's economic model, 120
State farm, 5
  definition, 8
Tang, Anthony, 56, 64
Technical change,
  definition, 84
  in USSR, 86
  neutral, 21

Technical efficiency, 18
Technical input, 31
Technological progress, 16
Three Red Flags, in China, 12
Total factor productivity,
  definition, 61
  trend, 62
Trade. See International market.
Transcendental Logarithmic function, 24
United Nations, 127
U.S.A., 101
Variable Elasticity of Substitution function (VES), 24, 30
Wadekin, Karl-Eugen, 66
Wage rate, 20
  in USSR, 55
Wheat unit, 10
Wong, Lung-Fai, 44, 119
Work point system in Chinese communes, 9
World economy, 120
Wyzan, Michael, 6, 33
Yamada, Saburo, 28, 43
Yearly shift factor, 68, 69(table)
  trends of, 70, 174-182(table)
Yugoslavia,
  agricultural growth, 10-13
  area, 7(table)
  labor productivity, 52-53(table)
  land productivity, 58-59(table)
  total factor productivity, 63-67(table)
  population, 7(table)
  technical change, 89(table)
  yearly shift factor, 69(table)